OFFICIAL GUIDEBOOK TO AMERICA'S STATE QUARTERS

DAVID L. GANZ

HOUSE OF COLLECTIBLES
THE CROWN PUBLISHING GROUP • NEW YORK

House of Collectibles and the HC colophon are trademarks of Random House, Inc.

Published by: House of Collectibles
             The Crown Publishing Group
             New York, NY

Distributed by The Crown Publishing Group, a division of Random House, Inc., New York, and simultaneously in Canada by Random House of Canada Limited, Toronto.

www.randomhouse.com

Manufactured in the United States of America

Library of Congress Cataloging-in-Publication Data
Ganz, David L. (1951–   )
The official guidebook to America's state quarters / by David L. Ganz.
Includes index.
1. Quarter-dollar—Collectors and collecting—Handbooks, manuals, etc.   2. Coins, American—Collectors and collecting—Handbooks, manuals, etc.   3. Commemorative coins—United States—Collectors and collecting—Handbooks, manuals, etc.   4. Emblems, State—United States—Miscellanea.   I. Title.

CJ1840.S73 G36 2000
737.4973'075—dc21
00-061318

ISBN 0-609-80770-6

10 9 8 7 6 5 4 3 2 1

First Edition: November 2000

To Michael Castle, John Lopez, and Philip N. Diehl, without whom there would never have been the America's State Quarters Program; to the members of the Citizens Commemorative Coin Advisory Committee, who became true believers before it became a reality; and for Kathy, who was present at the creation.

CONTENTS

ACKNOWLEDGMENTS

The Professional Coin Grading Service has given permission to quote from its Population Reports (April 2000 and June 2000 are utilized in the first edition of this book) for various grades and conditions concerning America's State Quarters. The book would be poorer but for their assistance.

Fred Weinberg of Encino, California, currently president of the Professional Numismatists Guild and a longtime dealer in not only rare coins but also in errors, was incredibly generous with his time and also his inventory. The error coin photos included in the book come largely from inventory that he simply sent me with a request that I send them back when I was done with them. As with many other error coins that Fred has shown me through the years, some wound up in my permanent collection. Permission to quote from and use his price lists was essential for accurate pricing of error pieces.

Alan Herbert, now an elected governor of the American Numismatic Association, provided valuable information about the errors for the State Quarters, as did William Fivaz, a former elected governor who served a single four-year term on the ANA Board that began when I took office. Bill was a good friend to me, and to all collectors on the Board, and his knowledge of the error field has made this book the stronger.

Scott Travers, my agent, is a well-known numismatic personality aside from the important role that he had in bringing this book to the marketplace. A coin dealer of considerable renown, and a consumer advocate before it became popular, he thought from the first that the topic was worthy of a book and persuaded Random House of its merits. He, too, is a former board member of the ANA (rising to vice president), and the author of a number of books in the rare coin field that are worthwhile reading. His comments on the manuscript were invaluable.

Ed Reiter first began to edit my writing when he was at *Numismatic News* in Iola, Wisconsin, more than a quarter-century ago. He does a lot more than add commas and remove dashes—he adds to the substance, and the accuracy, of any work. He edits my articles for *COINage* magazine every month (and has for the last 15 years or so), and the last coin book that I wrote, on U.S. commemorative coins, was so well edited by him that I would not have dreamed of doing this book without his help.

Sue Kohler of the federal Commission of Fine Arts was helpful beyond words, as was her colleague, commission secretary Charles Atherton, with whom I served over four separate years on the Citizens Commemorative Coin Advisory Committee (1993–96), where Charles is still a non-voting member. Sue culled through the archives of the Fine Arts Commission and pulled out relevant minutes relating to the State Quarters program; she also permitted copies to be made of designs that did not see the light of day, which have made this book the richer.

Staff members at the U.S. Mint could not have been more helpful in providing information about the State

Quarters program. Andrew Fishburn was able to provide relevant minutes from the CCCAC that related to the State Quarters program; Arnetta Cain, of the Office of Mint Director, provided some published official documents not otherwise easily obtainable; John Mitchell, deputy director of the Mint, spoke to me on several occasions providing support for the need to tell the story of how the 50 States program originated, and providing technical details on Mint operations; Ken Gubin, legal counsel, and Jean Gentry, his immediate successor, both of whom I have known for many years, lent their expertise in discussing some of the legal and legislative aspects of the underlying laws governing the program; Andrew Cosgarea, formerly assistant director for technology, and David Pickens, associate director for marketing, both spoke to me, at different times and at length, about various technical considerations in the manufacture and marketing of the state quarters. Needless to say, the information provided to me was synthesized by me, and the conclusions remain my own.

This book's first edition is intended to cover the circulating commemorative program, but I would be remiss if I did not mention the Mint's numismatic program (originally contemplated in my own plan for circulating commemorative coins), and my good friend Steven Grossman, who allowed me and Bob Leuver (ANA's former executive director and a past director of the Bureau of Engraving and Printing) the opportunity to witness firsthand and participate in formulating strategy for that program.

Thanks, also, to Steve Markoff, chairman of the A-Mark group, who lent his organization's experience and expertise in providing pricing and other data relative to this program—and the identity of holders of some of the high-grade certified State Quarter coins.

David Sundman of Littleton Coin Co., Littleton, New

Hampshire, was kind enough to provide me with his deluxe custom coin album, which I have used to hold circulation examples of the series as they have come to my attention.

David's Cookies, at Third Avenue and 79th Street in New York City, has a dedicated staff that is across the street from my law office, and ordinarily would have no place in this book except to thank them for supplying the coffee each day that has helped finish several of the chapters in timely fashion. But it turns out that three of the women who work there are also collectors of the State Quarters, and they look through their cash register not only for their collections, but also to allow me to exchange coin and currency to complete my own collection out of circulation.

Josie Harrington, who works for the Borough of Fair Lawn, New Jersey (where, at least at the time that I write this, I am the elected mayor), is also to be thanked. When I told her that I was unable to find a Connecticut (and later Maryland) quarter, she made certain that one showed up on my desk in Borough Hall. I still have it in my collection.

Philip Diehl, director of the Mint, has my profound thanks. Through his sponsorship, I was appointed to the Citizens Commemorative Coin Advisory Committee and, in that capacity, determined that a circulating coin was an issue. Despite what he himself called a "Johnny One Note" approach to the subject by me, he did not stifle the discussion (and he could have), but first encouraged a formal report, and gradually turned around his own views on the subject. After my tenure was complete, he invited me, and my wife Kathy, to many of the first-strike events for the coin program (and permitted me to start one of the presses for the Delaware coin issue). We have certainly worked together on many other issues, but on this, he took an idea, made it better, adopted it as his own, acknowledged the source, and created a growth industry in and of itself.

Julie Abrams, president of Teletrade, is thanked for her

willingness to share pricing data and auction frequency. (If you can find a phone or can access the Internet, you can bid in a Teletrade auction. Teletrade features "live" Internet bidding and bidding over its toll-free 800 lines using a Touch-Tone phone from anywhere in North America. All participants are brought together into one exciting, live auction. Teletrade auctions don't go on for days; they always end the day they start.)

The Numismatic Guaranty Corporation of America, in Parsippany, New Jersey, and its president, Mark Salzberg, are specifically thanked for providing up-to-date population reports on NGC-encapsulated coins that enabled valuable points of comparison to be made, allowing readers to draw their own conclusions as to the relative scarcity of some items.

Dennis Baker of NumisMedia, 21213-B Hawthorne Blvd., Suite 5658, Torrance, CA 90503 (*www.numismedia.com*) is a good friend and a true gem uncirculated guy. Although his price guide, available in print and online, does not yet carry information about the State Quarters, he did yeoman service when I asked for fair market values, searched them out, and reliably reported them so that they could be reprinted in this book. Originally, this is exclusive to the Official Guide; I hope that it spreads to his periodical and online version so that collectors everywhere can see the tremendous march of progress of this series for upper-grade coins. Dennis provided current fair market values for coins of Philadelphia (P or plain) and Denver (D mint marks) in superior grades (MS-65 and higher). Valuations are as of May 30, 2000 and are provided exclusively to *The Official Guide to America's State Quarters*. Fair market value prices listed are for certified coins only (usually PCGS, NGC, or ANACS). Raw coins may bring substantially less. Prices may fluctuate considerably as new issues are brought on the market and certified. As populations increase in a particular grade, coins may be easier to obtain and prices may fall. Where an asterisk appears for a grade, NumisMedia has not seen enough trading activity to establish a price at this time. (Valuations ©2000 by NumisMedia, Inc. All rights reserved. Used by permission.) A comprehensive listing of fair market values of American coins is found on the web site of Numis-Media, *http://www.numismedia.com*.

Randy Campbell of ANACS, 4150 Tuller Rd., Suite 210, Dublin, OH 43017, was kind enough to provide me with the highest grades assigned by ANACS on the BU State Quarters. My request came at an inconvenient time, when ANACS was about to go to press with its census report, but Randy put the information out, on time, to a grateful author and, I hope, readers.

The members of the Citizens Commemorative Coin Advisory Committee had a great deal to do with the ultimate product that was created, and while they are acknowledged by me, they should be thanked by all who collect these beautiful State Quarters: Philip Diehl, director of the Mint and chairman of the CCCAC; Charles Atherton (non-voting member), Elvira (Lisa) Clain-Stefanelli, Reed Hawn, Daniel Hoffman, Elsie Sterling Howard, and Thomas Shockley III.

I would surely be remiss if I did not extend a personal and formal acknowledgment to my wife, Kathy, in addition to the much more informal thanks that I have given her. Not only is she a good "first" editor, reader, and compiler, but she has the knack of asking critical questions that have made this book more focused and readable—especially since she is a non-collector. Many times she has accompanied me to the events that are discussed, and her photos are included elsewhere in the book. She devoted "our" time to talking shop about this book, and I want to repeat and reiterate, I owe you a "really expensive gift." I also thank you for all of your support in the very early days of the proposal to issue circulating commemorative coins, when I felt like the voice in the wilderness. In more ways than one, you made a dream come true.

John Lopez, formerly staff counsel to the Subcommittee on Domestic and International Monetary Policy of the House Banking, Finance & Urban Affairs Committee, now with the Federal Reserve, became an unstinting advocate of the State Quarters program some time after we first chatted with the other members of the Citizens Commemorative Coin Advisory Committee. He was an important source for government documents accumulated and there is little doubt, in my mind, as to who the key staffer was that made the proposal reality and, hence, made this book possible.

For nearly 30 years, I have had a good friend, and publisher, in the form of James L. Miller, whose *COINage* magazine ran regular stories on the monthly progress of the circulating commemorative coin effort. Although we see each other only once or twice a year, we speak regularly, and his encouragement of the idea, the articles, and ultimately this book helped make the program a reality, and this book possible. Without the material that I prepared for *COINage* magazine, this overall presentation would have been impossible to prepare.

David Harper, editor of *Numismatic News* (Krause Publications), is another good friend whose assistance in this book, and my earlier one on U.S. commemorative coins, was of invaluable assistance. His suggestions for columns for my long-running "Under the Glass" (which first appeared in *Numismatic News* in 1969) have been incorporated into this book severalfold, most recently with the chapter on designing your own State Quarter. Many years ago, from 1969–73, I was the Washington correspondent for *Numismatic News Weekly* (as it was then called), and eventually became an assistant editor living, and working, in Iola, Wisconsin, located about 60 miles west of Green Bay and Appleton in central Wisconsin. Chet Krause (the founder, and then the publisher) and Clifford Mishler (then the executive editor, and later president of the company) taught me a great deal about the true issues facing the coin hobby, and through the use of Clifford's raw materials on the American Revolution Bicentennial Commission's Coins & Medals Advisory Panel, I first learned of the need for circulating commemoratives—and the fight that the government would put up to prevent that singularly important action from taking place. Later, Burnett Anderson, a veteran news reporter, became Washington bureau chief for KP, and he was privy to many of the discussions about the circulating commemorative coin proposal, some of which he wrote about. His final illness and untimely death allowed me the brief respite of stepping back in time for several months to once again become KP's Washington correspondent, even as I had long since changed careers and become mayor of my own municipality of Fair Lawn, New Jersey, and a practicing lawyer in New York City. It also afforded me the opportunity to "cover" many of the events leading up to the successful conclusion of the legislative initiative, thanks to Dave Harper's confidence. Krause Publications has been supportive both in the publication of my columns and articles over the last 30 years and in providing photos of some of the commemorative pieces illustrated in this book. I appreciate its commitment to the coin hobby, and its assistance with this book.

The American Numismatic Association, the largest educational, non-profit organization of coin collectors in the world, has had a role in both the circulating commemorative coinage proposal and in what ultimately became this book. As the ANA legislative counsel (1981–82, 1983–1995), as a member of the ANA Board of Governors (1985–1995), and as the organization's president (1993–95), I did not operate in a vacuum, but relied on several staff members with whom I discussed legislative initiatives and reviewed congressional testimony for comment and advice, even (in some instances) to physically deliver bulky testimony to Washington. During my four years (1993–96) on the Citizens Advisory Committee, at least until my term of office as president ended, the ANA also involved itself in CCCAC activities, including the hosting of a historic meeting away from Washington (in Detroit, as part of the ANA convention that year) of the CCCAC and collectors. Some of this was reported in *The Numismatist,* ANA's monthly journal, edited by Barbara Gregory; others became grist for the publicity generated by Steve Bobbitt. Each is thanked for reviewing the text of speeches, testimonies, and even advocacy correspondence at the time. Bob Leuver, then ANA executive director, and formerly director of the Bureau of Engraving and Printing, also was essential to the success of the initiative, both from backing it in his appointive capacity and for overall guidance of the strategy that only a close Washington observer could suggest. Bob Hoge, ANA's museum curator, was particularly helpful in providing examples of past circulating commemorative coinage practice, and Lynn Chen, then ANA librarian, was resourceful in finding necessary backup and documentation to support the congressional testimony. Finally, Kathy Gotsch (as she was then known) was of immeasurable assistance in the simple mechanics of integrating the work of the ANA president with that of the ANA Board and the office of the executive director (where she was executive assistant and executive secretary). As you may have surmised, things worked out even better because we fell in love, and got married. This is the same Kathy who also is acknowledged elsewhere.

Beth Deisher, my editor at *Coin World* for many years, is acknowledged for her encouragement of my "Backgrounder" column (which ran for many years before having its scope changed to Law and Collectibles, a topic that grew too confining for me). A goodly number of my columns dealt with the circulating commemorative coinage theme. Beth was present at the July 1995 hearings offering her own view on the ills of modern commemorative coinage, but to her credit, and *Coin World*'s, even though she was not its originator, she has been a strong supporter of the State Quarters program.

There are a number of other individuals who provided me with ideas, drawings, or documents that ultimately found their way into this book. These include: Alan Stahl, Leslie Elam, Bob Korver, Jeri Hollinger, Teri Towe, Chuck Asay, Milt Priggee, Rep. Michael Castle, Elroy Young, Jason Russell, Wayne Pearson, LaVaughn Scott, Andrew Aslinger, Edward Ficht, Richard Lakatos, Kris Liaugminas, Michael White, and James Ruffin of the Office of Public Affairs, United States Mint HQ, Jon Turner of the Washington Mint (for State Quarter products), and Diane Wolf.

I am certain that I have left out in these acknowledgments individuals who were of immeasurable help and assistance. I am equally certain that future editions of this book will acknowledge the staffers of individual state commissions or groups who guided the design process and shared information. Some of them are mentioned by name elsewhere in the book, but all have my thanks.

The idea of a circulating commemorative has been around the hobby for decades, but frankly, good ideas are a dime a dozen. Far more rare is the ability to move an idea to reality, especially in the rough-and-tumble environment of Washington, D.C. From my vantage point, the lion's share of the credit for making the 50 States program a reality goes to David Ganz, for his persistence as an advocate, and Congressman Michael Castle for championing the proposal through Congress. David gradually persuaded me of the merits of the proposal, and we at the Mint, in turn, convinced Treasury and the Hill that it was doable. There are other claimants, to be sure, but the hobby owes a debt of gratitude to Congressman Castle and Mr. Ganz.

—PHILIP N. DIEHL,
DIRECTOR OF THE UNITED STATES MINT
(DECEMBER 11, 1998)

Reprinted by permission of *Numismatic News* (Krause Publications, Iola, Wisconsin).

David L. Ganz (L), the author, and (R) Philip Diehl, director of the Mint, at the July 1995 commemorative coinage hearing. At the time, I was president of the American Numismatic Association and also a member of the Citizens Commemorative Coin Advisory Committee. It marked the ninth time since 1974 that I had testified before Congress on coinage matters. I have known, and worked with, every Mint director since Eva Adams, who took office in 1961.

PROLOGUE

America's State Quarters already have their place in history.

Look in the Sunday supplement to your daily newspaper and you are likely to see a mail offer for the quarters that everyone is talking about.

Check your pocket change to see if you can find, and collect on the spot, a "finder's fee" of $500 for a Mint error that has been placed in circulation. (The error is hard to spot because the design is rotated 180 degrees; instead of being upside down, it is right side up.)

Seek out a more obvious Mint error where 10–15% of the design is off-center, caused by the Mint's rush to put hundreds of millions of pieces out into circulation throughout a 10-week production cycle. They're selling for hundreds of dollars to collectors.

Buy your proof sets from the Mint for $32, and find "perfect" or nearly perfect America's State Quarters. The certified version of some coins (privately encapsulated) is already selling for nearly the price of an entire proof set.

Check out your change drawer and see if you can find that uncirculated Delaware quarter that you set aside in 1999 out of pocket change. Coin dealers are already charging sophisticated coin collectors $1.75 for the Phila-delphia (P) or Denver Mint (D) specimens—an astonishing growth rate of 600% in a span of just 18 months. The expo-nential analysis (*see* Delaware Quarter chart) is promising and speaks of an upward trend-line for which the sky is the limit.

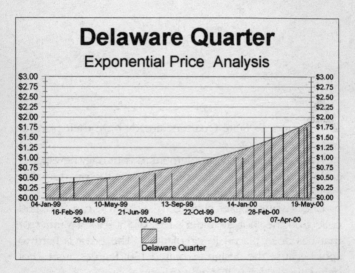

Compare these prices with the growth of Internet stocks on the NASDAQ, review the prices on the Dow Jones Indus-trial Average, and you start to get the idea that America's State Quarters are suddenly a hot topic, all across America.

They are the most widely collected new coin issue in a generation. There have been other first-issues in demand (the Lincoln cent of 1909, the Kennedy half dollar of 1964), but the sheer quantity of coins being minted (the average mintage is at least 800 million coins of the "P" and "D" Mints), and the number of known collectors (the U.S. Mint says that over 100 million Americans have been acquiring America's State Quarters), all suggest a long-term hit for this multiyear program. The State Quarters program is set to last until at least the year 2008, and more probably until the year 2009, if Congress, as expected, adds the District of Columbia, Puerto Rico, and several U.S. territories to the mix.

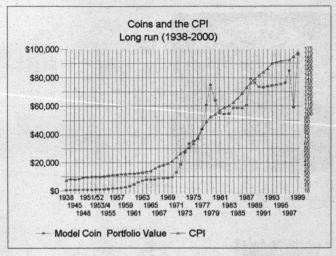

Coins and the CPI
Long run (1938-2000)

— Model Coin Portfolio Value — CPI

Rare coins have proven to be a good investment through the years (*see* the accompanying chart on coins and the CPI). No one can predict that State Quarters will fall into the same category, but the signs are all there.

This book is intended to be your Official Guide to America's State Quarters. You'll find out exciting information in this book about the brand-new error in which a coin die for the Sacagawea golden dollar was combined with the State Quarters' obverse—creating a great rarity in the process. This "mule" of two different designs, and denominations, is a major rarity and of such interest that it wound up as an Associated Press story as well as a television feature with Q. David Bowers appearing on nationwide television to show and tell about the coin found in ordinary pocket change.

It's also about merchandising, and the way that many new merchants are vending their wares—with philatelic-

Photo of Sacagawea dollar–State Quarter mule courtesy of Numismatic Guaranty Corporation (NGC).

Photo courtesy of The Washington Mint, Plymouth, Minnesota.

numismatic combinations being offered, State Quarters with enamel added, and many other coins and programs.

Relax and enjoy these coins as they come out every ten weeks for the next several years. Use this as an excuse to explore coin collecting if you've never tried it before; if you're already a collector, let it take you to new heights.

INTRODUCTION

Three shifts a day, seven days a week, the U.S. Mints at Philadelphia and Denver churn out America's quarters—coins destined to honor each of the states of the nation and, most likely, its territories and the District of Columbia. Fast forward a couple of days to a convenience store in New York City where a customer receives a new Massachusetts quarter, looks at the back with the Minuteman sentinel, and casually flips the coin over from the 12 o'clock position to the 6 o'clock position, only to find that George Washington is upside down. The coin is a mint error, a rotated die worth up to $500. The result of this is that the great chase to look at America's change has begun anew with nearly half the nation's population participating in the process.

Welcome to the New Age of American coin collecting, where every ten weeks, for at least ten years, a coin with a new design will leave the Mint for its rendevous with destiny. Most of the coins will not be errors—some of them will be, and that is why they are scarce and valuable—but each of them is part of an extraordinary series that began in 1999 and will collectively circulate for as long as there is American money.

These coins are legal tender—although there are other

collector versions of these coins that are never intended to reach circulation—and each has a face value of 25 cents, a quarter part of a dollar. You can use them to feed a parking meter, to make a down payment on a vending machine purchase, or in a hundred other ways where the design on the coin matters not a whit. That is what its legal-tender property endows it with. But the excitement of these coins goes well beyond a 25-cent face value, for even as the Mint sells these items by the $1,000 bagful, a secondary market has developed whereby even new issues are selling for double their face value or more as collector's items.

In the past, when the number of collectors was 2 or 3 million, or even 8 million—depending on what estimate you use—this didn't matter very much. There was always a sufficient supply to meet even high demand. Today, however, Mint statistics and marketing studies suggest persuasively that more than 140 million Americans—over 60% of the U.S. population—are actively collecting the 50-states quarters, and more than 85% of the country is aware that the coins are being produced in this manner.

How Successful Is the State Quarters Program?

Without question, this is the most ambitious and aggressive program that the U.S. Mint has ever undertaken—and its sole (but considerable) profit comes from the seigniorage, or difference between actual cost to manufacture and face value. This is nothing to sneeze at: The government will make profits well into the hundreds of millions of dollars each year. Deputy Mint Director John Mitchell disclosed to the House Banking subcommittee handling coinage matters on March 28, 2000, that U.S. Mint profits in 1999—largely fueled by the 50 State Quarters program—exceeded $1 billion.

If this unique, distinctive circulating commemorative

program had fallen flat, or been an also-ran instead of achieving success so early, it no doubt would be an orphan, but I would argue that its patrons, sponsors, and creators could nonetheless claim credit for a "good try" with an idea whose time had not yet come. It is doubtful, in such an instance, that anyone would have bothered to try to take credit for conceiving the program, or implementing it. There is no demand for progenitors of failed programs.

As it happens, the success of the State Quarters program knows almost no bounds. Consequently, it has a thousand fathers and mothers, each of whom qualifiedly, but unabashedly, claims credit for the idea of the year and the huge profits that the Mint is racking up. The program is so successful that the 50 State Quarters program has been trademarked by the Mint, and the marketplace simply adores the coins for the various ways that they can be sold and appreciate in value.

This is a program that goes beyond traditional coin collectors. *Parade* magazine, stuffer advertising, daily newspaper ads for a 50-state map that holds the coins, patents, copyrights, and trademarks all are part of the subsequent history of the 50 State Quarters program.

Although this was initiated as a 50 State Quarters program, there was almost immediate interest in expanding it to include the District of Columbia, Puerto Rico, and four American territories: Guam, American Samoa, the Virgin Islands, and the Northern Mariana Islands. Legislation was introduced in the 106th Congress to accomplish this.

Given the program's success, it seems obvious that before the end of the trail, it will be expanded to an 11th year with six more coins. For convenience, however, it is referred to as either the 50 State Commemorative Quarter Program, or simply America's State Quarters.

Why Collect State Quarters?

Three different factors make collecting America's Quarters so exciting. First, there is the random possibility of acquiring a mint error in change—and the instant profit that goes with finding such a coin. Second, there has been an increase in value for even the common coins in the series whose ten weeks in the sun have come and passed. For example, the Delaware quarter, depicting Caesar Rodney on horseback riding to sign the Declaration of Independence in Philadelphia, is already retailing for over $2.25 at this writing, even though it was first struck as recently as December 1998 and released during the first two months of 1999 (*see* Delaware Proofs chart).

The final reason is that coin collecting is fun, and it reminds us of history, economics, politics, religion, our nation's sociology, and its intellect. These all come together with coin designs that vary state-by-state, unified with a common obverse featuring our nation's first president, George Washington.

State Quarter Design Elements

Each of the coins in the series has a template. The obverse is identical, the reverse an ever-changing canvas whose top and bottom frame a different portrait every time. Significantly, all of the design elements, front and back (obverse and reverse), appear in a space of under 25 millimeters (24.6 millimeters, to be precise) utilizing a denomination whose history of service to its country dates back to 1796, a mere four years after the Mint was authorized by Congress on April 2, 1792.

Just what the coins contain is actually set down by law; only Congress has the power to coin money and regulate the value thereof (Article I, §8). And here, Congress was re-

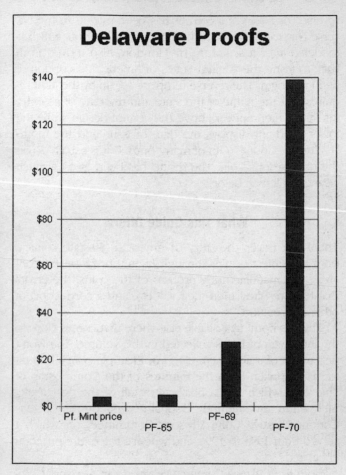

Delaware Proofs

quired to authorize the design twice. First, it set forth general parameters; when it found that these did not work, it allowed alteration of some elements: some previously required on the obverse were moved to the reverse, and vice versa.

Whereas the denomination usually appears on the

reverse (or back) of a coin, it has been moved to the obverse (or front), beneath the bust of Washington, which is modeled after a sculpture by Houdon. Also moved from back to front: the "United States of America" inscription of national origin. The reverse template set up by the Mint requires that the name of the state and the date of its entry into the Union appear above the central design while the lower quadrant displays the date of issue and the motto "E Pluribus Unum" (Out of many, one). Dates usually go on the obverse of a coin. The motto has been given a much cleaner look than before.

What This Guide Offers

This book traces the story of America's 50-state coinage from its earliest origins through its authorization by Congress, the manufacturing process of the coins, the errors that have resulted (and their values), and a cornucopia of other information.

There is nothing available elsewhere that comes close to the information that is collected in this volume. You won't find much of it anywhere else. For example, you'll find information taken from the minutes of the Commission of Fine Arts, which had a final say on all of the design elements. You also will find personal insights on the Citizens Commemorative Coin Advisory Committee, on which I served from 1993 to 1996, and whence the entire program emanated.

Both the Citizens Commemorative Coin Advisory Committee and the federal Commission of Fine Arts had important input on the design elements contained on each of the coins. The legislation surrounding America's State Quarters requires that the Fine Arts Commission review the designs, and there is almost always a modification suggested to make the designs artistically more pleasing. The Citizens

Commemorative Coin Advisory Committee has likewise made its mark on the reverse designs of the state commemoratives with modifications that have given them a more thematic approach.

Sometimes, it can be a technical suggestion, such as the matte finish on the map that is shown on the Massachusetts coin; other times, as in the case of the Delaware coin, it can be removing or altering lettering. Regardless, and overall, the contributions of each have made for a more artistically pleasing program—and that is important from a visual standpoint which, in turn, enhances collectibility. That a quarter taken from pocket change could have a value of $500 or more may seem astonishing; that new versions come on to the market every ten weeks is even more so.

For convenience, a template of a different sort is utilized to discuss the State Quarters designs. There are, as might be expected, certain common elements that coin collectors like to know about: what is depicted in the reverse design, what Mints have struck the coins, who is the sculptor of the obverse (William Cousins revised John Flanagan's original design from 1932) and reverse; what quantity was minted in regular quality, what number in proof, and what quantity in the silver version that is marketed to collectors.

The initial cost (whether 25 cents face value, or at a higher price from the Mint) is essential to know if you want to calculate appreciation in price since the time of issue. Quite naturally, there also is some basic information about the states, since this after all is a program about them and their history. Each coin bears the date that the given state ratified the U.S. Constitution (in the case of the 13 original states) or, in subsequent years, the date that it joined the Union.

Other portions of the template will include commentary on positions taken by the Commission of Fine Arts and the Citizens Commemorative Coin Advisory Committee. It is the intention of the author, and the publisher, for this to be a work in progress that is revised several times over the life of the program, adding information about designs, mintage figures, and price updates. That will clearly make this the definitive guidebook on the subject.

The hitherto unknown legal and legislative history of America's State Quarters program also is presented at length, along with a bibliographic essay to provide the reader with appropriate information and sources to consult for more information, should that be desired.

Being published so early in the program, this book should also provide guidance for states whose involvement isn't scheduled until the later years. If you want to know how to create a design and submit it to your governor, this book will tell you how to do it.

Mostly, this book is a labor of love about a program that seems destined to change the face of coin collecting and, in the process, provide an indelible, handheld record of American history that will stand for all time.

THE GENESIS
OF AMERICA'S
STATE QUARTERS

America's State Quarters are circulating the world over. Production began in December 1998 (with a Delaware coin bearing a 1999 date) and, in short order, they have captivated the public imagination.

Coin collecting was once an almost genteel hobby, sometimes referred to as the hobby of Kings (King Farouk of Egypt and King Victor Emanuel of Italy, to name two) and Presidents (John Adams, John Quincy Adams, and Franklin D. Roosevelt). The State Quarters program moved coin collecting from the hobby of between 3 and 5 million to one where more than 108 million Americans acknowledge that they are collecting the State Quarters coins.

Every ten weeks until at least the year 2008, the United States mints at Philadelphia and Denver intend to produce a series of new commemorative quarters that will circulate throughout the United States, and probably the world. All 50 states will be honored in the order in which they entered the Union.

Before the program is over in 2008, it is highly probable that the 50 states will be expanded, joined by Washington, D.C., Puerto Rico, the U.S. Virgin Islands, Guam, the Northern Mariana Islands, and American Samoa, making it a

56-coin-design program. This is certainly the largest and most ambitious commemorative coin program of any country, at any time in world history.

Delaware came first, both as a state to ratify the federal Constitution and as a commemorative coin in this program. The design recommended by its governor: a depiction honoring Caesar Rodney's historic 80-mile ride from Dover to Philadelphia, where he cast the decisive vote in favor of American independence from Great Britain in 1776.

That coin was first struck Dec. 7, 1998, in a ceremony at the Philadelphia Mint. The hydraulic presses doubly struck uncirculated specimens that were slightly more expressive in design than regular circulation strikes, but not quite proofs.

Next came the March 1999 striking of Pennsylvania's quarter, depicting an outline of the state, a keystone, and a Liberty figure. By May 10, 1999, New Jersey's coin depicting Washington crossing the Delaware River was introduced. That famous scene portrays the Christmas Eve crossing that surprised the mercenary Hessians in New Jersey in a rout for the Revolution.

About ten weeks after that, a Georgia coin showing a peach and a map of the state was produced, and before the end of the year, Connecticut's coin depicting the Charter Oak (the tree that hid the Royal Charter) followed. This theme, like many of those on the early coins, is steeped in both English and American history.

The success of the program was evident in its first weeks as 350 million pieces from the Philadelphia Mint and another 350 million pieces from the Denver Mint were produced of each coin type. The 700-million total yields the government a profit of 22 cents for every coin produced (or more than $150 million for each change of coin design). But the program proved so popular that by the time of the Connecticut issue, P-mint production was upped to 450 million, and 450 million Denver Mint coins were produced (the profit moves up to nearly $200 million). For 1999 alone, the Mint's profit—straight to the bottom line of reducing the national debt of the United States—amounts to $800 million. For the year 2000, it will be $1 billion or more. In 2000, more than 1.1 billion Massachusetts quarters were manufactured, and that was just the first of five issues.

The resulting coinage is a long way from what was originally contemplated, and even proposed, by the Citizens Commemorative Coin Advisory Committee, which began a drumbeat in 1993 that reached a crescendo at a Congressional coin hearing in the summer of 1995. What eventually emerged from a modest proposal to promote "our national ideals . . . and our esteem as a nation" grew into a proposal that was described as "the most tangible way to touch the lives of every American." Subsequent legislative history—how the Mint was required to first study the matter, then report back to Congress, and how three separate Congressional laws were required before it became reality—is well known to hobbyists (though it bears repeating for those who did not follow the issue closely).

What is less well known, however, is the inside maneuvering that went on in favor of the proposal, which ultimately was persuasive in turning around the position of the Treasury Department, the Mint, and Congress to favor circulating commemorative coinage.

An enterprising politician once said that "Victory has a thousand fathers, but defeat is an orphan." So, too, America's State Quarters program has a growing paternity with an ever-larger list of individuals who claim to have originated the idea, and to have single-handedly brought it to fruition. What actually happened is far more subtle, and there is more than enough credit to spread around.

Purpose of Commemoratives

American commemorative coinage began its long history in 1892 as part of the Columbian Exposition in Chicago. The coins were sold at a premium over their face value and intended primarily for collectors of memorabilia, not coin collectors, since there were millions of them made and hardly more than a handful of true coin collectors in the United States at the time.

From 1892 until 1954, the U.S. Mint produced 144 different commemorative coins in silver (when you count all of the dates, mint marks, and designs) in three denominations: one 25-cent coin, a silver dollar, and the rest 50-cent pieces. There were also nearly a dozen gold coins of various sizes and denominations.

Commemorative coins abused the purpose of coinage, but served a salutary purpose: commemoration and raising of funds for various groups and endeavors. That proved its undoing, and by 1930, President Herbert Hoover vetoed a commemorative coin bill passed by Congress. That set the stage for vetoes by all succeeding presidents through Dwight D. Eisenhower, though some measures made their way through.

The story of America's commemorative coinage is worthy of a book in and of itself. By coincidence, I wrote that book, *The Official Guide to U.S. Commemorative Coins* (Bonus Books, 1999) recently. Without elaborating extensively (because it takes up a full chapter in my earlier book), the commemorative coinage system of the 1930s and 1940s became so abused that it was shut down in 1954. The Treasury Department was so opposed that a generation later, when it should have been obvious that America's Bicentennial should be commemorated with circulating commemorative coins, the Treasury Department actively opposed the measure—though it allowed that noncirculating coins might be acceptable.

It's a fascinating story about how one person, Mint Director Mary T. Brooks, turned around a government department to sponsor noncirculating coin legislation, and how another person, John Jay Pittman, then president of the American Numismatic Association, persuaded Congress that a circulating quarter dollar that became the Colonial drummer boy coin, belonged in the mix. By another remarkable coincidence, I wrote a book about that, too, a quarter century ago, entitled *14 Bits: A Legal and Legislative History of America's Bicentennial Coins* (Three Continents Press, 1976).

The State Quarters program of 1999–2008 comes directly from the lessons learned from the earlier commemorative efforts as well as the Bicentennial program of 1975–76. I can say this authoritatively, because when I drafted my recommendations to the Citizens Commemorative Coin Advisory Committee and to the House coinage subcommittee, the facts from those days were never far from my mind.

Lessons Learned to Be Applied to State Quarters

Lessons learned from Bicentennial coin sales have become part of the legislative process and, ultimately, enshrined in the current silver proof coin program that augments the regular proof set program that the Mint has promoted since 1950. By my reckoning, at least six key lessons were derived from the Bicentennial circulating coin program and the numismatic products that it spawned:

- First, it was a mistake to produce a fixed number of coins (45 million silver pieces, split among three denominations), rather than establish a maximum and produce only as many as there was demand for. This was particularly painful, because hundreds of thousands of silver proofs and silver uncirculated Bicentennial coin issues sat in mildewed bags. Many eventually had to be melted because they had suffered damage and were unsalable.

• Second, the Mint learned the marketing ratio that is preferred by collectors: proofs, overwhelmingly, over the identical uncirculated coins.

• Third, it witnessed the usefulness of a copper-nickel–clad commemorative coin that circulated. Jack Ahr's Colonial drummer boy, a quarter century after the last coin was placed into circulation, still can be found as a permanent reminder of the Bicentennial.

• Fourth, without special interests benefiting from the merchandising of the program, it could nonetheless be a highly successful endeavor—and there could be considerable involvement of the community at large in the program.

• Fifth, a wide-open design competition, however interesting, produces only a small percentage of useful designs—and a high percentage of those entering did so for a variety of reasons that had little to do with artistic ability.

• Finally, the lesson that should have been learned either hasn't been, or has been ignored. That is that absent some assistance to the marketplace, the price of the commemoratives cannot be sustained once interest in the program moves on.

When Treasury Secretary George Shultz, who had previously been director of the Office of Management and Budget (OMB), and served as Secretary of Labor in the Nixon Administration, signed off on the transmittal letter in March 1973, no one could have predicted the eventual result. Indeed, by the time that Shultz became Secretary of State in the Reagan Administration in 1982, a U.S. Olympic commemorative program was about to become one of the most successful merchandising programs in direct-mail history. That was a long way from the minds of the framers when the original legislation was proposed in the winter of 1973.

First of the more recent commemorative coin bills began when Rep. Doug Barnard, D-Ga., a member of the House coinage subcommittee since its inception, decided that the 250th anniversary of the birth of George Washington merited a special effort on the part of the Mint. A staff member who happened to be a coin collector guided him.

No one thought the proposal had a ghost of a chance, least of all Washington insiders, because of the adamant opposition that the Treasury Department in general, and the Mint in particular, had toward commemorative coins. In Treasury's view coinage was for circulation, not for amusement or commemoration. It argued that increased counterfeiting was a possibility with commemorative coins, and it denounced private profits being made as constituting a "misuse of the coinage system."

Casting aside the opinions of the past, U.S. Treasurer Angela M. ("Bay") Buchanan (sister of Patrick Buchanan, a onetime White House speech writer who subsequently ran for president several times) came out foursquare in favor of the Washington commemorative piece—and almost immediately, plans started to hatch for other events.

First of those following the Washington 90% silver half dollar was the Los Angeles Olympic coin program, consisting of two silver dollars of traditional size and weight plus a gold eagle. That was followed by the Statue of Liberty coin program with gold, silver, and copper-nickel coins. The Constitution program of a silver dollar and $5 gold piece then followed.

By 1992, issuance of non-circulating U.S. commemorative coinage had exploded out of control. These were special

coins, intended primarily for collectors and souvenir seek-
ers, produced by the U.S. Mint with a legal-tender value, but
never intended for circulation.

Coins honoring Columbus's 500th anniversary (three
different denominations), the 25th Olympiad (three different coin designs), and the White House Bicentennial were
authorized by Congress, as other bills were introduced. It
became almost impossible to deal with, something that I
predicted back in July 1987, writing as a contributing editor
to *COINage* magazine.

I wrote:

> What really remains as a problem, however, is decid-
> ing what new coin issues ought to be produced by
> the Mint—in other words, making the initial recom-
> mendation as to which events are to be commemo-
> rated, and which more properly should be ignored,
> or subject to national medals.
>
> National medals, once the be-all, and end-all (from
> 1954 to 1980, they were the only real chance that
> most groups had) have now fallen into eclipse. One
> benefit that they did have, though, was that they
> were a good catchall for ideas, and offered a large size
> for attractive designs.
>
> Determining what commemorative coin pro-
> grams ought to be created should not be left in the
> hands of Chief Justice Burger, however well inten-
> tioned (or even correct) his assertion that the Bill of
> Rights is America's legacy to the world.
>
> Nor should it be left in the hands of Congressman
> Annunzio, whose efforts have in fact revitalized the
> coinage program of the U.S. Mint and made it world-
> class in terms of competing with other countries'
> commemorative programs.
>
> The reason for this was well stated by the late

sculptor Ralph Menconi, then a member of the
American Revolution Bicentennial Commission's
Coins and Medals Advisory Panel, which ultimately
suggested that a distinctive numismatic commemoration of the Bicentennial be done with several
coins.

Toward an Advisory Committee

At the 1972 [Coin and Medals] Advisory Panel [of
the Bicentennial Commission] meeting at which time
the concept of multiple coins were discussed, Menconi criticized Congressional involvement in the design process, stating "every congressman . . . is an
artist. . . . Going with three coins may be insolvable.
You need two Michelangelos and a Botticelli."
   A better answer, it would seem, would be the
creation of a citizens advisory panel to make formal
recommendations to the Mint, and to the Treasury
Department, and to coordinate efforts with the Fine
Arts Commission.

Eventually, this became a legislative reality. *Coin World*'s
editor, Beth Deisher, shares her observations of the 1992
law signed by President George Bush, but hardly his
initiative:

If you check the record and with Rep. Esteban E.
Torres, D-Calif., you will find that the Bush Administration had little or nothing to do with the creation of
the CCCAC. True, President Bush did sign the legislation into law. However, Torres was sponsor of the reform legislation. His staff (Roddey Young) drafted the
language from his notes of a session that included
Torres, Young, and me. I had requested a meeting

with Torres for the purpose of an interview (story published in *Coin World*) about the proliferation of commemorative proposals before his committee (he was the new chairman of the subcommittee). He and Young had obviously done their homework and commented specifically on an editorial I had written that suggested a commission or committee similar to what the Postal Service has for stamps. After the interview was complete, the three of us spent more than an hour talking exclusively about the scope of such a committee, the types of background and experience its members should have, terms of service, etc. I presumed the topic would be the subject of a public hearing at some later date. A couple of months later, when the reform legislation had been put together as an omnibus bill, Roddey called and had a couple of points he wanted to clarify. He was referring to the notes from our meeting. It was at that time I learned they had drafted a separate title and were creating the CCCAC within legislation they felt sure would pass.

The point here is not to get personal credit, but rather to point out that a Democratic chairman of the subcommittee, Esteban E. Torres, initiated the CCCAC. Had it not been for Torres, I do not believe the CCCAC would have been formed. David Ryder did nothing to implement the CCCAC. (He was still angry that a Democrat [Alan Cranston] had held up his Senate confirmation as Mint Director.) It wasn't until Philip Diehl came into office and understood the usefulness of the CCCAC that implementation got under way.

If and when a definitive history of the CCCAC is done, Torres should get the credit for its creation. Not the Bush Administration.

Congress Acts Even Before
the Advisory Committee Meets

Even as the Citizens Commemorative Coin Advisory Committee was slated to meet in mid-December 1993, seemingly chartered by Congress to limit non-circulating commemorative coin issues, Congress authorized five new commemorative coin programs to be issued in 1994. Coins honoring Thomas Jefferson, the U.S. Capitol, and various military matters created 10 new coins (in proof and uncirculated qualities) to go alongside the existing six-coin World Soccer Cup commemorative coin issues. Waiting in the wings were still more commemoratives, namely those already authorized in 1992 to commemoratve the Civil War battlefields, together with the Olympic issues scheduled for 1995–96.

Altogether, before the Citizens Advisory Committee had even met, there were eight different commemorative coins struck and sold by the Mint in two different conditions in 1994. This would then be closely followed by three different designs for the Civil War battlefields, in 1995, sold together with eight Olympic coin designs also struck in proof and uncirculated. For 1996, eight more Olympic coin designs were authorized. These moves came as Congress also debated passage of the Brady gun control bill, causing at least one hobby leader to remark that passage of the bill was unnecessary because collectors had already been killed by the onslaught of new coins.

Although the new programs had relatively modest mintages contemplated, the primary purchasers of the coins still were the nation's coin collectors, who had been the principal purchasers in the past of every major coin program except that honoring the centennial of the Statue of Liberty. All told, in 1994, 1995, and 1996, if a collector at the time had wanted to buy all of the available current-year proof and uncirculated commemorative coin issues, that

would have come to a total of 27 different designs (and
54 total coins), or about a third of all the 144 silver pieces
produced from 1892 to 1954 in all dates, mint marks, and
varieties.

Programs approved in November 1993 included three
honoring military veterans, one honoring the bisesquicentennial of the birth of Thomas Jefferson, and one honoring
the Capitol building itself. They passed in the wee hours of
the morning in vintage Washington style. Since President
Clinton had vetoed no legislation in his first year in office,
passage was assured.

Approved were up to 500,000 silver dollars honoring
prisoners of war; up to 500,000 silver dollars commemorating the 10th anniversary of the Vietnam Veterans
Memorial, and 500,000 silver dollars honoring American
servicewomen. Also authorized were up to 600,000 Jefferson silver dollars and 500,000 silver dollars honoring the
bicentennial of the Capitol. All of these coins would carry a
pricing surcharge designed to benefit a worthy cause.

Significantly, and relevant to the future agenda of the
Citizens Advisory Committee, the legislation also contained
a non-binding "Sense of Congress" resolution that claimed
that there were too many commemorative coins being authorized for the marketplace to absorb, and directing that
Congress approve no more than two programs each year
unless the newly constituted Citizens Advisory Committee
on Coins certified that there was a compelling need.

Hearings on most of the legislative proposals were held
Nov. 10, 1993, before the House Banking subcommittee
on Consumer Credit and Insurance, which had jurisdiction
over coinage matters. The subcommittee previously handling this was Consumer Affairs and Coinage. The committee chairman, Rep. Joseph P. Kennedy, Jr., D-Mass., scheduled
the hearing after all of the bills, but the Capitol commemo-

rative proposal received more than 218 co-sponsors, a majority in the House of Representatives.

Under the rules of the parent Banking Committee, no hearing on commemorative coinage matters could be scheduled unless a majority of the House had already signed on to the legislation. The theory was that this would ensure its eventual passage, though this is not always the case, since co-sponsors can change their votes at a later time.

Kennedy's opening remarks in the form of a prepared statement excoriated sponsors who were seeking to flood the market with commemorative coins, and gave no hint that less than a fortnight later, both the House and Senate would send those proposals on to President Clinton for certain signature. Politics was obviously the impetus, and what propelled each of the proposals toward passage. The military-related proposals had the strong backing of Rep. Sonny Montgomery, D-Miss., chairman of the House Veterans Affairs Committee, where Kennedy also served.

It is hard for members of Congress to resist the appeal of backing a commemorative coin package honoring the servicemen and women who were in the Armed Forces, if only because there are so many of them who are potential voters, if not coin purchasers.

In the two weeks following the hearing at which Kennedy appeared to oppose the commemorative package, he changed his mind—no doubt influenced by the events that showed an overwhelming majority of his colleagues favored passage. He introduced the legislation in the form of a single joint bill that covered all of the ground. The identical version went forth in the Senate, where Sen. Robert Byrd, D-W.Va., former majority leader and then president pro tempore of the Senate, tacked on the Capitol commemorative coin bill.

Overall, the legislation did a substantial injustice to the

coinage system, making the Mint strike the Thomas Jefferson bisesquicentennial coins in 1994 but bearing a 1993 date. Proceeds benefited the restoration of Monticello.

Debate on the floor of the House on the proposal proved interesting. After briefly reciting the history and purpose of the various bills, Kennedy got to the matter at hand:

> During my brief service as chairman of the subcommittee that is responsible for coinage matters, I have learned more than I ever thought there was to learn about coins.
>
> Thanks to the efforts of the coin collecting community, I have become aware of the need to reform the commemorative coin process. This legislation attempts to respond to their concerns. It expresses the sense of the Congress that no more than two coin programs should be enacted in any one year.
>
> [In particular, he continued] This limit will help to ensure that the coin market does not become saturated, so that coins like the ones we are voting on today will continue to be bought by coin collectors, who purchase an average of 90 percent of all commemorative coins.

Rep. Al McCandless, R-Calif., ranking minority member of the House coinage subcommittee, added his thoughts on why limitations on commemoratives were "absolutely essential to ensuring the continued success of commemorative coin programs."

"Congress should not pass enabling legislation for more than two commemorative coin programs per year unless otherwise advised by the Citizens Commemorative Coin Advisory Committee," he declared. Explaining the origins of that group, McCandless noted that "The committee was established in the 102nd Congress to comment on the selection of subjects and designs for commemorative coins." As to its real rationale, he postulated that "this provision recognizes the limited manufacturing capability of the Mint and the limited purchasing power of those who are interested and purchase commemorative coins."

Meanwhile, in the Senate, the proposal was also advancing—together with a request from the Mount Rushmore group, whose commemorative program had been approved by Congress several years earlier, to receive an additional portion of the proceeds from the surcharges and purchase prices paid. Rumors were rife of other members tacking a Christmas tree of amendments onto the legislation for their own favorite coin proposals. But in the final analysis, only Senator Byrd had the sway to add a coin—for the benefit of the U.S. Capitol, which he held near and dear.

As Congress rushed toward its annual Thanksgiving recess and adjournment for the year, that spelled the end of David Ryder's tenure as director of the U.S. Mint. Given a rare recess appointment by President Bush, he was permitted by law to serve only until the recess of the next Congress.

Though the Citizens Advisory Committee had been created on his watch, he had stalled on implementing it, using "austerity" in government as a rationale. As a result, he had been frozen out of the process while a career civil servant, Eugene Essner, ran the Mint on a day-to-day basis as deputy director. A political appointee, Philip N. Diehl (formerly chief of staff to Senator, and then Secretary of the Treasury, Lloyd Bentsen) became executive deputy director, superseding Essner. Diehl would ultimately make the suggested appointments to the Citizens Advisory Committee to Bentsen, who approved the nominations.

All of this had the practical effect of giving the Mint interim leadership but the equally regrettable result of leaving

Deputy Director Gene Essner to defend the Mint and oppose the new legislative proposals. He failed.

Further complicating the picture was a proposal on the boards to restructure the way that the Mint operates. Under the Clinton Administration plan, the positions of superintendent of the Mint at Philadelphia, Denver, San Francisco, and West Point would be abolished. A career civil servant would handle management. Also slated for abolition was the post of chief engraver, which has existed since passage of the original Mint Act of April 2, 1792. The post had been vacant since Elizabeth Jones resigned in a dispute with Mint Director Donna Pope several years earlier.

Potentially crippling was the mandate to produce all of the commemorative coins in both uncirculated and proof versions; the Mint was also directed to market the military coin commemoratives individually as well as in one or more sets. In addition to the new coins Congress had authorized, the Mint's mandate was to manufacture six different designs in proof and uncirculated for the World Soccer Cup bearing a 1994 date, and a host of other coins.

Surcharges were imposed erratically and included $1 on clad issues for the World Cup, $7 for World Cup silver dollars, and $35 for World Cup gold. The Jefferson silver dollar had a $10 surcharge, as did the military coins. The Capitol silver dollar surcharge was $15. Totaled, this meant that a coin collector who wanted to have each of the coins in uncirculated and proof would have to pay a coin collector's tax (surcharge) totaling $181 on top of the suggested selling prices.

The $3,500 figure for total cost of all these coins was, and is, about double the amount that typical collectors spend each year on all of their coin acquisitions, including those from dealers. However unwittingly, the Mint had set the stage for a fundamental change in the way that people collect coins. Instead of striving for one of each date, mint

The Citizens Commemorative Coin Advisory Committee meets at U.S. Mint headquarters in Washington. Left side of table (front): Reed Hawn, Elvira (Lisa) Clain-Stefanelli, Elsie Sterling Howard, Thomas V. Shockley, III; John Mitchell, deputy director of the Mint; Philip Diehl, director (front at rear). Right side: front, Charles Atherton, rear Dan Hoffman. Missing: the cameraman, author David L. Ganz. Newsman Burnett Anderson is at side, above Elsie Howard.

mark, and method of strike (proof or uncirculated at the present time), those who choose to purchase the commemorative coin extravaganza are forced to make a choice. For the time being, most choose proof.

That, in turn, has set in place an anomaly: The Mint strikes more proofs than uncirculated coins (and charges more, because they cost more to produce), yet the less expensive uncirculated issues have a greater overall market potential because of their lower mintages.

With this as a background, in early December 1993, Philip Diehl started making telephone calls to individuals he thought would make good members of the Citizens Advisory Committee. One of those calls was to me. At the time, I was in my twelfth year as a member of the board of directors of the Industry Council for Tangible Assets, and my eighth year as a member of the Board of Governors of the American Numismatic Association (in the first year of a two-year term as president of the not-for-profit organization chartered by Congress back in 1912 for the purpose of advancing the science of numismatics). I accepted with alacrity.

I cannot, of course, speak for the other members of the Advisory Committee. They read their agenda books prepared by the Mint, and they applied the knowledge that they had about coinage (or what they learned). My approach was different, and perhaps that is because I had a different agenda. As a writer in the field for more than 30 years, and as president of the largest national association of coin collectors in the world, my view was (and had been for some time) that contemporary commemorative coinage could avoid the abuses of the past only if there were no surcharges imposed on the sales, or no beneficiaries for the largesse of the program involved—and if there were circulating coins. It was my feeling that it was absolutely essential to "grow" the Mint's market by introducing circulating commemorative coinage so that it would appeal to those on limited income (mainly young adults and seniors) as well as children—all of whom were marketing segments that the Mint had all but ignored (perhaps justifiably) because of high product cost. Furthermore, a circulating commemorative program would open up wholly different marketing segments to the Mint, and wind up being highly beneficial to not only the manufacturer, but coin collecting in general—and eventually help to increase membership in numismatic organizations such as the American Numismatic Association and local coin clubs.

Even though I had reported on, and was familiar with, the legislative history of the Citizens Advisory Committee, the general mantra was that the Advisory Committee was supposed to deal only with the problem of non-circulating legal-tender commemorative coins, i.e., those that the Mint had recently been producing, and which then were facing a crisis. This seemed to be a prevailing view at the Mint, and certainly with the individuals who were initially appointed to the committee.

My view was different, however, and to get there, I fell back on my training as a practicing lawyer to look at the text of the statute authorizing the Advisory Committee, to see precisely what Congress specified, and then to see if the envelope could be stretched to support a different meaning.

The applicable section of law is found in Title 31 of the U.S. Code (Money and Finance) in section 5135.

From my reading of the law, there were several areas that could be utilized—if there was an effective advocate—to advance a slightly different cause. First was in subparagraph (b)(1)(A) of the title, which required a designation of the event to be commemorated. If the event was not related to a "funding" mission, then it might be possible to remove one of the key objections. The second related to subparagraph (b)(2)(B) to make recommendations as to the mintage level for any commemorative coin recommended (from the earlier paragraph). This became the no-brainer: Pick a topic, and then set the mintage at 350, 500, or 750 million pieces—enough to make sure that the coin would truly circulate, just as the Bicentennial coins did a generation earlier.

To be certain that the recommendations were not received perfunctorily, the statute required that the theme be conveyed in a report to Congress together with the mintage level and, most important, "the committee's reasons for such recommendations."

A briefing book for the meeting, prepared by the Mint staff, arrived a week or so before and I had pored over its contents, which consisted of about an inch-full of papers in nine separate tabs that had been placed in a white spiral binder.

Inside the binder, I covered my top page with just two notes of reminder to me: The first said "Don't forget camera," to be sure that there would be a photo record of the event, and "circulating comm. cn.," for circulating commemorative coin, which I intended from the first meeting to bring to the committee's attention.

Also inside the binder was a proposed "Charter for the Citizens Commemorative Coin Advisory Committee," which had a different view of the job responsibilities of the group, except that it specified in broad language that the committee was to comment on "any commemorative" that it recommended, a mandate I took very broadly.

All of us introduced ourselves at that first meeting, and I used that opportunity, as I did with each successive meeting over the next couple of days, to make a point: The committee's mandate was to cover all commemorative coins, and the starting point for that was a circulating commemorative coin that had no cost but its face value.

Citizens Advisory Committee Participates

I was honored to be appointed as one of the first members on that new Citizens Commemorative Coin Advisory Committee, pleased to move from attacking the problem in print as a columnist first for *Numismatic News,* later *Coin World,* and as a contributing editor to *COINage* magazine, to becoming a part of the solution—which in my view then, earlier, and now, can be summarized as trying to help the Mint "grow the market."

At the panel's first meeting in Washington on Dec. 14, 1993, the Mint and some of the committee members tried to define the mandate of the group as safely deciding how to lower mintages of existing non-circulating legal-tender issues and set design themes for the future which would be more limited than the present. As I stated earlier, I did my research and concluded that the committee's mandate was broader, and that Congress intended—and expected—innovative proposals that would help the Mint's commemorative coin program, as it was then constituted, and as it might be authorized in the future. Sitting in the seventh-floor conference room at the Mint headquarters then located at 633 Third St., N.W., in Washington, I faced colleagues with differing views, some of whom thought that my idea for a circulating commemorative coin was well outside the committee's mandate.

From my many years of involvement in organized numismatics, I had long known Elvira (Lisa) Clain-Stefanelli, executive director of the national numismatic collection at the Smithsonian Institution; I was also acquainted casually with Reed Hawn, a Texas businessman who collected coins with a passion and a fine eye for value. I had previously met Charles Atherton, secretary of the Fine Arts Commission, whose historical and artistic expertise has been an important (but hitherto unrecorded and underappreciated) component in coinage design for many years. The unknowns to me were Thomas Shockley, a utilities executive from Texas; Dan Hoffman, then a 16-year-old from South Carolina, and Elsie Sterling Howard, a community activist from Miami.

From the Mint side of the equation, I had just become acquainted with Philip Diehl, then executive deputy director of the Mint (who had been announced, but not yet confirmed, as director). The Mint staff consisted of many people with whom I was more than casually acquainted over a period of more than 30 years, dating to the time that I started working as a "stringer" and later Washington correspondent for *Numismatic News,* during the time that I was in college at Georgetown University's School of Foreign Service (1969–73). Though members of the Mint staff were friends, they were also schooled in the tradition that generally opposed commemorative coins and, not that many years earlier, had been nearly unanimous in opposing circulating Bicentennial commemorative coinage.

Nonetheless, as part of my introductory remarks to the new Citizens Commemorative Coin Advisory Committee, I made a formal recommendation that the committee take its mandate from Congress seriously, explore the idea of circulating commemorative coins, and make an affirmative recommendation in its annual report to Congress favoring such a proposal. It was a drumbeat that I did not stop during the three years that I served on the committee.

Initial response to the proposal was less than lukewarm. It was downright chilly. My notes from that first meeting held at the Mint headquarters in Washington reflected significant opposition from Philip Diehl. "It's not within our mandate," was the substance of what he said at that first meeting, a view echoed by Tom Shockley, who was a lover of Buffalo nickels and had been a coin collector for many years. This appeared to me to be based on advice from longtime Mint staffers who still recalled 50 years of opposition within the Treasury Department to commemorative coins. This was useful, I remember thinking, because an executive may initially take up and agree with a staff position, listen to the merits of a sound proposal, and change his mind—whereupon the staff's recommendations themselves can change.

But on that cold December day it seemed colder, indeed frosty, and looked like it was going nowhere. The official "Minutes of the Regular Meeting of the Citizens Commemorative Coin Advisory Committee, December 13, 1993 at 9:00 a.m." merely recited laconically: "The possibility of producing a commemorative coin for general circulation was also discussed."

As its primary (and initially only) advocate, the discussion was my initiative and the opposition was that of the Mint and my colleagues. The next meeting of the Advisory

Committee was slated for February 1994 in Washington, but there were two interim telephone meetings. Somewhere along the line Philip Diehl got so tired of hearing about circulating commemorative coins that he suggested that if I felt strongly about it, a report could be presented to the committee at its next meeting. In Washington-speak, that's sometimes a kiss of death. Without staff, without advisers, and without assistance—and the Advisory Committee members were on their own—a report that is requested is often not written. Or, if it is, it becomes something that is commissioned, tossed aside, never read, and forgotten. The lack of professional staffing aside from a Mint liaison was only partially troublesome; fortunately, my law partners, associates, and my secretary gave me the necessary backup that allowed its timely completion.

Also fortunate: The other members of the Committee didn't know that Washington rule. And Philip Diehl, as he immersed himself into the subject, learning about coin collecting and commemorative coins, came to recognize— long before his staff did—that circulating commemoratives were essential to the long-term survival of the Mint's for-profit programs.

For the Feb. 22, 1994, meeting, several presentations were slated for the afternoon. First was the Mint's outreach program with a dynamite educational video program. Then came an invitation that I had tendered, as president of the American Numismatic Association, to have the first public outreach—a CCCAC meeting at the ANA convention in Detroit that summer. Dan Hoffman then was to present a discussion on a young collector's views on commemorative coin themes, while at 3 p.m., my presentation was slated for "concepts and options for a circulating commemorative coin."

During the month of January 1994, I worked on a report that covered commemorative coinage in several different contexts, the most important of which was how circulating commemoratives took their place beside non-circulating legal-tender coins. By Jan. 27, a 5,000-word report was completed and shipped off to the Mint for inclusion in the binder going to each of the committee members. There were 42 separately numbered footnotes in the report and some illustrations that were thought to be helpful to those who were not experienced in the history of commemorative coinage. The opportunity to make a report and oral presentation to the committee was what really excited me, because that made it plain that the idea would be the subject of debate, discussion, and possibly action.

Years of attending hearings at the Senate and House Banking committees as a witness testifying, as well as in the capacity of a reporter, taught me that a written report should be complete, but that an oral presentation should be quick, precise, and to the point.

> At our last meeting, I reiterated the importance in my view of making a fundamental change in the way that commemorative coins are thought of, and are issued. I brought this point home several times because I believe, sincerely, that if we are to meet our mandate, it is essential that we consider not only themes for coin designs, but also how those coins will be marketed.
>
> Phil Diehl was kind enough to ask me to formalize my views and commit them to a presentation to you. I have already sent to you a 5,000-word essay on the subject, and I don't think it is necessary for me to read that formal presentation to you.
>
> Instead, I'd like to take just about five minutes of your time to briefly discuss the issue as I see it, and to tell you why I believe that the subject of circulating commemorative coins is within our statutory mandate.

More important, I want to tell you why it is essential that our report at the end of 1994 advise the Secretary [of the Treasury], and the Congress, that it is our view as a committee that circulating commemorative coinage (with collector versions as a bonus) is essential if the next dozen years are to be as fruitful as the past dozen have for coin issues.

If we suggested that 1.5 billion quarters . . . be produced commemorating some subject or the other, it would be obvious enough that the only way that this could be absorbed in the marketplace would be by making the coin a circulating one.

So whether we proceed directly or indirectly, it is my view that we must ultimately cross that Rubicon and systematically back circulating coins as a means of saving commemorative coins from themselves.

Minutes later, I wound toward my conclusion by mentioning Canada's 10-province and two-territory program, which had been a significant success. "The circulating counterpart did not detract from the sale of the collector coins," I said, "It heightened the interest. The bottom line to this is profit to the Mint, and more new coins to the general public."

I concluded by saying:

It would be naive of me to suggest that only commemoratives worthy of circulating in pocket change ought to be produced by the United States Mint, or indeed, any world minting authority. However, as the evidence shows, there is a strong history in many countries outside the United States that utilizes coinage as a medium of expression to the population as a whole for certain commemorative themes that are deemed worthy (by the issuing authorities) of seeking popular support.

I suggest to you as a guidepost that the Citizens Commemorative Coin Advisory Committee adopt as a recommendation for a resolution providing that at least one (1) coin issue each year be produced as a circulating commemorative coin issue; that a sufficient quantity be produced to effectively circulate the coin; that a special collector version (in precious metal, as a proof issue; or in base metal, as a proof issue, or both) be produced; and that any design or theme chosen be of a character of sufficient importance as an event to warrant its introduction into commerce as a circulating commemorative coin.

At each meeting of the Citizens Commemorative Coin Advisory Committee that was held that year—and there were five or six more—the topic of circulating commemorative coinage came from me with repetitive regularity. For a time, it was like a traveling salesmen's convention where jokes are identified by number, to save time. I simply had to ask for the floor and say "circulating commemorative coin" to hear the groan. I continued to advocate this view at each CCCAC meeting held throughout the year. Philip Diehl, reflecting on this in an interview with another reporter, Kari Stone, editor of the monthly *COINage* magazine, called me "Johnny One-Note" on that subject.

Near the end of the government's fiscal year, as the committee met to consider its annual report to Congress, I drafted a proposed chapter that was faxed to each member strongly advocating that we propose a circulating commemorative coin. Sent Sept. 18, 1994, my fax to each committee member suggested that we state that "In making this report to Congress, the Committee does so with the recommendation that at least one commemorative coin, every two years, be produced in sub-

stantial quantity, and utilized in circulation, as well as being offered to collectors."

But as the year moved on, as members of the committee
broke bread together before and during each meeting, the
idea began to catch on for all the right reasons. It was eco-
nomically beneficial to the Mint and the country, and more
important, worked to support the Mint's other programs.

Annual Report to Congress

The next real fight was the test of the Annual Report, the
first that the committee was charged with developing for
Congress. It was drafted for us by the Mint's helpful professional staff after listening to our discussions and views.

To a point, it was accurate; but at a fall meeting, the committee had agreed that we would formally recommend to
Congress the creation of circulating commemorative coinage. The Mint staff simply omitted it, perhaps unintention-
ally, perhaps because members of the staff opposed it.
Some Washington turf battles are won by attrition, some by
hoping that small details will slip through the cracks—and
some by simply trying to gloss over differences between
staff and committee members.

I pounced on this omission at the next committee meeting and drew my line in the sand: Either the committee's
report made favorable mention of circulating commemorative coinage, as we had agreed to, or I would file a formal
dissent in the report which would state my position explic-
itly, and at length, together with a rebuttal of the committee's position. It would also be apparent, in such case, that
my one-year term on the Advisory Committee would come
to an end, with the appointment simply not renewed.
Those who do not go along don't stay long either.

Fortunately for me, Philip Diehl had become a convert,
even if his staff had not, and ordered a rewrite. I volunteered

to do a draft, and initially worked up 500 words or so as to why it was worthwhile, and why it would work. I ultimately edited this to 250 words and presented it to our group.

My draft began:

> The Committee strongly endorses issuance by the Mint of a circulating commemorative coin. Coinage is the most tangible way to touch the lives of every American. Circulating coinage promotes our national ideals, builds pride in being an American and our esteem as a nation, and also reaches millions of visitors whose lives each coin touches.
>
> A circulating commemorative coin is a regular, legal-tender coin issued with a distinctive design, but without surcharge. It is used in circulation. All profits from the sale of the coins go to the Treasury as an off-budget item.
>
> Congress directed by the Act of Mar. 4, 1931, ch. 505, 46 Stat. 1523, that the Bicentennial of George Washington's birth be remembered with a circulating commemorative coin, and the quarter dollar designed for that remains in circulation to this day.
>
> In 1973, Congress enacted Pub. L. 93–127, 87 Stat. 456 (Oct. 18, 1973) which caused a commemorative quarter, half dollar, and dollar reverse to be issued by the Mints, which replaced, for 18 months, the familiar design on the back of the Washington quarter, the Kennedy half and Eisenhower dollars.
>
> Canada, in 1992, successfully issued a series of 12 circulating commemorative quarters (one for each province), that stimulated demand; attracted new collectors to acquire the coins (and, subsequently, other mint products); and generally called attention to the national coinage to the population of the nation as a whole.

The Committee believes that the U.S. Mint should do no less, picking at least one coin every two years that is intended to circulate in the coinage system, but bears a commemorative theme. The seigniorage on the coin (the profit between its metal cost and all Mint overhead, and nominal face value) would accrue strictly to the Treasury, as now, as an off-budget item.

Three coins could lend themselves to such a program: the quarter, half dollar, or dollar coin. To accomplish this within the scope of any programs already authorized would require a new legislative initiative, approved by Congress, since the Act of Sept. 26, 1890, otherwise precludes design changes more frequently than once in 25 years. (That is the reason for the 1931 and 1973 legislation.)

If it were to be implemented for a coin not yet authorized, then the Committee recommends that Congress give strong consideration to choosing either the quarter, or a new small-sized dollar coin.

If the quarter is chosen, instead of typical annual production of about 1.5 billion coins, the Mint would probably have to manufacture about 2 billion coins to accommodate demand. The seigniorage on this would also be about $100 million more than at present from existing quarter production. (Mint seigniorage on *all* coins presently totals about $700 million annually, all "off-budget" items.)

If a small-sized dollar were chosen, it would be introduced as a new denomination, since the Susan B. Anthony dollar last circulated a dozen years ago. It is reasonable to conclude that between 500 million and 750 million of such coins would be required in the first eight months of production. Seigniorage or profit to the government on this would be a minimum of $400 million, and could be as high as $650 million.

Then, everyone began to work on the edit, and the final version—four paragraphs in the First Annual Report—truly incorporated all of our views, even if many of the surviving words were originally mine:

> Finally, the CCCAC endorses issuance by the Mint of a circulating commemorative coin. Coinage is a tangible way to touch the lives of every American. Circulating coinage promotes our national ideals, builds awareness and pride in our history, and informs millions of foreign visitors who use U.S. coins.
>
> A circulating commemorative coin is a regular legal-tender coin issued with a distinctive design but without a surcharge. American taxpayers would be the only financial beneficiaries of the issuance of the coin . . . Two modern precedents. . . . are the George Washington quarter authorized in 1931 (still in circulation today) and the Bicentennial [coins]. . . .
>
> The CCCAC recommends that Congress authorize the Secretary of the Treasury to issue a circulating commemorative coin. . . . The coin would continue to circulate as a medium of exchange but would also become a collector item.

Diehl's subsequent espousal of that position (which came in late 1994, after it had been advanced time and time again by me at every single meeting of the Citizens Commemorative Coin Advisory Committee) made all the difference. Ultimately, all of the members came around, and by the time that the CCCAC filed its first report to Congress in December 1994, there was a sincere consensus that circulating, legal-tender commemoratives should become part of the U.S. coinage scene.

From the time that the Citizens Commemorative Coin Advisory Committee threw down the gauntlet in its December 1994 report, the idea of a circulating commemorative coin was no longer a voice in the wilderness, but rather something that was moving toward the mainstream.

Hearings Before the House Coinage Subcommittee

After the CCCAC's report to Congress, there remained opposition to the concept within the Treasury Department itself—though increasingly, Mint staff members who opposed the change of position either retired, or decided it was in their best interest to change their views to accommodate a majority position. By the summer of 1995, it was clear enough that there were other problems with the overall commemorative coinage program—in particular the gold and silver non-circulating legal-tender programs—that had caused mintages to drop precipitously and had made virtually every program a hard sell.

Hearings were scheduled before the House coinage subcommittee, chaired by Rep. Michael Castle, R-Del., with Rep. Floyd Flake, D-N.Y., serving as ranking minority member. Those invited to testify included Mint Director Diehl, and several hobby leaders, among them Beth Deisher, Harvey Stack, Alan Stahl, and me. The scope of the hearings was to reform the non-circulating commemorative coins.

For those who have never testified before a congressional committee, it can be a heady experience—one that is at once humbling and a bit mysterious. I had first testified before the coinage subcommittee nearly a quarter century earlier, in 1974, and had done so many times since. My approach was the same as it was for the advisory committee:

Witness table at the July 1995 hearing. Closest at the table (right, front) is Philip Diehl, Mint director. I am seated next to him. To my right, Harvey G. Stack, Alan Stahl, Beth Deisher. Visible at the rear of Diehl: CCCAC member Reed Hawn.

have long, extended remarks with lots of background and details in an appendix to pique the interest of staffers, and possibly members—and then have a very brief oral presentation that highlights the testimony, but with a focus on only two or three key points. Despite the intent of some to keep the focus on problems of non-circulating legal-tender coins, I took the same approach that I did before the Citizens Advisory Committee—the bulk of my focus, my testimony, and the exhibits all had to do with the need for a circulating commemorative coin.

The testimony of the other witnesses took a different approach. *Coin World* editor Beth Deisher called for elimination of surcharges, but acknowledged that "it would be unrealistic to expect the U.S. Mint to sell modern commemoratives at face value. . . ." Dr. Alan Stahl, a curator at the American Numismatic Society, focused his prepared remarks on the need to have beautiful designs and the importance of involving outside artists in design competitions. Harvey Stack, a coin dealer from New York City representing the Professional Numismatists Guild, used his prepared remarks to rail against unconscionable pricing by the Mint and the authorization of too many coins by Congress. Mint Director Diehl's prepared testimony covered a panoply of issues—though not a circulating commemorative coin.

My remarks focused almost exclusively on the need for circulating commemorative coinage available at face value. Not only was the entire 5,000-word report to the Citizens Advisory Committee included as an attachment, but I summarized the Advisory Committee's position, reciting that the CCCAC not only wanted to see lower mintages for non-circulating legal-tender coins but "made a unanimous recommendation signed by all voting members of the Committee that Congress give serious consideration to the issuance of a circulating, legal-tender commemorative coin—a coin without surcharge—which would have its designs regularly changed to exemplify contemporary commemorative themes. The purpose of this would be to stimulate the general public to look at their coins, and their pocket change. . . ."

In the extemporaneous part of the hearing, Chairman Castle said: "Interest groups supported by Congress have progressively expanded the program both in numbers of coins and mintage levels beyond the ability of collectors to absorb these issues." Castle referred in his introductory statement to "generous surcharges awarded to the beneficiary organizations" and the need to change a "recipe for disaster" consisting of existing commemorative programs.

Rep. Flake, who arrived after the hearing had started and left for a meeting at the Justice Department before it was concluded, had also studied the prepared remarks and deplored the politicizing of our decision-making process which, he said, "has produced a glut of over 17 million coins for one event," the Olympics, and "coin collectors [who] are so dissatisfied with our commemorative process that they are boycotting some of the most recent coins."

First oral mention at the hearing on the topic of circulating commemorative coins came from Dr. Alan Stahl, then a curator at the American Numismatic Society who is a true historian (with a Ph.D. in history from the University of Pennsylvania), an excellent lecturer, and able to put commemorative coinage into a historical context. He closed his oral presentation "with a few thoughts on the relation of commemorative coinage to circulating coinage." He observed that "to many Americans, the only true commemorative coin issued in their lifetimes is the Bicentennial quarter, as it was the only one which circulated."

Next came Harvey Stack, the New York dealer, whose oral remarks made a small but important mention: "I, as the others, have advocated a circulating commemorative which would cost nothing to the people, but would project history."

My opportunity came to speak after a brief committee recess on which a vote was taken on the House floor. My oral remarks were far more pointed than the prepared remarks, and though they may have given the impression of being extemporaneous, they were meticulously edited to make a key point: "It is time to issue circulating legal-tender commemorative coins with no surcharges." I noted that "as Mr. Diehl and my colleagues [on the Citizens Advisory Committee] sitting behind me would tell you, it is a theme that I have repeated and reiterated at every meeting of the Citizens Advisory Committee." The reason for this was clear to me: "There is no better means of . . . promot[ing] public awareness of coin collecting . . . than with a new circulating commemorative coin, emblematic of the very values that have made our country great."

On page 40 of the hearing's printed transcript, at the end of a rambling monologue on commemorative coinage history, Harvey Stack stumbled onto a proposal he had made to the Citizens Advisory Committee earlier in the year: "We could do the first 13 states and issue new commemorative coins every year or two that would commemorate the other states as they came into the Union, and then cover at least the first 50 states."

Chairman Castle, who represents Delaware (the first state to ratify the U.S. Constitution) called it "a brilliant idea," adding: "Delaware was the first state."

I then added that "I think it is viable, that it would work, and Mr. Stack's idea for the 13 original colonies, starting first with Delaware, Mr. Chairman, is a wonderful idea."

By page 45 of the transcript, Chairman Castle said he was going to ask me a question. "I think everybody has mentioned it. You mentioned it first . . .a circulating commemorative coin . . . would this be in lieu of the commemorative coins we presently do, or in addition to them, or how would that work?"

Boy, what a slow pitch, right over the heart of the plate! It was no doubt thanks to good staff work by John Lopez, the committee's chief counsel, who had been talking with the CCCAC about circulating commemoratives for more than a year. (I had mentioned the idea to Lopez when the CCCAC first went to Capitol Hill to pay a courtesy call on the members of the coinage committees and their staffs, and the idea took hold. Like many ideas propounded that way, it took on a life of its own.)

The softball crossed the center part of the plate and I sprang to hit it with the meatiest part of my verbal bat, talking first about the Washington quarter circulating commemorative of 1932 (authorized as a one-year commemorative in 1931), and then going on to the Bicentennial coin

Rep. Michael Castle, R-Del. (center, right of flag), Chairman of the Subcommittee, at the seminal July 1995 hearing before the House coinage subcommittee. To his left, Rep. Floyd Flake, D-N.Y., ranking minority member. To the right of Castle: John Lopez, counsel to the committee. Painting at left: former House Banking Committee chairman Wright Patman, D-Texas, who was instrumental in creating America's Bicentennial commemorative coinage in 1973.

program. "It circulated. It was pocket change. But there was also a collector's version that was available in silver. . . . So this would really be in addition to a scaled-down version of the programs that are existing right now. . . ."

By the end of 1995, the Citizens Advisory Committee had another annual report to make to Congress, and this time, "circulating commemorative coins" took up all of page 16 of the report. It clarified that "The CCCAC unanimously endorses the issuance of a circulating legal-tender commemorative coin"—a face-value commemorative. Since the director of the Mint is a statutory member of the committee, that completed the cycle and brought it the full circle—to support from within the Mint.

There would be other rows to hoe, and legislation to accomplish the goal which became a 50-state commemorative coin program spread over 10 years would not become reality until late 1997. First would come the legislative proposal to order a true study on the efficacy of the proposal; the Mint supported the idea, the main Treasury opposed it, and even with the favorable outcome, the Treasury Secretary seemed to withhold support. Philip Diehl, John Lopez, the staff counsel to the House coinage subcommittee, and Rep. Castle took charge and moved through yet another piece of legislation designed to implement the proposal.

There are those who will claim that they merely mentioned the idea and it became reality, but the parties carrying the real load were Philip Diehl at the Mint, John Lopez at a staff level on Capitol Hill, and Mike Castle at the high-end legislative locus. In truth, without John Lopez, Philip Diehl, and Rep. Michael Castle, this would have been just one more good idea whose time never came.

Legislative Maneuvering Begins

Every good idea that becomes reality has a hundred fathers. In my view, Congressman Michael Castle, R-Del., then chairman of the House Banking subcommittee that dealt with coinage matters, is the legislative father, and it was his proposal, H.R. 3793, legislation directing the Mint to strike 50 different coin designs—one for each state over the next 10 years—that was introduced July 11, 1996. The occasion marked the one-year anniversary of hearings held before the subcommittee on Domestic and International Monetary Policy of the House Banking and Financial Services Committee, which Castle then chaired.

The July 1995 hearing put the cart before the horse, for even though the legislator was there, the rest of Congress

July 1995 hearing before the House coinage subcommittee. During a break, I spoke with Congressman Castle, the chairman. John Lopez, subcommittee counsel, is standing in the center (bearded).

and a recalcitrant bureaucracy had to be persuaded that the proposal made sense and was viable. Castle's 1996 legislation took the concept from the July 1995 hearing and went to its logical conclusion: a continuity program of five coins per year, issued over a 10-year period of time. A silver version would also be produced for collectors.

The bill began with legislative findings. Among them: that "a circulating commemorative coin could produce earnings of $110 million" and produce indirect earnings to the Treasury of $3.4 billion. It then went on to state that "It is appropriate to launch a commemorative circulating coin program that encourages young people and their families to collect memorable tokens of all the States for the face value of the coins."

This traces its financial projections to recommendations made a year earlier by the Citizens Commemorative Coin

Advisory Committee, which in turn relied on the experience of America's Bicentennial coin program.

The theme for the Castle program is written broadly as the 50 states of the Union, their rich history, geography, and rich diversity. But the politics of how it moved to fruition is somewhat less obvious. Although the proposal moving toward resolution made the decision seem obvious, it initially faced intense opposition within the Mint and the Treasury Department, based in large part on bureaucratic inertia. Only the steady reassurance from Castle, Lopez, and Diehl, and their combined persistence, made it possible for the program to truly proceed.

Altogether, it took three separate laws before the circulating commemorative program could achieve reality. First of these was Public Law 104-329, enacted Oct. 24, 1996, which created a host of non-circulating commemorative coins, restructured the CCCAC, and called for a study of the circulating coin proposal.

That study was actually intended to kill the measure, for in between the time that the CCCAC endorsed it formally, opposition to it arose high in the Treasury Department among political appointees near the top, principally individuals opposed to Diehl's success record. These were no longer Mint career servants, but political appointees in the Main Treasury Building located across the street from the White House.

The week following Labor Day 1996 was slated to mark the occasion of the House passing historic legislation that would create a 10-year-long continuity program of circulating 25-cent commemorative coins. A House vote was scheduled for Sept. 4. Circulating commemorative coinage honoring all 50 states inched toward reality as the Senate and House of Representatives, in early October 1996, directed the Secretary of the Treasury to study its implementation.

A day before Congress adjourned for the year, and months after both houses had passed commemorative coin reform legislation, a spate of bills came before the House and Senate to work on before the 104th Congress adjourned, sine die, into history.

On Sept. 30, 1996, President Clinton signed into law the commemorative reform legislation limiting new non-circulating commemorative coin issues to two per year, maximum. Of course, since Congress made the law, it could change it at any time, a fact not lost on the sponsors. On Oct. 3, Sen. Alfonse D'Amato, R-N.Y., chair of the Senate Banking Committee, rammed through legislation that authorized seven new commemorative coin issues and directed study of the 50-state circulating coin proposal that had already passed the House unanimously.

The House had previously taken no action on the majority of the Senate's proposals to commemorate the 125th anniversary of Yellowstone National Park; the Bicentennial of the death of George Washington; black Revolutionary War patriots including Crispus Attucks, the first African American to be killed in the war for independence; the National Law Enforcement Officers Memorial commemorative; the Franklin D. Roosevelt commemorative coin benefiting his new monument in Washington; Dolley Madison, first lady in the Jefferson and Madison administrations; and Jackie Robinson and the 50th anniversary of the breaking of baseball's color barrier.

The Senate version also called for the Treasury Secretary to study and report by June 1, 1997, on the feasibility of a 50-state circulating commemorative coinage program. Specifically, "The study shall assess likely public acceptance of and consumer demand for different coins that might be issued in connection with such a program (taking into consideration the pace of issuance of coins and the length of such a program)." Also ordered: "a comparison of the costs of producing coins issued under the program and the revenue that the program would generate, the impact on coin distribution systems, the advantages and disadvantages of different approaches to selecting designs for coins in such a program," and other factors.

While this was going on, the numismatic trade press began its own campaign among readers. *COINage* magazine organized an informal contest among its readers to see what they could come up with for the various states. Response to the informal contest was overwhelming, and suggested that if the Treasury ultimately recommended the proposal and called for a publicized national design competition, there would be plenty of interest. As events turned out, it would be the nation's governors who would benefit from this, and many subsequently held design competitions or contests.

Elroy Young of Bethlehem, Pennsylvania, suggested a quarter dollar depicting the bust of Benjamin Franklin on the obverse. From the looks of the submission, the hundred-dollar design portrait would be utilized. The reverse was a bit more crude, depicting a small eagle in the sky and the discovery of electricity by the inventor.

Jason Russell, a Missouri resident, sought to honor his home state with a skyline view of St. Louis featuring the great arch that marks the gateway to the West, together with the state motto, "Let the Welfare of the People Be the Supreme Law."

Wayne Pearson would have used an equestrian portrait of George Washington on one side, and the Great Seal of the State of Delaware on the reverse, with the addition of "E Pluribus Unum" to meet statutory requirements.

LaVaughn Scott of Gainesville, Florida, honored the "Birthplace of Our Nation—1513" with a depiction of the state of Florida, a portrait of Ponce de Leon, and some fauna that are typical to the Sunshine State.

Andrew Aslinger, a 14-year-old *COINage* reader from Montclair, Virginia, made a moving sketch of a cannon astride water that "could be the Rappahonnock or the Potomac" honoring the Commonwealth that represents the "Foundation of Our Nation's Independence." Andrew also did one for Tennessee, featuring the "Origin of Great Music." For this one, the quarter is made to look like an old phonograph record complete with jukebox and guitars and microphone, and the name "Nashville."

Edward V. Ficht of Washington, Illinois, based his obverse on a portrait of Washington (not provided) and a drawn reverse featuring a rendering based on the Illinois State Seal. The 13-year-old *COINage* reader depicted an eagle with a ribbon in its beak representing "State Sovereignty, National Union."

Richard J. Lakatos had a great idea for the Big Apple; his New York commemorative, bearing a 1998 date, depicts an apple embracing Liberty, while the reverse is an eagle straight on, coming out of the Adirondack Mountains.

Mike Cortozzo would honor Tennessee with two portraits—one on the obverse, the other on the reverse. Andrew Jackson together with the state outline and the year 2001 grace the obverse; Elvis Presley would be on the reverse of this coin for "The Volunteer State."

Wayne Pearson of Union City, Indiana, utilized a variation on the Indiana State Seal for both the obverse and reverse of his design, featuring the additional motto "Hoosier Crossroads of America." Also shown: the peony (state flower), a cardinal (state bird), and a buffalo.

An evidently younger reader, Kris Liaugminas, thought Ulysses S. Grant should be on the "front" of the coin intended for commemoration, and another reader whose signature is difficult to read thought "Illinois—Land of Lincoln" with a portrait of the 16th president on the obverse would work, with a state outline for the 21st state on the reverse.

There were differences between the houses of Congress. Normally, that is cause for a conference for the two bodies to work out their differences. Late in the session, the choice is agreement and passage, or disagreement, with the proposals all dying. The House chose compromise, and the Senate version of H.R. 1776 prevailed.

As finally agreed upon, the bill gave a clear mandate to the Secretary of the Treasury: report to Congress by Aug. 1, 1997, as to the viability of a circulating commemorative coin program using 50 different coins—one for each state. One key issue: the U.S. Mint already was slated to produce 16 billion coins in 1999 before considering the commemorative proposal. If the final determination was a positive one, the program would start up on Jan. 1, 1999—unless the Secretary of the Treasury postponed that date of commencement. But if he did, he would still have to prescribe a different date.

Of course, there was the possibility that Secretary Robert Rubin would say no—though in hindsight, many would wonder why. But there was intrigue, backstabbing, and a sense of drama right until the end. I can recall writing a news story about the decision with two separate leads—one where the Secretary supported the measure, one where he called it out on strikes.

Setting up the mission for Secretary Rubin and the Mint was Congress itself, by Public Law 104-329, passed at the urging of Congressman Castle. This move derailed an otherwise steamroller that seemed to ensure passage of the proposal. Castle evidently acted because of concerns on the part of the Mint that it would be unable to meet its statutory mandate of providing the nation with sufficient circulating coins if it were also required to manufacture a new series of commemorative coins intended to honor each of the 50 states in the Union.

In reality, two forces were at work: that portion of the Mint bureaucracy that did not want the program to proceed, and the bureaucrats over at the main Treasury building, next to the White House, that had some of the same concerns, and also a political agenda.

The underlying proposal called for the coins to be struck at the rate of five per year for the next decade in the order that the states were admitted to the Union. Specific requirements of the examination procedure by the Secretary of the Treasury are set out in the statute. He was required to assess "likely public acceptance of and consumer demand for different coins that might be issued in connection with such a program (taking into consideration the pace of issuance of coins and the length of such a program)." He was also required to prepare "a comparison of the costs of producing coins issued under the program and the revenue that the program would generate, the impact on coin distribution systems, the advantages and disadvantages of different approaches to selecting designs for coins in such a program."

The task was a daunting one—particularly since a circulating commemorative coinage program of this magnitude had never been undertaken before. The easy part would be the designs, because Congress directed that they relate to the states of the Union in their order of entry.

First of the states, not surprisingly, was Delaware, which ratified the Constitution on Dec. 7, 1787. The succeeding order over the next two years would include Pennsylvania, New Jersey, Georgia, Connecticut, Massachusetts, Maryland, South Carolina, New Hampshire, and Virginia. The rest followed through Hawaii, which achieved statehood in 1959 (Year Ten of the program).

Three times between 1995 and 1996, portions of the government shut down as both houses of Congress were unable to reach agreement on simple proposals to fund the various working branches. The State Quarters program became bogged down again, this time caught up in the snarl of national politics—a nearly impenetrable maze. Late in the session, as a host of other commemorative coin proposals started moving from the drawing board to political reality, the circulating coin proposal advanced and was nearly enacted.

Evidently, at that point in time, the Mint staff began to have attacks of apoplexy, recognizing that a circulating commemorative coin might add 700 million production units to an already heavy workload and that five new coins per year could add upwards of three to four billion new pieces. On that basis, the Mint prevailed upon the sponsors to suggest a study of the problem first, in order to make sure that the result could in fact be achieved. That's what the final law said.

That the U.S. Mint is capable of producing large quantities of coins is beyond cavil. Its production facilities at Philadelphia, Denver, San Francisco, and West Point, whose physical plants are designed to produce 13 to 15 billion pieces a year, can turn out 17 to 19 billion pieces with a bit of hard work. The issue was whether other coinage demand had slacked off sufficiently in order to permit the Mint to produce 3 or 4 billion coins beyond the cent, nickel, dime, and half dollar that were already planned. No quarter dollars would be produced with the Washington design of 1932, and the heraldic eagle on the reverse; the concept would be five circulating legal-tender coin designs, one from each state, which would be rotated in approximately every two-and-a-half months.

That the Mint would oppose new circulating commemorative coins was not especially surprising to most close observers. Treasury officials vehemently opposed the creation of a circulating Bicentennial commemorative coin. Initially, they sought to block the American Revolution Bicentennial Commission from even dealing with the subject.

As the Mint raced to complete the study mandated by Congress, I predicted that the bureaucrats were going to report the same tired facts, slanted against circulating commemorative coins, cloaked in production arguments.

I wrote:

> They'll cite coinage demand studies and projections that show that the Mint won't be able to keep up with the demand for circulating coinage. (The record, to the contrary, shows that the Mint and the Fed don't have a good track record in forecasting long-term coinage needs.)
>
> It's likely that they'll also claim that there will be a problem of hoarding of new circulating commemorative coins, and that millions will be withdrawn from circulation—unspent—by the nation's coin collectors.
>
> There is a partial truth to that, but all manufacturers should be this lucky, to produce a widget at a cost of three cents that has a wholesale (and retail) value of more than eight times cost, or 25 cents.
>
> The more that the Mint produces, the more profit that they make. That's pretty simple. The more profit (even off budget), the greater the economic benefit.

By the late spring-early summer of 1997, it was unclear what was going to happen. It was learned, as I wrote in an article in *COINage* magazine, that despite some bureaucratic snafus and opposition from professional staff, the Mint was prepared to endorse the program that Congress mandated—with one coin for each of the 50 states, produced five coins a year for a total of 10 years.

Although it was thought that the Mint would have a

problem producing an extra three to four billion coins annually to encompass the program, principally because of production capacity requirements at the Philadelphia, Denver, and San Francisco mints, the report concluded that the program could be accomplished. The source for the information was none other than Mint Director Philip Diehl, who told reporters at the West Point, New York, Mint that the production capacity issue had been resolved, pointing the way for the program's endorsement. It also showed that Diehl had come full circle, from active opponent to active proponent.

Publication of the initial confirmation came in *Coin World*, a weekly hobby newspaper, but without any details as to how it could be accomplished. That's in part because the Mint already was operating on three shifts and producing about 19 billion coins a year. The problem was that the production capacity of the four U.S. mints is only about 15 billion coins—meaning that a superhuman effort is required to increase this by 25%, and to sustain the level for a prolonged period of time is difficult because of maintenance requirements.

Nonetheless, the Mint was committed to a circulating commemorative coin program, just as it was committed to expanding its physical plant to permit it to strike needed coinage of the realm together with the commemoratives.

Even before Congress passed legislation favoring a circulating commemorative coin program and required the Mint's considered opinion on its viability, the Mint recognized that its production requirements and forecasting abilities for future coinage needs had been called into question. It responded in March 1996 with a document entitled "Strategic Plan"—a secret, generally unpublished report which defined the problem as having "aging manufacturing equipment, loss of experienced work force, and uncertainty regarding raw material cost [which] pose threats to our ability to meet escalating demand for our product."

The Mint set goals to accomplish this. One was to "develop production capacity to meet projected demand of 24 billion coins by the year 2002." The objective way of doing this, it said: "By 1997, perform necessary architectural/engineering studies for increased capacity and production" and also "develop schedules and budget plans for purchase of additional equipment."

For the goal defined as being "prepared to produce circulating commemoratives as approved by Congress by 1998," the plan was to "assist the Citizens Commemorative Coin Advisory Committee and Congressional banking committees in designing a circulating commemorative coin program compatible with our circulating coin production mission."

Diehl's words suggested that Mint officialdom had come down on the side of common sense, and good politics—and that a circulating commemorative coin program would soon be in the offing.

An important public study of the utility of circulating commemorative coins, undertaken on behalf of the Treasury Department by the "Big–8" accounting firm of Coopers & Lybrand, was then released by the Treasury and sent to Capitol Hill on June 10. Its key findings, based on a statistically sound survey and focus group, were announced 10 days later than the statute which ordered the examination had requested. The delay was worthwhile, because the startling results showed that only 11% of those surveyed opposed a 50-state commemorative coin program. More significant was that 75% of those polled declared that they would be "almost certain" to start collecting the series, or minimally that there was a "good possibility" that they would do so.

Each coin that is collected and removed from circulation represents a 22-cent profit for the government, meaning that hundreds of millions of dollars in seigniorage profit were likely to accrue in any lengthy program stretching over 10 years' time.

"I am very pleased about the study, and hope that this positive report means the Treasury will 'green-light' my proposal to give the quarter a new look," Congressman Castle said.

"This proposal has many benefits," he explained. "By placing a symbol of each state on one side of the quarter, we are paying tribute to our country as a whole and commemorating each of our 50 very different states."

Significantly, Castle said, we also would be "saving the taxpayer money we otherwise would be paying on the U.S. debt and making the process of getting change more educational and a lot more fun."

Commemorative coinage that functions as coinage of the realm seemed on the verge of being authorized to make pocket change. Many felt that this was the most likely way to hook an entirely new generation on the joys of coin collecting. It also was the way to salvage an otherwise over-burdened series of coin issues that constituted little more than a tax on the nation's coin collectors—the modern commemorative coins issued since 1982.

The report by Coopers & Lybrand totaled more than 80 pages; more than 2,000 individuals were interviewed by telephone to develop a valid random statistical sampling or model that could form the basis of a public-opinion poll. It was required to be completed by June 1, 1997, because by Aug. 1, the same law required that the Secretary of the Treasury make a determination or finding as to whether the results of the study justified the program. What Coopers & Lybrand did went well beyond the mandate, and appears to have become involved in a political turf battle between the Mint and the main Treasury—which apparently opposed some aspects of the circulating coin plan.

Resulting from this was a comment in the report that is

simply historically wrong, and could only have been inserted to give the Treasury secretary the ability to deny the proposal in its entirety if he wanted to. What Coopers & Lybrand wrote is that "The U.S. Government has always considered changes to the face of its coinage and currency. Historically, the Government has always required a clear, direct link to a single event or memorial date to change circulating coin designs."

The statement is ludicrous on its face, and was either based on sloppy work by the accounting firm's consulting division, or based on a request from the Treasury Department to find a means—any means—to show why the government shouldn't go for a $2-billion-plus profit. The statement may have been true in recent times, but the U.S. Mint is now more than 200 years old, and the tradition that Coopers & Lybrand appeared to be reporting on was precisely the opposite of what it represented.

Take the simple cent, first issued in 1793. In that first year of issue alone, there were eight major design varieties ranging from the Flowing Hair Chain-type reverse to the Wreath reverse and Liberty with Liberty pole and Phrygian cap. A Draped Bust was introduced in 1796, and in 1808 the so-called "Classic Head" made its debut. The Coronet Liberty began in 1816 with a mature Liberty, but by 1835 a younger head for Liberty was chosen. The year 1856 saw a Flying Eagle cent, 1859 an Indian Head cent, and 1909 a Lincoln cent—the latter being the only coin issue tied to an event (the centennial of Lincoln's birth).

The coins under consideration were to be quarters, and that denomination showed major changes, too—especially among the eagles on the reverse. The 1796 Draped Bust has a puny eagle; by 1804, it was a heraldic eagle. The portrait changed again in 1815, as did the eagle. A Seated Liberty design was added in 1838, the classic Barber-designed Liberty was introduced in 1892, the Standing Liberty design in 1916, and the Washington commemorative (for the Bicentennial of the birth of George Washington) in 1932.

The 1976 Bicentennial coin reverse of the Colonial drummer boy was, of course, specifically picked for a very precise event—even though the Treasury Department initially opposed changing the quarter dollar, or any other coins for that matter, to commemorate such a prestigious event.

The task then facing Secretary Robert Rubin, who was required to make the decision by Aug. 1, 1997, of whether or not to go ahead, was therefore a daunting one—particularly since a circulating commemorative coinage program of this magnitude had never been undertaken before.

The forces that sought delay in implementation appear to have been political appointees inside the main Treasury building. What evidently occurred was a turf battle between Mint Director Diehl, who was first appointed by President Clinton with the support of Treasury Secretary Lloyd Bentsen, and Diehl's superiors in the Treasury Department who were allied with Bentsen's successor, Rubin.

With the outcome of the proposal hanging in the balance, the consensus of observers, including some knowledgeable staff members on Capitol Hill, was that the Administration's decision would have little to do with the merits of the proposal—which was nearly universally acknowledged to have merit—but on raw intra-party politics.

The Coopers & Lybrand report transmitted to the Secretary said that there was an evident omission of the District of Columbia, territories, and U.S. possessions. "The act is silent" on these, it said, adding that "There are political and pragmatic implications of including or excluding the District and territories in or from the Program," ignoring that Congress is a legislative body that took those very things into account.

My view was that this was a red herring inserted at the request of opponents within the Secretary of the Treasury's office, seeking to find a means to derail an otherwise fine program—one that would save the taxpayers billions. It was also correctable by legislation, which has been pending in each succeeding Congress. My strong guess remains, in early 2000, that Washington, D.C., Puerto Rico, and the four American trust territories (Guam, Northern Mariana, Virgin Islands, and American Samoa) will be included before the program ends. On Sept. 7, 2000, the House coinage subcommitee approved legistation to do just that.

Secretary of the Treasury Rubin Acts

Treasury Secretary Rubin finally did give his mandate for change. Your pocket change, that is. Directed by Congress to report by Aug. 1, 1997, as to whether or not he approved or disapproved of the congressional plan to have the Mint produce circulating commemorative coinage honoring each of the 50 states, he gave a thumbs-up.

What finally moved the program from conceptual idea to reality was the push given by Congressman Castle's office in the face of opposition by the Treasury Department. As little as a week before the final decision was made, oddsmakers said the decision could go either way. With the decision hanging in the balance, Castle sprang into action, soliciting a letter that went from the speaker of the House, Newt Gingrich; to the majority leader, Dick Armey; to the majority whip, Tom DeLay; to the chairman of the House Banking Committee, James A.S. Leach, and himself; to Rubin asking for the change in our change.

Rubin's July 31 response followed wherein his approval was tepid, and appeared to require congressional reapproval, which was all but certain to succeed. In a July 31, 1997, "Dear Mike" letter, signed "Bob," Rubin stated:

> [I have] reviewed the proposal for a fifty-state circulating commemorative quarter program and the

Rep. Michael Castle, R-Del. chair of the House coinage subcommittee, in front of a coinage press at the Philadelphia Mint, December 1998. The picture, at left, shows the Delaware quarter about to be struck; the monitor at center connects to a computer designed to keep the pressure of the coining press accurate. A news crew records the event.

study that the Treasury Department commissioned from Coopers & Lybrand.

The study, through extensive polling and market research, concluded that while there is a substantial degree of interest in the program, there is also a large percentage of people who are indifferent to the program or are unfavorably disposed toward it. I am concerned that this program could affect the public's perception of our coinage. [He therefore asked for legislation to assure that] our money includes elements symbolic of the basic principles of our nation . . . for the full consideration of these and related issues by requiring design review by the Citizens Commemorative Coin Advisory Committee and the Fine Arts Commission, [plus the Treasury chief,] to ensure that no frivolous or inappropriate designs are implemented.

That meant that starting in 1999, the reverse of each quarter dollar entering circulation would bear a design emblematic of one of the 50 states, starting with Delaware and continuing at the rate of five per year until the program was completed in 2008.

Rep. Castle, the chairman of the House coinage subcommittee, was immediately enthusiastic, promising through staff aide John Lopez to seek legislation at the conclusion of the August congressional recess to do just that. Sen. Alfonse D'Amato, R-N.Y., chairman of the Senate Banking Committee, which has jurisdiction over coinage, was likewise bullish. The legislation to finish the process was enacted expeditiously.

Each of the coins would be struck by the U.S. mints at Philadelphia, Denver, San Francisco, and West Point, and then placed in circulation just as ordinary pocket change is today, through the Federal Reserve System and your local banks.

Mint Director Diehl, speaking at the American Numismatic Association convention in New York City, explained in August 1997 that it was likely there would be two mint-mark varieties per coin, meaning a complete set would contain 100 coins—two for each of the 50 states. All coins would be produced in sufficient quantities to assure an adequate supply to meet the needs of commerce—the Mint's first responsibility—with a secondary effort to assure that the nation's current coin collectors, as well as prospective ones, had the opportunity to acquire one or more.

Early estimates were that the Mint would have to produce around 2.5 billion quarters in 1999 to meet all commercial needs and still allow for about three coins for every American to be withdrawn from circulation. That meant about a half-billion coins of each design would be produced—relatively low by previous standards. Not since 1972 had as few as 500 million quarters (from all Mint facilities) been produced.

That the U.S. Mint was prepared to endorse the program that Congress mandated—with one coin for each of the 50 states, producing five coins a year for a total of 10 years—was nothing short of amazing. It contradicted the history of the Mint as a bureaucratic organization opposed to change, which spent more than half a century opposing issuance of any commemorative coins, even the non-circulating legal-tender type.

Where it was thought that the Mint would have a problem producing an extra three to four billion coins annually to accommodate the program, principally because of production capacity requirements at the Philadelphia, Denver, and San Francisco mints, the Mint concluded that the program could be accomplished.

Time Line

A multistep process was required before newly minted 25-cent commemorative coins could be issued by the Mint. Here's how Coopers & Lybrand saw the process in its May 29, 1997, report:

1. 8/1/97 Program announced
2. 8/29/97 Competition announced
3. 9/1–10/24/97 Public prepares designs
4. 10/27–11/21/97 Central body determines design
5. 10/27–11/21/97 Central body determines finalists
6. 11/24–1/2/98 Public votes on finalists
7. 1/5–1/30/98 States vote on winning designs
8. 2/2/98 States submit designs to Director of the Mint
9. 2/3/98 Mint director submits to Citizens Commemorative Coin Advisory Committee and Fine Arts Commission
10. 4/28–5/28/98 Treasury Secretary reviews designs
11. 5/26/98 Treasury Secretary approves designs

12. 5/27/98 Production process begins at the Mint
13. 5/27–6/16/98 Plaster models developed
14. 6/17–6/30/98 Reduction hubs developed
15. 7/1–8/18/98 Test and trial strikes conducted
16. 8/19–9/15/98 Produce dies
17. 9/16–12/1/98 Pre-production procedures
18. 12/2/98 Live production begins
19. 1/4/99 Launch date
20. 1/4/99 First coins delivered to Federal Reserve Banks

1   20
8/1/97   1/4/99

What About Those Designs?

There was uncertainty at first as to how the Mint would handle designs. It determined early on that this was a political hot potato, and decided to punt to the nation's governors.

A private design contest, or a public one, would have its own advantages, and the Cooper's & Lybrand report suggested that either approach could be taken within the same time parameters contemplated. The real question was who would participate.

In Illinois, one official proclaimed that Michael Jordan of the Chicago Bulls was the perfect representative to appear on the Illinois commemorative, which wouldn't be produced until the fifth year of the program. A state representative from West Virginia, otherwise stumped for design ideas, thought that the State Seal would prevent the legislature from being caught up in a "very long" debate on a reverse design for the quarter. And in New Jersey, a local political candidate thought that the Statue of Liberty belonged on that state's coinage "because it's ours anyway." At the time, there was a lengthy legal battle pending between New York and New Jersey over who owned Bedloes and Ellis islands, homes of the statue and the immigration museum, respectively.

If the Mint controlled the contest, there would likely be up to a dozen artists invited to participate in the design process for each state—with the possibility that each could offer several alternatives for the quarter reverse.

Public competition, on the other hand, could mean thousands of designs—and that would significantly broaden the appeal of the coin, its collectibility, and its desirability among children as well as all voting-age citizens.

When the Coins Will Be Struck

As noted, the coins have been entering circulation at a rate of five coins per year since Jan. 1, 1999, with production runs of about ten weeks apiece (starting in December, February, May, August, and October). Under existing law and regulations, the Mint could produce each of the coin designs throughout the calendar year; their release, however, is mandated by statute to provide for issuance in the order that each state entered the Union.

Here is the order that the coins are being struck, along with the dates that will appear on them:

1999 (Date Production Commences)

1. Delaware (December 1998)
2. Pennsylvania (February 1999)
3. New Jersey (May 1999)
4. Georgia (August 1999)
5. Connecticut (October 1999)

2000

6. Massachusetts (December 1999)
7. Maryland (February 2000)
8. South Carolina (May 2000)
9. New Hampshire (August 2000)
10. Virginia (October 2000)

2001

11. New York (December 2000)
12. North Carolina (February 2001)
13. Rhode Island (May 2001)
14. Vermont (August 2001)
15. Kentucky (October 2001)

2002

16. Tennessee (December 2001)
17. Ohio (February 2002)
18. Louisiana (May 2002)
19. Indiana (August 2002)
20. Mississippi (October 2002)

2003

21. Illinois (December 2002)
22. Alabama (February 2003)
23. Maine (May 2003)
24. Missouri (August 2003)
25. Arkansas (October 2003)

2004

26. Michigan (December 2003)
27. Florida (February 2004)
28. Texas (May 2004)
29. Iowa (August 2004)

30. Wisconsin (October 2004)

2005

31. California (December 2004)
32. Minnesota (February 2005)
33. Oregon (May 2005)
34. Kansas (August 2005)
35. West Virginia (October 2005)

2006

36. Nevada (December 2005)
37. Nebraska (February 2006)
38. Colorado (May 2006)
39. North Dakota (August 2006)
40. South Dakota (October 2006)

2007

41. Montana (December 2006)
42. Washington (February 2007)
43. Idaho (May 2007)
44. Wyoming (August 2007)
45. Utah (October 2007)

2008

46. Oklahoma (December 2007)
47. New Mexico (February 2008)
48. Arizona (May 2008)
49. Alaska (August 2008)
50. Hawaii (October 2008)

Victory for Diehl

Action by Treasury Secretary Robert Rubin to mandate design changes for circulating quarters, starting in 1997, was a victory for Mint Director Philip Diehl over opposition high in the Treasury Department.

The loser in the decision was Assistant Secretary of the Treasury for Management George Muñoz, who turned the circulating coin debate into a power struggle with Diehl over the perception that he has been remarkably successful over the last four years in achieving legislative victories.

Muñoz was reported to have opposed the circulating coinage proposal, pushed by Diehl, because it had Republican authors and because of Diehl's remarkable track record of achieving the needs of the Mint.

Diehl's recommendations, which paralleled those of Congressman Castle and Senator D'Amato, were predicated on his own analysis that the ideas made sense. Diehl is a Democrat who was sponsored for the Mint job by former Treasury Secretary Lloyd Bentsen.

The Law Seemingly Finalized

With the stroke of a pen on Dec. 1, 1997, President Clinton signed The 50 States Commemorative Coin Act into law, moving into the mainstream an idea that was once in the wasteland, validating the Citizens Commemorative Coin

Advisory Committee in the process. This marked the second law needed for the program. There were many changes from the time the idea was first proposed at a 1993 Citizens Advisory Committee meeting in Washington, D.C., to the time it began to seriously percolate in Congress over the summer of 1997.

Taking the CCCAC viewpoint, Congress has declared through the new law that "it is appropriate to launch a commemorative circulating coin program that encourages young people and their families to collect memorable tokens of all of the States for the face value of the coins." With this, the federal government has become the friend of coin collecting, which was once such an anathema that Eva B. Adams, while director of the Mint, tried to make collecting coins illegal—and that failing, persuaded Congress to freeze the dates on coins in the 1964–65 period.

The CCCAC had advocated the program as a billion-dollar budget maker. In the text of the law, Congress concurred with this, stating that the circulating commemoratives "could produce earnings of $110 million from the sale of silver proof coins and sets over the 10-year period of issuance, and would produce indirect earnings of an estimated $2.6 billion to $5.1 billion to the United States Treasury."

To help prepare for the program, the Mint was allowed to produce coins with the existing Washington quarter design by John Flanagan, issued originally in 1932 as part of a one-year circulating commemorative for the Bicentennial of George Washington's birth, throughout calendar year 1999, even though they might bear the 1998 date. A comparable freeze in designs was permitted when the Mint produced hundreds of millions of Bicentennial quarters in the 1975–76 period. It was explained then, as now, as a means of preventing a shortage of coins.

Just what would appear on the coins remained subject

initially to pervasive speculation, though Congress imposed certain restrictions and limitations to be certain that the coins wouldn't become the tools for commercial endorsements or political statements. That's something that the Citizens Advisory Committee did not address during its four years of advocacy, but something the law did, since it requires that the designs be run past the CCCAC for its comments.

Design selection involves the Secretary of the Treasury consulting with the governor of the state being commemorated, or "such other state officials or group as the State may designate for such purpose." Also required to be consulted: the federal Commission of Fine Arts. Each design must be reviewed by the Citizens Commemorative Coin Advisory Committee, but neither it nor the Fine Arts Commission—or even the state itself—has veto power over a coin's design.

When Treasury Secretary Rubin first came out in favor of the 50-state commemorative proposal in the summer of 1997, he wrote to Congressman Castle, chairman of the House coinage subcommittee, that he hoped that the designs would not include some of the proposals that had already been raised, such as Michael Jordan for Illinois, or Adidas tennis sneakers. The legislation responded to that concern by declaring that "Because it is important that the Nation's coinage and currency bear dignified designs of which the citizens of the United States can be proud, the Secretary shall not select any frivolous or inappropriate design for any quarter dollar minted."

To that end, the law also was changed to require scenic or pictorial depictions, rather than individuals that a state might choose to honor. That is accomplished by the clause requiring that "No head and shoulders portrait or bust of any person, living or dead, and no portrait of a living person may be included in the design of any quarter dollar."

The nation's editorial cartoonists have had a field day in

With a push of a button, the Grabener press starts churning out coins; here, Mint Director Diehl picks up some of the new Delaware quarters as they exit the press.

designing pseudo-coins. One, from the *Cincinnati Enquirer,* depicts an Arkansas coin with "We're Not Really Crooks." Another shows a state referred to as "staythehellaway from Montana." One of my favorites is the well-researched editorial cartoon of Chuck Asay in the Colorado Springs *Gazette-Telegraph.* He drew "The Clinton Commemorative Coin" in which the president's face appeared to be doubled; the new national motto read "In Rhetoric we trust," while in the lower righthand corner, a suited lawyer resembling me in physical appearance exclaims, "Hey! That's a double-die coin. Its worth a lot of money," only to have someone else exclaim, "No: They're all like this!"

Wilkinson, editorial cartoonist in the Philadelphia *Daily News*, referring to the police arrest of some Amish people for drug possession, offered the inscription: "Pennsylvania—where even the Amish know how to party." Like Milt Prigee in the *Seattle Times*, Wilkinson also allowed for a "write-in" to reflect readers' votes.

Jim Borgman in the *Cincinnati Enquirer*. Reprinted by permission of the artist and King Features Syndicate.

Even under existing law, living people can appear on commemorative coinage—though this has been rare. In 1926, President Calvin Coolidge appeared on the sesquicentennial half dollar, issued to mark the 150th anniversary of American independence. In 1936, Sen. Carter Glass and Sen. Joseph Robinson appeared on Virginia and Arkansas issues. And more recently, Eunice Kennedy Shriver appeared on the Special Olympics coin issued in conjunction with the 1996 Olympic Games in Atlanta.

The Countdown

The U.S. Mint started the countdown to the year of circulating coins. Its plan moved full tilt at an almost frenetic pace, in a rush to issue the first 5 coins of a 50-state program that Congress had ordered to start in 1999.

In mid-January 1998, Treasury Secretary Rubin wrote to the governors of all 50 states advising them of Public Law 105-124 enacted the previous Dec. 1, telling them that the first five states had less than 180 days to make their design recommendations. Under the terms of the law, the states recommend designs to the Treasury chief. The design recommendations are then passed on for analysis by the Citizens Commemorative Coin Advisory Committee and the federal Fine Arts Commission. Charles Atherton, secretary of the Fine Arts group, has been an overlapping member on the CCCAC.

The statehood coins are intended to circulate, augmenting the existing money supply of a widely used denomination—the quarter. Initially, the Mint estimated that the program would increase overall production by about 6 billion coins per year. But Mint Director Diehl, in an interview with me, said that long-range forecasts projected lower coinage demand for other denominations starting in 1999, and predicted the circulating commemorative package could fill the void. Diehl left office in March 2000, before completion of the program.

His prediction was borne out in 1997 when, after three consecutive years of mintages exceeding 19 billion coins

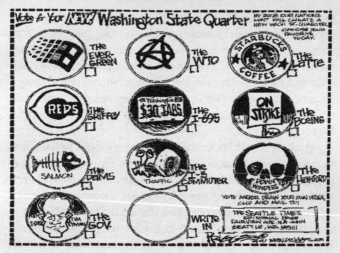

From the *Seattle Times*. © Milt Priggee. Reprinted by permission.

Reprinted by permission. Chuck Asay and Creators Syndicate, Inc. The bearded guy in the lower righthand corner is the author, David L. Ganz.

from all facilities, Mint production slipped more than 6 billion pieces to the 13-billion mark—a doughnut hole that could be filled nicely with the circulating quarter program. Some 1.19 billion quarters were produced at the Philadelphia and Denver mints in 1997 using the traditional design by John Flanagan. The art community reacted enthusiastically to news that the State Quarters program would go forward.

"Possibly it will show the Mint that it would be possible to have a whole new set of designs for our circulating coinage," said Patricia Verani, the Londonderry, New Hampshire, sculptor whose artwork appears on several modern U.S. commemorative coins. But she added her real hope: "I also hope that they would consider using Laura Gardin Fraser's portrait of Washington on the obverse," a universally acclaimed design that the Commission of Fine Arts approved in 1931, but which Treasury Secretary Andrew W. Mellon vetoed. Instead, that would be utilized for the 1999 $5 gold piece issued on the 200th anniversary of George Washington's death.

Treasury Secretary Rubin had the authority to change the Washington portrait because it had been used for more than 25 years and the Act of Sept. 26, 1890, authorized him to replace it administratively. But there had been resistance to the creation of an independent series for the 50 states, perhaps because of a fear—however irrational—that it could cause additional demand for the coinage, and hence strain Mint production capacity.

Action by the first five states was proceeding apace in early January 1998, with New Jersey being the best prepared. Its Assembly and Senate passed legislation, signed into law by Gov. Christine Todd Whitman, to create a 15-member commission to work out design recommendations. This was considered remarkable, because New Jersey has spent more than 38 years debating what should be the state song, and a comparable period trying to decide whether the Jersey tomato should be the state's official fruit or official vegetable.

In Delaware, the governor's office was aware of the federal law, and as of early February 1998 had begun implementation. The *Atlanta Constitution* reported in late December 1997 that Georgia had begun consideration, but surprisingly, nationwide, only about five stories had appeared in the daily press about the program according to the Lexis-Nexis computerized data base.

On Feb. 1, 1998, the Richmond *Times-Dispatch* reported that Gov. Jim Gilmore was on the verge of selecting a reverse design for the Virginia quarter and sending the proposal on to the Mint for action. The same article suggested that persons with design ideas should write directly to the governor in Richmond.

Pennsylvania Gov. Tom Ridge announced on Feb. 27, 1998, that through Internet technology, petitions, classroom projects, and the U.S. mail, more than 5,300 Pennsylvanians had answered his call for ideas for Pennsylvania's commemorative quarter. "We asked Pennsylvanians for their ideas, and they have responded," Ridge said. "From our youngest to our oldest, Pennsylvanians are proud and eager to show off our state on an American coin."

Pennsylvania's experience could well be the nation's as its citizens grappled with what should be placed on the tiny 26-millimeter surface—a design that is intended to symbolize the state for posterity.

Gov. Ridge said the most nominated concepts included the keystone, the State Seal, an Amish horse and buggy, the Liberty Bell, the State Capitol's Commonwealth statue, and the ruffed grouse as the state bird. Also included: the mountain laurel as the state flower, Independence Hall in

Philadelphia, the Capitol Building, and the nation's first oil-drilling well in Titusville. Many entries suggested multiple concepts, and many entrants suggested similar concepts.

Responses came by U.S. mail, which has existed since the United States began as a nation, as well as modern electronic mail. Submissions from 20 elementary school class projects also were included.

"Pennsylvania long has been admired nationally for our robust and forerunning leadership in industry, labor, the arts, literature, transportation, architecture, business, natural resources, education, technology, and community," Gov. Ridge said, surrounded by schoolchildren at the State Museum of Pennsylvania in January 1998 when he announced the quarter campaign. "It is only fitting that all Pennsylvanians have the opportunity to suggest an image that will be cherished and collected for centuries to come."

Ridge was required to submit his endorsed Pennsylvania coin concepts to the Treasury by March 13, 1998, almost a year before its quarter would be coined. The U.S. Mint then would draft visual design concepts for approved themes and send them back to the state for the governor's final selection in July.

For its part, the *Boston Globe* took the view that its readers were qualified to come up with the design concept. The *Globe* invited its readers "to sketch an image of what you believe would best represent Massachusetts on a 25-cent coin. Remember, no portraits and keep it appropriate (OK, OK, we're always up for a chuckle). An impartial jury of journalists will judge content, not presentation, to select a winner. A *Globe* illustrator will then create a rendition suitable for printing in the newspaper and forwarding to the acting governor's office. No promises, no fortune, just a fleeting moment of fame."

For Rhode Island, the 13th state to ratify the U.S. Constitution, there was a misunderstanding as to what could be included in the design, for its senior senator, Republican John Chaffee, suggested various portraitures. That was specifically prohibited under the law, thus sandbagging the suggestion that the Seals of the 50 states might be utilized (since the state of Washington has a frontal portrait of George Washington in its seal). Chaffee also suggested that an ocean scene be used—and it is a fair bet that at least one of the 50 states will utilize such a scene.

Many other states jumped at the opportunity for early action. Indiana's First Lady made it a personal project and her husband, the governor, introduced a statewide design competition that brought out thousands of entries two years before the coin would be produced. In all, the excitement and electricity reached a crescendo that was felt nationwide.

Just where the designs are going is another story. The prohibition against portraiture, however well conceived, is limiting. Some states, such as New Jersey, have highly allegorical State Seals; others are less lucky and have Seals that are functional if not beautiful.

It's fair to say that the design specifications for these circulating quarter dollars are far more stringent than those for non-circulating, legal-tender commemorative coinage that the U.S. Mint has issued with increasing regularity since 1982. And for good reason—non-circulating commemoratives are seen principally by collectors; this money will be coin of the realm, and will be the stuff by which history judges America's coinage, and its civilization. Eons from now, it is improbable that a Special Olympics coin will be found buried, and a question raised as to who Eunice Kennedy Shriver was, or what she accomplished in her lifetime. Her achievements, so very sincere and genuine, and indeed good works, simply have little long-term historical import.

Several members of the New Jersey state coinage design committee at the Philadelphia Mint, December 1998, with the design of the New Jersey quarter.

Perhaps because of the Shriver coin, the legislation creating the 50-state circulating commemorative coins specifies that "no portrait of a living person shall be included in any design," together with a specific prohibition against using even a head-and-shoulders portrait or bust of any person, living or dead.

"Suitable subject matter for design concepts include State landmarks (natural and man-made), landscapes, historically significant symbols of State resources or industries," flora, fauna, icons, and even outlines of the state boundaries, one Treasury Department guideline says. Not suitable: "state flags and seals," though some emblems from them are so highly symbolic that they will no doubt make the final cut and appear on the national coinage, and move into history. (Many of these are listed in the catalog portion of this book.)

As events turned out, the tentative designs from the first of the states showed that problems were being caused by the statutory requirements to use certain inscriptions on the coin, thus limiting the space for state-related designs.

Enter Congressman Castle yet again with the third law directed specifically to this circulating commemorative coin program, this time changing Mint practices (and existing laws) that date back to the founding of the Mint in 1792.

The inscription "United States of America," long a dominant part of the reverse of the quarter dollar (and, indeed, all U.S. coins), was authorized for placement on the obverse. The value (quarter dollar) also was moved from the reverse to the obverse. By contrast, the four-digit date which has been on nearly every coin's obverse, except for the $1 and $3 gold pieces, was shifted to the reverse, where it could be worked into the historical or allegorical design.

"I want to express our thanks to Chairman Castle and all members of Congress who moved so expeditiously on this issue," said Mint Director Diehl, a strong proponent of "the new balanced design" that, he said, allowed engravers "the artistic freedom needed for the statehood designs on the reverse."

Expeditious it was, for the legislation to allow for the design change was introduced after the Mint had begun to solicit "design concepts" from the governors of the first five states. The new legislation was introduced by Rep. Castle on March 2, 1998, and the House passed it by voice vote on March 27. Senate consideration came May 19, and President Clinton signed Public Law 105-176 on May 29, 1998.

Friday, June 12, 1998, was the date that Delaware made its design recommendation at a press briefing held in

Dover, the state capital. Its choice: patriot Caesar Rodney astride the horse carrying him from Dover to Philadelphia with the deciding vote in favor of signing the Declaration of Independence. Close second in the design concept competition, in which hundreds of Delaware citizens participated: an allegorical figure bearing a torch with the outline of Delaware and the inscription "The First State." Another also ran: a quill and parchment document with the same inscription.

There are two intriguing developments that have yet to achieve widespread media attention, but which will likely coalesce and result in expansion of the program beyond the 50 states.

First was the complaint by Washington, D.C., congressional delegate Eleanor Holmes Norton, D-D.C., that the Capitol District is ignored in the program (because it is not a state). The second is the possible addition over the next 10 years of another state, possibly Puerto Rico. Norton threatened to put a hold on the bill as it rushed toward a unanimous consent passage if the District of Columbia was not included. She was persuaded by Congressman Castle that a Washington, D.C., addition would be given consideration at a later date.

Some would argue that the more compelling issue is why Washington, D.C., with a population larger than Delaware, South Dakota, North Dakota, and Wyoming is not a state with full rights to representation in Congress, but Holmes Norton believes that, too, is an issue for another day. Watch for the 51st coin to be authorized, however.

The second element relates to U.S. territories: The Commonwealth of Puerto Rico, Guam, American Samoa, the Virgin Islands, and Northern Mariana. Legislation to add them to the program, along with Washington, D.C., has been introduced in Congress. My strong guess is that the program will be at least 56 coins before long.

The Mint has created special collector sets (you can still add your name to the Mint's list for future sets by calling it at 202-283-2646).

Congress began moving toward adding the District of Columbia, Puerto Rico, and the territories of Guam, Virgin Islands, Northern Marianas, and American Samoa late in the second session of the 106th Congress. Legislation was introduced by the chairman of the House coinage subcommittee, Rep. Spencer Bacchus, R-Alabama, cosponsored by the delegates to Congress from each of the represented areas. On Sept. 7, 2000, the coinage subcommittee held hearings, and markup of the legislation, recommending its passage by the full House. Action there was anticipated, as well as in the Senate, before the year's end. Signature into law by President Clinton would follow. The program is a separate one, though it would follow the 50-state program in 2010 with six additional coins in a single year—making an integrated 56-coin program to collect.

GRADING

Circulated Coins

 ost of America's State Quarters have gone directly into the circulation pool. The coining presses churn out hundreds of coins a minute per press, thousands of coins per hour, and in the aggregate, more than a hundred million coins each week during the production cycle of about two-and-a-half months per coin at both the Philadelphia and Denver mints.

Once the coin is struck, it is ejected into a bucket attached to each coining press, and, ker-plink by ker-plink, the bucket fills until it is dumped onto a conveyor belt that takes it to the coin counting machines.

Throughout this process, the coins come in contact with other coins, and tiny contact marks, or chinks in the metal, are found to occur. The coin counting machine is gentle, but it is nonetheless metal against metal, allowing for more minute abrasion. Sometimes these marks go into the "field" or undesigned, flat surface on each coin. A nick or a scratch there, or perhaps on a high point of the design, is bound to happen.

A small percentage of the coins that go through this process receive no metal damage, or perhaps pick up a nick or a scratch that coincides with a curl on Washington's hair lock, so it simply does not show. Perhaps another has simply had the chink of the metal hit at a rate that is less damaging. Regardless, those who examine the America's State Quarters in depth are aware that a high percentage of these coins have minor marks, abrasions, metallic chinks, or other minor surface damage on each coin. The number of specimens that are truly unimpaired and visually pleasing, even under a 5- or 10-powered magnifying glass, is few.

In January 1999, when America's State Quarters program was in its infancy, *Numismatic News* editor David Harper and I performed an admittedly unscientific experiment at the Florida United Numismatists (FUN) show, held each year in January in Orlando, Florida. We looked at hundreds of Delaware coins to try to assemble four or five coins from circulation that could be photographed in order to show the new design. After several hundred specimens were examined, we were astonished to find that only about five pieces merited photography, and that even here there was typically one side that was better than the other, with none reaching that ethereal perfection that many collectors crave.

Of course, this is anecdotal rather than scientific research, but the near universal anecdotal experience with the America's State Quarters program is that the rim has been lowered, and the basin for the coin design upon which the features appear has been raised. The consequence of these technical details is that the coins get banged up rather easily and their designs marred.

This does not say that the coins are still not uncirculated, for they are; uncirculated is an art, and a defined term, rather than a scientific or precise meaning of "not in circulation," which by definition a coin obtained in change cannot be.

Don Ketterling, director of numismatics at Goldline

International, an A-Mark subsidiary, has been promoting the statehood quarters by giving them to customers with each order since the original release of the Delaware coins. He comments on the scarcity of high-condition specimens: "Along the way, we have gleaned a few examples of the best in quality and have certified some. You should know, that as of now and to the best of my knowledge, there have been NO business-strike examples of any of the statehood quarters which have graded MS-68 or higher. There have been precious few that have graded 67. I am using the PCGS population report as reference. The NGC report shows none graded 67 or higher."

The reference to the grading scale will be explained momentarily, but the scale runs from 1 (worst) to 70 (best), and these last few numbers of 66, 67, 68, 69, and 70 are extraordinarily well-preserved coins, and even though modern, they are scarce and relatively valuable.

Ketterling continues: "We have an MS-67 example of the Massachusetts and all the other issues have only one or two examples in that grade thus far. For reference, the other Mass 67 sold on Teletrade at $260 plus the buyer's fee. . . . In general, the quality of the business-strike specimens are quite abysmal, which will only continue as production increases with subsequent issues. We are currently perusing original bags of Maryland coins and have found scarcely an MS-66, if that!"

Verbal descriptions of uncirculated and other conditions were utilized first by collectors, but a numerical method of grading has been in use for more than a half century—and, in the last 15 or 20 years, this has come to predominate as the method of describing coins' conditions, and ultimately their value.

If you are not a collector, you would probably assume that coins were graded on the same numerical scale that all of us were used to from the time we were in grammar school: 1 to 100. That might make a lot of sense, and coins certainly could be graded that way, but the coins that form the basis for numerical grading are old U.S. large cents and half cents, and the grading of these was not so much descriptive, initially, but was a set of numbers reflecting basal value. A scale of 1 to 70 was utilized. A coin in poor condition, with a basal value of 1, would cost 1/60th of the amount of the same coin in uncirculated (Mint State-60). A coin in uncirculated condition but of a better grade (Gem or Mint State-65) according to this theory should have had a price of about 5% more than an MS-60 example of the same coin.

The inventor of the system, Dr. William Sheldon, was a Yale professor and mathematical genius who was also famous for advancing a theory that by studying bare anatomy, it was possible to predict intelligence. Like the concept of mathematical pricing through grading, the physiological photographs are part of a discredited theory.

Even though the theory is long since gone, numerical grading is here to stay using a 1 to 70 scale, and all coins are graded and described using these numbers. Because the value of all of America's State Quarters depends so much on their grade or condition, it is important to understand coin grading in its historical context—for it is that very format that serves as the underlying basis for grading all coins today. Put differently, if you understand the concept of how a coin is graded, it does not matter whether you are grading America's State Quarters or a rare old silver dollar. The principles are identical.

Coin collecting is sometimes termed a precise and exacting science but coin grading is an imprecise form of it at best. This is because coin grading offers a succinct definition or interpretation of the state of preservation, and the relative condition, of one or more coins.

This is done through an examination of the surfaces of

the metal, the strength of the strike, the luster or sheen that time has given the piece, and the rendering of an opinion of these factors coupled with eye appeal. This is as true for America's State Quarters as it is for an Indian Head cent made prior to the start of the 20th century.

Having said that in the abstract, the lack of a definite, fixed standard has a great deal to do with the comparative nature of grading—the examination of one coin, and the inevitable mental image or physical comparison of that coin to another specimen. To that extent, grading is personal, and not unlike comparing great wines, where adjectives— or even numbers alone— cannot adequately convey a subjective impression.

Many times, a grader will examine a coin and conclude that it is "the best" example that is known. Comparisons of lesser specimens are automatically drawn to that coin. If, at a later time, a different and better specimen becomes known to a grader or cataloger, so inevitably does the point of comparison.

In one case where the Federal Trade Commission was bringing claim against the grading practices of a dealer who sold rare and other coins, its experts (renowned coin dealers) were asked to grade the identical set of coins, piece by piece. The supervising federal District Court judge was astonished to find that they disagreed as to the grades of nearly half of them, and in several instances by more than one grading description or numerical point.

That coin grading is imprecise in the abstract does not mean that a dealer, whose livelihood depends on the grade—or a trained collector—cannot uniformly apply a personal standard. They do, every day. In a world of subjectivity, where each element is inherently non-objective, amid the imprecision and lack of consistent, objective standards or means of interpretation, it is nonetheless important to collectors and coin buyers to have in some concrete form the fundamental basis under which a system of comparative evaluation can operate. Dozens of articles, and a number of books, have attempted to do this with respect to the grading of numismatic items. Some exist prior to the 20th century, others are far more current.

The least common denominator is that in describing the condition of a coin or grading, it continues to be what it always has been—a highly subjective opinion that offers an interpretation of the particular state of preservation of a coin.

Rudiments of coin-grading standards or methodologies were quite limited even as short a time as three decades ago. They can best be summarized by stating that except for early American copper coins (thanks to Sheldon's *Penny Whimsy*), adjectival descriptions were widely utilized by collectors and dealers alike in a very general way. Coins were principally termed Good, Very Good, Fine, Very Fine, Extremely Fine, About Uncirculated, or Uncirculated, or defined as being struck as a proof or specimen coin intended for collectors.

In 1997, the Professional Coin Grading Service oversaw preparation of the *Official Guide to Coin Grading and Counterfeit Detection,* edited by Scott A. Travers. The significance of this book is enormous. Particularly, it sets forth grading standards for contemporary and earlier coinage—the same standards that are employed by PCGS as it encapsulates hundreds of thousands of coins in sealed plastic with a printed grade attributed to each coin.

Actually, there is nothing terribly remarkable about the contents of the *A.N.A. Grading Guide,* or some other books that describe grading techniques and attempt to quantify the condition of a coin. Its verbal equivalents to numerical grading have changed since the first few editions. The verbiage that it uses to describe a typical Uncirculated coin (usually referred to as MS-60), a Choice Uncirculated coin (once referred to in the guide as MS-65, but usually referred to in the trade as MS-63), and a Gem coin (once referred to in the guidebook as MS-67, but uniformly called in the trade MS-65) is hardly innovative at all. Rather, the *A.N.A. Grading Guide* starts with a conceptually perfect coin and then adds or subtracts a series of detractions in the form of scratches, marks, bag marks or contact marks, and other flaws which tend to make the coin appear to be less than perfect on a declining scale.

The initial *A.N.A. Grading Guide* was systematic, offered extensive analysis, and had good drawings of what coins in various states of preservation look like. The 1987 *A.N.A. Guide* introduced photographs to accompany the verbal descriptions. But these books do not yet show in any type of detail what many collectors and investors need to know: where a coin has its high spots, which is to say the point and places on which wear is most likely to appear.

The original Sheldon parameters of 1 to 70 are widely followed, as originally stated in *Penny Whimsy* in 1948: Good condition starts at 3; Fine condition is 12; Extremely Fine is 40; About Uncirculated starts at 50; and Uncirculated is between 60 and 70. However, wide differences have developed among mint-state coins, where specimens are now being graded on a single-digit basis between 60 and 70.

Most experienced collectors and dealers can differentiate between a typical Uncirculated coin and a Choice Uncirculated specimen. Most can also distinguish between a technically graded MS-65 and an MS-63 coin. There are those who believe they can identify, time after time, without error, intermediate grades such as MS-61, MS-62, and MS-64 (without confusing an MS-64 with an MS-63 or MS-65, for example). This is unlikely, however, for even the best graders and catalogers frequently will admit that they may view a point differently in the morning than they will at the end of a tired day, and that the perception of whether or not a coin is MS-63 or MS-64 (representing a significant price difference in the marketplace) often will depend on demand in the market—which means that grading is market-driven.

The *Official A.N.A. Grading Standards for United States Coins* acknowledges that "grading can never be completely scientific in all areas . . . there are no scientific means available to measure the surface condition—the amount of wear—of a coin."

Still, several points must be emphasized about the grades of uncirculated coins. First, although the difference between an MS-65 and an MS-67 is only two points, the difference in the monetary value of coins in these two grades can be great, even for America's State Quarters, which are so new. For some of America's State Quarters, an MS-68 may have a value of several hundred dollars, while an MS-65 may be worth just 10 times face value.

A large private company, the Professional Coin Grading Service (PCGS) offers grading opinions about coins owned by dealers and consumers. It requires that four graders view each coin to determine its final grade. It uses an 11-point standard, from MS-60 to MS-70, for all uncirculated coins. This is true for America's State Quarters, whose Uncirculated condition is described as MS-60, MS-61, MS-62, and so forth, all the way to MS-70. The second-largest grading company is the Numismatic Guaranty Corporation of America (NGC), located in Parsippany, New Jersey.

These various grading services do not necessarily agree on the state of preservation of a particular coin. Q. David Bowers, a respected expert in the coin industry, states in *Adventures With Rare Coins* (1979) that: "Often five different sellers will assign different grades to the same coin, perhaps differing just slightly but still differing, often with important financial consequences. . . ."

For the time being, it seems likely that most of America's

A pristine coin, with fine-line detail for the hair, at the ears, chin, and lettering. This coin would grade 65 or better on the 1-to-70 scale.

State Quarters will be called either About Uncirculated (grading AU-50, AU-53, AU-55, or AU-58) or various gradations of Uncirculated, starting at MS-60 and continuing sequentially through MS-70. There are also proof examples, encased by the government, which could theoretically be as low as Proof-60 (or running sequentially through Proof 70), but more likely will minimally grade Proof-65 (or Gem status).

Circulation has been simulated on this State Quarter obverse. Notice how Washington's hair lacks the fine detail of an uncirculated coin and how, beneath the cheek, there are signs of wear. There is also some wear on the lettering.

The way to imagine what each grade represents, even in Uncirculated, is often described as the visualization of a 12" ruler. At the "1" end of the ruler is a coin in Poor condition; at the "11," Uncirculated starts and each of the minor lines of an eighth or sixteenth of an inch constitutes a different Uncirculated grade (Uncirculated 60, Uncirculated 61, Uncirculated 62, and so forth). For purposes of the America's State Quarters program, it is perhaps more useful to focus on *how* a coin is graded, and *why* a coin might be classified as MS-62, MS-63, MS-64, or MS-65, since these are the coins that are most likely to be encountered.

Grading is a form of shorthand, with a numerical or adjectival basis that is intended to describe the overall appearance and condition of a coin. It takes into account luster, the condition of the planchet, distractions on the surface such as scratches or minor chinks in the metal, signs of surface wear, the natural sheen that the coin exudes, and its overall visual appearance contrasted with that of other coins. As a coin enters commerce, it quite naturally comes in contact not only with other coins, but with machinery that counts it, bags it, rolls it, and separates it, together with the hands of consumers that rub it, jingle it, and otherwise handle it. All of this creates a minor residue of metal that is removed from the surface, altering the "perfect" state of preservation that a coin typically starts with when it is produced by the U.S. Mint.

The minting process is a harsh one; strips of metal of about 3 inches in width and many feet in length are fed into a blanking press which punches out a planchet that is blank on both sides. The metal at this point is too hard to be struck into a coin, so it has be annealed, or heat-treated, in ovens that reach temperatures of thousands of degrees. The heat-treated metal is then cleaned in a soapy solution and tumbled with ball bearings to clean off the surfaces. This already impregnates the surface with imperfections, but the next step in the process which transforms the blank into a coin both beautifies it and entombs the imperfections for eternity.

Blanks are placed in a hopper and fed into a coining press that provides several hundred tons of pressure to a planchet (or coin blank) where an obverse or front die meets a reverse die. The metal blank in the middle, when struck under pressure, flows outward to a collar. The edge is then reeded, if applicable, the design struck up, and the coin ejected.

Assuming that there is not an error on the planchet, at this point in time the coin is pristine, but each ker-plink or ker-chunk that involves one coin coming into contact with another creates a flaw, and the minor flaws gradually, but cumulatively, start to detract from its overall condition.

As they enter the circulation pool, the vast majority of the uncirculated coins would be called somewhere between MS-60 and MS-63, fewer yet MS-65, and even fewer MS-67 or above. Of course, some fit grades that are in between, and some coins actually seem to be struck "Uncirculated" with discernible wear, or with marks all over the planchet that bring down its overall condition. As coins remain in circulation, the metal begins to wear more subtly on the surface. For example, on the Delaware quarter, the head of Caesar Rodney or his knee, both high points in the design, may begin to flatten out, and other fine details may become obliterated. The curls on George Washington's wig or his chin may begin to show signs of blurring in the metal. All of these elements conspire to reduce the grade (and ultimately the value) of the coin.

There are certain common elements of the obverse design (the constant in the series) where wear is likely to be seen. The same is true for each of the other coins, though they must be described separately because their designs are different. On the reverse (the "state" side of the quarter), the date and "E Pluribus Unum" (Latin for "Out of many, one") always appear at the 6 o'clock position of the coin, while the name of the state appears at the top or 12 o'clock position, together with the date the state ratified the U.S. Constitution or joined the Union. The obverse with Washington's portrait will be the constant in the series, and its signs of wear will be evident in the field opposite Washington's nose and and above the national motto, "In God We Trust."

Regardless of which side of the coin is involved, there are certain general principles that are nearly universal. First, it is inevitably the high point of the coin design that will first show signs of wear, and will pick up the nicks and scrapes and minute metal particle alterations that change the condition of the coin. There is probably an easy way to visualize what takes place. Imagine that you have taken an 8½" × 11" sheet of paper and drawn a circle on it along with a design of George Washington. This is a "pure" MS-70 coin. Take an 8½" × 11" sheet of tracing paper and put it over George Washington's face and take a light No. 2 pencil and shade a portion of his jaw and a portion of his curls. This is designed to simulate minor portions of wear. Next, take another sheet of tracing paper and put five or six dots in the left field opposite Washington's eyes. This is designed to simulate metal fatigue where the design has been lightly damaged by contact marks. Looking at the coin overall, it is not especially displeasing; it is probably the equivalent of Uncirculated condition. If you remove the tracing paper with the shading on the chin and ear, it is now somewhere between MS-63 and MS-65, since there is no wear on the coin but some design damage of an infinitesimal degree.

The grading of the America's State Quarters is important and, ultimately, in future years, will have a substantial impact on their value. Indeed it already has a significant impact even now. For example, the Delaware quarter that remains in change is probably in Extremely Fine condition at this point in time. It has little more value than its nominal legal-tender worth. Meanwhile, a better Uncirculated coin (MS-65) is selling a year-and-a-half after issue at $1.75 per coin. Examples in MS-68 and even MS-70, taken right from change, were selling at $27.50 or more a mere 18 months after the government decreed that the lump of metal had a worth of 25 cents.

Proof Coins

Quite unlike the process of examining circulated coins for minor defects, proof coinage is made differently, looks very different, and in at least one respect is much easier to grade. Proof coins are struck on specially selected planchets that were previously cleaned in a cream of tartar solution that leaves them with a mirrorlike sheen. They are produced on a hydraulic press that can strike several coins a minute at a maximum, contrasted with hundreds of coins a minute on a regular production press. Regular coins are struck just once, while proof coins are struck twice (or more) to bring up the design while simultaneously maintaining a mirrorlike finish in the fields. Sometimes the design elements are struck in a mirrorlike manner; other times they have a "matte" finish because of a production technique that has no effect on condition.

In the 21st century, virtually all proof coins, off the press and into the packet, will have a grade of at least Proof-65, and some will go higher quite easily. At an earlier time, even in the modern era of the 20th century, Mint production, storage, and coin interaction many times lowered the grade into the Proof-62 or Proof-63 range. It is always useful to remember that when it comes to the grades Proof-68, Proof-69, and Proof-70, there really aren't a lot of coins that merit these descriptions. Hence, even though the Mint might offer a proof set at $32.50 complete with the 50 State coins, a single 50 State coin 18 months out of production in Proof-68 condition typically had a $30 price tag, which means a fivefold return on the investment if all coins in the set were of the same grade and condition.

In the catalog section of the book, grading hints have been supplied for each coin that is in Uncirculated condition. Generally, this section focuses on the high points of the coins, and shows how they wear. Even with this good

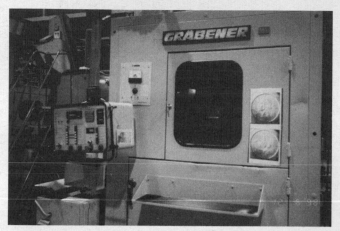

This Grabener press at the Philadelphia Mint is utilized to strike State Quarters for circulation. The picture on the front of the press is of the Delaware coin. Because so many different coins are struck now, the design is duplicated and placed on the front to assist pressmen looking for errors.

information comes an important caveat: When coins are in circulation or come in contact with people or other coins, the mars, nicks, scratches, digs, and contact marks can show up in the darnedest places. The third edge of a coin is its rim; it should always be examined for contact marks, although to be candid, a small "ding" on the rim has far less effect on the value of a coin than does one on the facial element, in the field opposite the face, or in the large reverse field.

Traditionally, collectors have emphasized the condition of the obverse over the condition of the reverse. Thus, if a coin was MS-65 grade on the obverse and not quite as nice on the reverse, it probably would get a higher designation of MS-65. On the other hand, historically, if the reverse was MS-65 and the obverse was MS-63 or MS-64, it would *never* achieve an MS-65 grade.

The verdict is not in on this yet, but it is apparent because of the heavy focus on the 50 States portion of the program, that collectors will give far more emphasis to the reverse side of the series than to the obverse. The little "scratch" or the little "ding" or contact mark on the reverse will more likely have a greater substantive effect on condition than before.

STATE QUARTER ISSUES FOR COLLECTORS INVESTING IN THE NUMISMATIC ECONOMY

A substantial and worthwhile collection of America's State Quarters can be assembled from coins produced by the U.S. Mint as proof or specimen coinage, and also in high-grade (MS-66 and above) uncirculated issues. The proofs are intended primarily for coin collectors, and the uncirculated versions are taken carefully from circulation—but even if you aren't a collector now, it's a series that you ought to give consideration to. Two different versions of proofs are available—one in copper-nickel clad, the other in coin silver (90% fine); each is sold initially only by the U.S. Mint at a fixed price. A substantial secondary market has developed, based primarily on the condition of the coins. These coins—and the very high-grade uncirculated pieces as well—have significant investment potential that some have already realized and others may seek to examine or at least consider in the coming years.

Created and sold by the Mint in sets, the coins have been broken out of the holders of issue and submitted to one or more independent grading services, where the better ones have been found to be Proof-65 at a minimum, all the way up to Proof-70 (the best grade). They have then been re-marketed to the collecting public and those interested in making an investment choice in America's State Quarters, at prices substantially in excess of the initial offering price from the Mint.

All proof coins are not created equal; most produced by the U.S. Mint today grade a minimum of Proof-65 on the grading scale (Proof-60 to Proof-70 is what is generally used; if a proof coin goes into circulation, it can grade Proof-58 or lower; at least in the year 2000, none of the proof coins produced had entered circulation, and in any event, circulated modern proof coins are generally not collectible, absent a mint error to substantially enhance their value).

Prices for the proof coins being sold on the secondary market are extraordinary, not only in advertisements found in the commercial trade press such as *Numismatic News, Coin World, COINage* magazine, and *Coins* magazine, but also in online auctions such as Teletrade (the oldest service of its kind, which has more than 300 auctions involving more than 300,000 coins).

About Proof Grades

It is a common misnomer to term *proof* a condition. Proof is actually a method of manufacture. The typical coining press today produces coins at a capacity of about 600 per minute and perhaps operates more typically at a bit less than a third of that level. By contrast, proof coins are produced on hydraulic presses operating at much slower rates, and in a way that allows the coins to be struck with two blows from the die, rather than the single blow that is typical of circulation strikes. On some models, coin blanks are hand-fed to the press; on others, they are machine-fed and gently removed on an air blanket that prevents the planchet or the struck coin from coming into contact with other metal that could damage the coin or cause small abrasions. The planchets are highly polished beforehand, the dies see limited use, and also are polished to assure that the end product is a work of art, a thing of beauty, that can be appreciated not only by a collector, but also by a casual viewer.

Proof coins, like uncirculated coins, have different gradations. Generally, proof coins might be described as a Typical proof, a Choice proof, or a Gem proof, with numerical gradations only at the major demarcations (Proof-60, 63, 65, 67, and 70). There are numerical gradations at each unit from 60 to 70 (i.e., 61, 62, 63, etc.). The difference between Proof-63 and Proof-64 is difficult for the novice to tell, and sometimes the experienced collector as well. For that reason, many collectors, and investors, have come to rely on third-party grading services which, for a fee, will examine a coin, grade it, and then permanently encapsulate it in a hard plastic holder that allows the viewer to see both sides without physically touching the coin (which, of itself, could cause damage from finger oils or mishandling).

Among modern coin issues, collectors overwhelmingly prefer proof coins to their uncirculated counterparts, but the irony is that better-grade uncirculated coins are, as a result, generally much scarcer. For example, among the U.S. Mint's contemporary commemorative coin issues, more proof coins are struck than uncirculated versions by a more than 3:1 ratio (more than 75% of the coins are proof, the remaining portion uncirculated). As the mintage figures in the catalog section of this book show, and as the coins certified by third-party grading services prove, high-end uncirculated State Quarters are downright rare. But if that is true, it is also the case that very high-grade proof State Quarters are scarce, and quite valuable, because there are enough of them to make them collectible, desirable, and marketable.

Perhaps the easiest way to explain this unusual distinction is to offer an example with a rare coin such as the Brasher doubloon. In the mid-1970s, none had been sold publicly in more than a half century (the last one at the

Jenks Collection sale of 1921). Only a few existed, and no one was quite sure what they were worth. Capitol Coin Company had acquired its specimen nearly 20 years earlier from the Virgil Brand collection, and when it offered it at public auction in the Rare Coin Company of America (RARCOA) section of Auction '79, no one truly knew what the coin might bring. It opened on the bidding floor at $210,000, and ultimately sold for $435,000—with perhaps a dozen bidders interested even as it crossed the $400,000 mark to become, in its day, the most expensive coin ever sold at public auction. (The mark has since been surpassed many times over.)

At the same auction sale, two examples of the 1904-S Morgan silver dollar were sold—one by RARCOA described as Gem Uncirculated, the other by Superior Galleries (termed MS-60 or Typical Uncirculated). About 2.3 million of these silver dollars were struck at the San Francisco Mint about a century ago, and few survived in superior states of preservation. The MS-60 version sold for $2,400 and the Gem (at least MS-65) sold for $4,000.

To give some measure of the availability of the 1904-S silver dollar, the Numismatic Guaranty Corporation (NGC), as of May 2000, had encapsulated nearly 500 examples, of which 109 were MS-63, 117 were MS-64, and 17 were MS-65 (there were two that were MS-66 and one that was MS-67). The Professional Coin Grading Service (PCGS) had encapsulated and graded about a thousand coins, with 252 in MS-63, 220 in MS-63, and 67 in MS-65. (There were also four in MS-66 and two in MS-67.)

Because of the quantity available, the 1904-S is actively collected by many collectors and investors. The Brasher doubloon is simply outside the reach of all but the upper echelons of those who collect, or invest in, coins.

If you have occasion to independently buy a proof coin or a proof set containing the State Quarters, you may wish to have some general guidelines to assist you in grading and evaluating them and their condition.

It is important to recognize that over the course of the last 30 years, the way that proof coins have been described, and the way that collectors grade these coins, have changed significantly—and it could well continue to evolve. There have not been significant deviations from the general principles involved in evaluating the grade of a proof coin. Originally, however, standards as set forth in the original *A.N.A. Grading Guide* for proof coins were divided into three classifications:

PROOF-60 (PROOF). Proof-60 refers to a Proof with some scattered handling marks and hair lines which will be visible to the unaided eye.

PROOF-65 (CHOICE PROOF). Proof-65 or Choice Proof refers to a proof which may show some very fine hair lines, usually from friction-type cleaning or friction-type drying or rubbing after dipping. To the unaided eye, a Proof-65 or a Choice Proof will appear to be virtually perfect. However, 5x magnification will reveal some minute lines. Such hair lines are best seen under strong incandescent light.

PROOF-70 (PERFECT PROOF). A Proof-70 or Perfect Proof is a coin with no hair lines, handling marks, or other defects; in other words, a flawless coin. Such a coin may be brilliant or may have natural toning.

In his introduction to the second edition (1984) of the ANA grading guidebook, Q. David Bowers, who was then president of the American Numismatic Association as well as the Professional Numismatists Guild, and a respected dealer in his own right, observed that "the situation of intermediate grades among Mint State [and proof] coins is taken care of nicely by the five numerical grades available in the *Official A.N.A. Grading* system: MS-60, MS-63, MS-65,

MS-67, and MS-70." (The same applies to Proof-60, Proof-63, and so forth.)

Bowers went on to note that "A.N.A. consultants feel that such minor divisions as MS-61, MS-62, and so on cannot be adhered to with consistency. For this reason, the only grades recognized in the *Official A.N.A. Grading* system are as indicated: MS-60, MS-63, MS-65, MS-67, and MS-70."

Expanding upon this slightly, the introduction continued that "the insertion of the new MS-63 and MS-67 grades can also generally be agreed upon by numismatists who are experienced. However, it is the opinion of the A.N.A. that not even the most advanced numismatists could consistently agree on such minute classifications as MS-61, MS-62, MS-64, and so on, and for this reason minute distinctions of this nature are not incorporated in the text. These distinctions would simply be too minute to permit accuracy."

The Official Guide to Coin Grading and Counterfeit Detection (edited by Scott A. Travers, House of Collectibles, 1997) utilizes adjectives and numbers to describe proof grading, and is regarded today as the authoritative reference work on the subject. It grades from Proof-50 (Circulated Proof) by degrees to Proof-60 (Proof), and includes numbers through Proof-63 and Proof-64 (Choice Proof), Proof-65 and Proof-66 (Gem Proof), Proof-67, Proof-68, and Proof-69 (Superb Gem Proof), and Proof-70 (Perfect Proof).

For purposes of collecting State Quarters, the following general descriptions are relevant. These characterizations are taken from the text of *The Official Guide to Coin Grading and Counterfeit Detection*:

PROOF-65 (GEM) Sharply struck, with a high degree of luster and average-to-superior eye appeal (which nearly everyone finds attractive). There may be light hair lines or contact marks and there may be unobtrusive planchet flaws.

PROOF-66 (GEM) Exceptionally sharp strike, excellent reflectivity, overall high eye appeal. Any surface defects must be minor and not detracting from overall appearance.

PROOF-67 (SUPERB GEM) Defects to the unaided eye are minor, unobtrusive hair lines, sharp strike. If the eye is drawn to a defect, it is unlikely to reach this grade. Superb eye appeal, nearly full reflectivity.

PROOF-68 (SUPERB GEM) Virtually undetectable hair lines or other defects; full strike and detail; fully reflective and exceptional eye appeal.

PROOF-69 (SUPERB GEM) Appears perfect to the unaided eye. On magnification, a minor hair line or planchet flake may be visible. Full strike, fully reflective, superb eye appeal.

PROOF-70 (PERFECT). There can be no defects visible with a 5-power glass, free of hair lines or mint-caused post-striking defects. Fully reflective surface, spectacular appearance.

Here are some prices that give a general sense of this end of the State Quarters market for proof coins as reported by Teletrade[1] in its auctions, which have had over 40,000 participants over the past dozen or so years:

---

[1] Since 1986, Teletrade has been a leading auctioneer, servicing and protecting both buyers and sellers. Buyers can always depend on Teletrade to deliver exceptional service. Teletrade takes possession of all lots offered in their auctions, describes each lot (which is always graded by a major service, and encapsulated, eliminating any grading disputes), professionally packages, fully insures, and ships all winning bids, and offers among the best online images in the industry. Consignors can count on a "good" check from Teletrade. Generous cash advances are also available. Whether you are at home, at work, or on the road, with or without a computer, all services at Teletrade's web site are free. You only pay a fee when you buy or sell an item. You can reach Teletrade at 800-232-1132 or at its web site at http://www.teletrade.com.

DATE	TYPE	GRADING SERVICE	HIGH BID	SALE DATE
1999-S	CT cu-ni	PCGS-69	$39	SEP 99
1999-S	CT deep cameo	PCGS-69	$85	DEC 99
1999-S	DE deep cameo	PCGS-68	$33	DEC 99
1999-S	DE deep cameo	PCGS-69	$90	DEC 99
1999-S	GA cameo cu-ni	PCGS-69	$30	DEC 99
1999-S	GA deep cameo	PCGS-69	$60	DEC 99
1999-S	PA deep cameo	PCGS-69	$60	DEC 99

There also are a number of examples of individual coins in Proof-69 or Proof-70 selling for $129 or more—impressive, considering the original cost per set. The 1999 silver proof set (which includes silver versions of the Kennedy half dollar and Roosevelt dime in addition to the five State Quarters) had a $31.95 issue price. That averages about $6.40 per State Quarter if you discard entirely any cost associated with the other coins. The Mint estimated that production limits of 800,000 would be imposed for these coins.

Regular proof sets, which cost $12.50 through 1998, and $19.95 in 1999, had a limit of about 2.5 million sets estimated initially by the Mint. There, the five copper-nickel–clad quarters had a cost of about $4 apiece, again excluding the value of any of the other coins. Encapsulation also has a cost (figure it at around $2 to $20 per coin)—but at the end of the day, the overall investment is quite minimal and the return potential substantial, depending on the numismatic economy.

The result of all this can be quite pleasing, and offer an unexpected gain. NumisMedia regularly publishes a *Fair Market Value Price Guide* through the Numismatic Interactive network, available both online and in a print edition. Dennis Baker, who for many years was editor of *The Coin Dealer Newsletter,* is senior editor of NumisMedia, and uses the term "fair market value" to refer to "the price a dealer is asking for a coin, which is a reasonable charge over a dealer's wholesale price." Baker's reputation, over a period of many years, is for solid, conservative pricing. His report as of May 30, 2000, for the State Quarters program is necessarily limited—prices for coins only up to Maryland issues are included—but they are dead-on when considering the future of the series:

WASHINGTON QUARTERS	MS-65	MS-66	MS-67
1999-P Delaware	20	36	144
1999-D Delaware	24	37	180
1999-P Pennsylvania	20	32	—
1999-D Pennsylvania	23	54	—
1999-P New Jersey	23	37	—
1999-D New Jersey	19	37	222
1999-P Georgia	19	42	300
1999-D Georgia	23	54	—
1999-P Connecticut	26	35	—
1999-D Connecticut	16	24	162
2000-P Massachusetts	17	25	66
2000-D Massachusetts	16	24	53
2000-P Maryland	24	60	180
2000-D Maryland	—	—	—

In the catalog portion of this book, current fair market value in superior grade (MS-65 and higher) condition appears. Valuations are courtesy of Dennis Baker and Numismedia, as of May 30, 2000, and are provided exclusively to *The Official Guide to America's State Quarters*. Fair market value prices listed are for certified coins only (usually PCGS, NGC, or ANACS). Raw coins may bring substantially less. Prices may fluctuate considerably as new issues are brought on the market and certified. As populations increase in a particular grade, coins may be easier to obtain and prices may fall. Where an asterisk appears for a grade, Numismedia has not seen enough trading activity to establish a

AMERICA'S NEW STATE QUARTERS

The Washington Mint, a private facility, produced this philatelic-numismatic combination with a first-day cover.

price at this time. (Valuations ©2000 by Numismedia, Inc. All rights reserved. Used by permission.) A comprehensive listing of fair market value of U.S. coins is found on the website of Numismedia, *http://www.numismedia.com.*

The Numismatic Economy

There's a numismatic economy, all right. Collectors see it every time they want to buy a new issue that has sold out and have to go into the secondary market and acquire it at a higher price. It's especially true with the State Quarters proof coinage. Investors become aware of the numismatic economy when they see gold or silver prices take a jump, expect their coins to do the same, and find that the two markets, however parallel, don't always follow the same track.

Even dealers learn that there are economic laws that function—like trying to deal with a changing system of values, and grades, over a period of time and witnessing how traditional supply-and-demand economics function differently in numismatics. That's one of the reasons why third-party grading for the State Quarters program, especially for higher proof grades, is so essential.

Anyone who is involved in the buying, selling, and trading of coins learns about the numismatic economy fairly quickly—or else is in for a rude awakening when, relying on what might otherwise be common sense, they take an action that is contrary to the rules of the game. Some of the stakes seem like hardball. Perhaps for that reason it is of paramount importance for someone involved in coins to like what they're doing, instead of just being a glutton for the potential profits.

Some of the aspects almost resemble a board game like Monopoly, the classic Parker Brothers board game that cheered America through a Depression and later gave several generations a roll of the dice for their money. Think about it: Roll the dice, buy a coin, put it in your vault, and wait for two years. On your next turn, you get to try to sell the coin, only to discover that what was MS-65 when you bought it has now turned into an MS-63 or lower coin. What about rolling snake eyes and advancing to the card that says 1960 Small Date cents or 1950-D nickels, each touted as an "investment" in its time and spoken of as the one item to bet the bank on. Perhaps it is a 1999 Delaware quarter. Or perhaps times have truly changed.

If you make the wrong choice, you get to tie up your money for a couple of years and then sell at a substantial loss. Despite the relative rarity of each piece—the '50-D nickel at a mere 2.6 million pieces, the Small Date cent estimated at several thousand as a proof, several hundred thousand in uncirculated—none ever took off. The reason: either the market is a lot thinner than many thought or no one was really interested in modern rarities.

The author with a Mint technician after striking by hand on a hydraulic press a new Delaware coin on Dec. 8, 1998. The Delaware coin, in uncirculated condition (MS-65 or better), sells for eight times face value less than a year-and-a-half after issue.

That's probably not the case with the State Quarters, because all evidence suggest that there are more than 100 million people actively collecting these unique and distinctive coins. Only a small portion could ever hope to acquire the proof coins (because of their mintage); in turn, only a fraction of that small portion is holding truly high-grade (Proof-67, Proof-68, Proof-69, and Proof-70) material.

Roll the dice again and you land on Bahamian proof sets, produced by The Franklin Mint. It tells you to pick a card, so you can see which one you get to purchase. What you find is that the early sets attracted collectors, and supplies were lower than demand; prices jumped accordingly.

Later issues saw people jump in who missed the boat the first time and hoped to make a killing. They paid double the price for the earlier sets, and found little liquidity in the marketplace—a pattern that continued with many other

Franklin Mint items produced later. That is something worth watching with the State Quarters, and is a strong reason to follow mintage figures and other similar announcements of availability.

Grading, of course, is a part of the game on one square; you get to buy an MS-65 coin with ANACS papers at the full *Greysheet* price (the price quoted in *The Coin Dealer Newsletter*), and say who sold it to you. A few squares later, you're required to have it sent in for regrading at ANACS, which now takes strike into account as well as eye appeal. (If the coin doesn't pass muster, you're required to sell it at a loss, but with the certificate, so that the next person to buy it will know what someone once thought it was.)

You're a collector who likes coins with a colorama surface—iridescent toning, sunbursts, and other hues in an array of delightful colors. In fact, you like them so much you pay extra for them (nearly everyone does). So roll the dice and land on Chemical City, where every coin that you get to buy is dipped. The directions tell you that some pros do it, adding color through chemicals and baking. So, because you won the toss, you can have it done to your coins for free. Some winning throw!

The next square is a logical corollary to this, best told in the words of James L. Halperin, whose *NCI Grading Guide* tells more about "real world grading" than most of us will ever know. The coin involved is a 1795 Bust dollar with hideous toning—a coin that "simply lacked eye appeal."

"I had some reservations about dipping the coin . . . [but] a quick dip in Jewel Luster produced one of the most stunning, blazing white, semi-proof-like gem, early U.S. silver coins I had ever seen. Really, nothing had changed except the eye appeal. . . ." The postscript to this story is that the coin changed from $33,500 to $137,000 in short order.

For every good point, there's a bad one; the next square

is where you dip a coin and it comes out with noticeable flaws, flaws that the toning was intended to hide in the first place.

If perchance you're a dealer and playing this board game, we'll add a wild card—the Federales. This can be anyone in the alphabet soup of government agencies that has an interest in coins these days: the Federal Trade Commission, the Internal Revenue Service, or the Securities and Exchange Commission. The U.S. Postal Office also can be included.

This board game is for everyone, so let's add just a couple of accurate plays in the numismatic economy. Let's say you roll and land on "Apply for a No-Action Letter to the SEC," so that you know what you're doing doesn't violate the securities laws. You find, to your chagrin, that they're no longer issuing no-action letters to those in the coin field. Proceed at your peril and take another spin of the dice.

This time, you land on an IRS square which says simply to select a card. Among the choices: "Provide 1099 forms for everyone you purchased coins from last year." While you're at it, try to explain why meals you eat on the road— the crummy hamburgers and greasy fries with a soft drink— are only 80% deductible. (Does the government take 20% of the indigestion?)

Are you bored yet?

This is only part of the numismatic economy. There are lots of fun things about coins and coin collecting, buying and selling them. Those are the reasons that you ought to be collecting or acquiring coins.

But if you're a buyer, or a seller, or a dealer for other reasons—such as a belief that it is an attractive investment vehicle—take solace in your roll that says "Salomon Brothers Survey." You know, the one that has gone up steadily year after year. It tells you to draw a card, and you do. Surprise. This is one that the Federal Trade Commission wants revealed: that Salomon is only a market basket, and that none of the coins that you purchased are in it. Too bad.

There are those who will say that this numismatic economy board game seems to be predicated on Murphy's Law—things don't get bad, they get worse. Well, there are those who seek to acquire coins only for the money, and the profit (and not for any enjoyment or other pleasure), who learn to their sorrow that Murphy was an optimist.

Some Perspective

For some 35 years, I have been writing about the economics of numismatics—and how the events of our everyday lives impact on a hobby, and the coin industry taken as a whole. This includes rises and falls in the stock market, changes in the Consumer Price Index, and announcements of changes in the gross national product of Pakistan.

In the backwater years, economic news was located in the daily newspapers' financial section, usually at the rear, often incorporated into stock tables. It made the front page when the Dow Jones Industrial Average went up 10 points in a single day. Yes, 10 points was significant back in 1965. The whole Dow Jones was under 1,000 (it was 910 that year, declining to 792 in 1966—and the rate of change for that 10 points was over 1 percent). It is today's equivalent of a change of more than 100 points on a daily basis, but that's become so common that it doesn't even make the front page of the financial section of the dailies.

Back in 1965, the price of gold was immutably held at $35 an ounce by force of government intervention. Much earlier, in 1933, at the end of the Hoover Administration, it had been pegged at $20.67 an ounce, the same rate it had been stabilized at, irregularly, since 1837. (At that rate, a $20 gold piece had $19.99 worth of gold metal in it.)

All of these numbers tie together eventually, and point to the interrelationship between all sectors of the economy, whether they be statehood quarters, the stock market, or precious-metal prices. In October 1999, for example, IBM saw a major loss of $23 per share in a single day's trading. Because 1.8 billion shares are held by the public, the loss for that single day aggregated about $35 billion, which is about half of Pakistan's gross national product for an entire year.

But the shock of that is that gold—and, for that matter, platinum and silver—simply did not react. Statehood quarters in Uncirculated condition increased modestly, and proof versions (silver and clad) showed that they are independent of this and began what eventually could be characterized as a meteoric rise.

Gold did not react as expected when there was a suspected coup d'état in the Soviet Union. Instead of going through the roof, it notched down more than a peg, and the effect was the same when Saddam Hussein sent chemical rockets toward Tel Aviv. Gold simply took to the tank and dropped another $50 an ounce.

Economics, from my perspective, is different now from what it was 35 years ago when I first started writing about coins. What is the same is that as the numbers are announced, they have an effect on coin prices—and on the coin industry—even if it is not necessarily what would have been predicted in the past. This makes charts and other analysis more significant, because in part it allows for trendlines to be created, and to get a general sense of where coin prices are going. What it also does is make periodic reviews and commentary essential, and make price guides published in *Numismatic News* and other periodicals useful tools in understanding the process.

With the new millennium upon us, it seems clear enough that the universe of collectors is expanding. The Mint's 50-state commemorative coin program alone has seen to that. So have efforts by the American Numismatic

Association and the Professional Numismatists Guild. What that may well translate to, if it can be marketed properly, is a change of the economics of the new millennium to move the market in rare gold coins—those left from the major melts of the Thirties—and the contemporary modern issues that are perhaps even scarcer than the melted-down remnants of a century ago and more.

Look at your *Guidebook* or *Standard Catalogue* and compare the mintages. Economics 101 tells you that supply and demand will set the price. There's an increasingly smaller supply and a higher demand. Let's wait and see if the traditional laws still work here.

Charts, Graphs, and Overview

The Dow Jones Industrial Average turned 100 years of age on May 26, 1996, and the Salomon Brothers index of rare coin values would have been 22 years old in June 2000. A surprising correlation of these two prestigious indices shows that rare coins have outpaced the stock market, even now as records are broken daily.

Equally interesting is a comparison of the Dow Jones, the Nasdaq Composite index, and other rare coin prices, with the progress that has been made with the State Quarters—both as common-grade uncirculated coins (better condition), and as proof specimens (superior states of preservation, Proof-67 and above as a grade).

Rooted to an 11-stock average that covered railroads, and was first published by Charles H. Dow in 1886 in his *Customer's Afternoon Letter* (the forerunner of *The Wall Street Journal*), the Dow as an industrial average of 12 stocks was first begun on May 26, 1896. New records are set and smashed on a daily basis as the Dow has gone up, and down, rising above 10,000, then to even higher extremes, rising and falling at a rapid rate of change. It makes other investments look less than stellar.

But when rare coins are compared with the Dow, what it has done recently, how it has performed in the last three decades—indeed, how it has performed over the past half century—the surprising results are highly favorable to the coins.

Even more startling is the comparison that can be seen with the State Quarters taken from pocket change and matching the rate of return with the Dow, the Nasdaq, and even the old Salomon Brothers survey of rare numismatic items. Remember, these quarters are plucked from pocket change, with 25 cents as the basic cost, and in some cases, their rate of return over significant periods exceeds the Dow and the Nasdaq. They also show that rare coins remain a valuable investment vehicle in their own right.

Rare coins, by comparison, don't have a daily index, but, for a number of years, they had an annual one—prepared by the prestigious Wall Street investment banking house of Salomon Brothers, which surveyed coins and other collectibles starting in 1978 and continuing for a dozen years. The State Quarters have no index at all, but do have price quotes that can be found weekly in *Numismatic News* and *Coin World*, two trade periodicals that run extensive advertising of all sorts of rare coin items. A number of other periodicals also track their progress.

There is also *A Guide Book of United States Coins*, commonly known as the "Red Book" after the color of its cover, which has been published through more than 50 annual editions starting with a cover date of 1947. Inside are the grades and prices of thousands of coins; it lists recent prices for the State Quarters, as well as prices for other rarities. By looking at older editions of this *Guide*, it is possible to ascertain reliably how the numismatic market has progressed through the years.

The Salomon Survey, the Dow Jones Industrial Average, and the Nasdaq Composite are market baskets, designed as consumer research tools to be used to get a quick fix on the financial health of the marketplace. By contrast, the Red Book is simply like *The Wall Street Journal, The Coin Dealer Newsletter,* or NumisMedia's *Fair Market Guide* in that it reports the editor's impression of various transactions and what those do to overall prices.

Starting with a dozen stocks in 1896 (only one of which, General Electric, is still easily recognizable today), the Dow Jones Industrial Average expanded to 20 stocks in 1916, and on Oct. 1, 1928, to 30 stocks—the same number utilized today.

Through the years, the components have changed in the Dow Jones Average for a variety of reasons. In 1928, AT&T was dropped and replaced by IBM. In 1939, IBM's fast growth made it a target for elimination from the Dow, and AT&T was brought back. On March 24, 1997, four stocks that had long been Dow components were removed and replaced by newer issues that were deemed more representative of the market as a whole. Since then, Microsoft has been added and there have been other changes.

Today, AT&T (owned by more shareholders than any other company in America) and IBM are used as a barometer along with American Express, Boeing, Coca-Cola, Disney, DuPont, Kodak, Exxon, General Electric, General Motors, 3M, Procter & Gamble, Sears Roebuck, and others to measure the nation's economic health.

The comparable market basket used to measure the state of the numismatic economy includes a 1794 half cent, an 1873 two-cent piece, an 1866 nickel, an 1862 silver three-cent piece, an 1862 half dime, an 1807 Bust dime, an 1866 Liberty Seated dime, an 1876 quarter, an 1873 quarter, an 1896 Barber quarter, and a 1916 Liberty Standing quarter. Other coins rounding out the portfolio of what would constitute a nice type set of minor, subsidiary, and dollar coinage include the 1815 and 1834 half dollars, the 1855-O

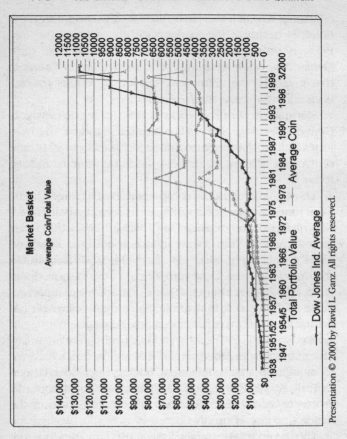

Liberty Seated half dollar, the 1921 Walking Liberty half dollar, the 1795 Draped Bust dollar, the 1847 Seated Liberty dollar, the 1881 Trade dollar, the 1884-S Morgan dollar, and the 1928 Hawaiian commemorative half dollar.

There is no comparable market basket for State Quarters, but there are few enough of them that they can be individually graphed, or perhaps even charted, against the various indices based upon their own prices and performance. Individual price charts are found in the catalog section of this book, showing price charts against the Nasdaq, the Dow, or other vehicles.

All of the coins in the Salomon Brothers portfolio were chosen by Harvey Stack and the late Norman Stack of Stack's Rare Coins, New York City, the auctioneers and coin dealers who created the portfolio and monitored its progress.

"We chose these coins because they were representative of the kind of coins that were widely collected," Harvey Stack said in an early, explanatory interview in which he noted that the collection was intended to represent a nice type coin collection. That meant, in 1978, that most were Choice Uncirculated (the equivalent of MS-63 today), rather than Gem Uncirculated. But, as events clearly show, that didn't mean that the coins weren't of investment quality.

No gold coins were included. This was not because they were not regarded as type coins, but because Salomon Brothers believed that including them would cause an unnatural result based on the price changes in the world gold market.

It's easy to argue that the Dow is not the most accurate of barometers; just 30 stocks (which themselves have been weighted to account for stock splits) may not necessarily represent an entire marketplace. The same is true of the Nasdaq, whose components are heavily weighted in the technology area. Astonishingly, however, for extended periods of time, State Quarters have run ahead of all of these indices.

Yet it is the Dow that is reported daily in the newspapers, in the government's annual publication *The Statistical Abstract of the United States,* and is even available, historically back to its origins, on the Internet. Graphically, the Dow Jones Industrials are easily compared to the Salomon Brothers index, and to State Quarters, as well. The result

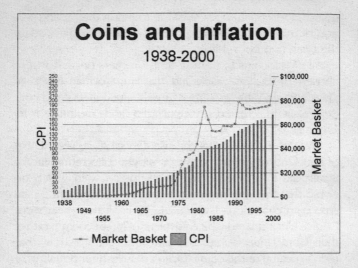

may surprise some who thought that the rare coin market was more than a little dormant over the past several years. What the bottom line shows is a vibrant market for rare coins that has continued to grow—at times far better than the equities market, or other more traditional investment media.

Using data supplied by *Numismatic News,* and earlier pricing guides from the old Wayte Raymond *Standard Catalogues,* as well as interpreting data from *A Guidebook of United States Coins* (the Red Book) and NumisMedia, we find that through about 1972 there was a close correlation between the two, with price changes moving almost in tandem. That is, from 1947 to 1972, a purchase in rare coins or a purchase in Dow Industrial stocks would have yielded the same approximate rate of return.

The explosiveness of inflation, most of which was an accompaniment of the Vietnam War, resulted in wage and price controls starting Aug. 15, 1971. This had a profound effect on the stock market: it was part of an overall slump that lasted for years.

By contrast, the collectibles market jumped dramatically, though after 1979–80 a peak led to a long valley before prices began to make a recovery in the form of a dramatic march back to the top.

In 1972, the Dow Jones Industrial Average ended the year above 1,000 for the first time; earlier in the year, to commemorate the occasion, The Franklin Mint sent as a present to all of its shareholders an ingot recalling the instant historical event of the breakthrough to the 1,000 mark.

It has hardly been a steady progression since then; there has been lots of slippage. There have been ups, and downs—a high rate of change. The following year, the Dow had declined to 851, and the year after that (1974) to 604. By 1982, the Reagan presidency revitalized the economy and stock market, turning around the high inflation of the Carter years, and the Dow closed at 1,046 for the year. It progressed steadily upward after that, as the previous graph shows.

More recently, the market movements ended the year at 3,168 in 1991, and above 5,100 in 1995. The next doubling took much less time. As a dual graph depicting the Dow and some of the coins in the Salomon Brothers portfolio shows, coins and the Dow progressed nicely—often at the same time, and in tandem.

Volatility has been significant in the current market, with slides of 50 or 100 points in a single day becoming almost routine; in the past, such a gain or loss was sufficient to trigger dramatic consequences, even headlines in the daily press. Now, the market is so high that the rate of change represents a modest percentage, and hence is not looked upon as significantly as it might have been, had the percentage been higher. Put differently, when the market is valued at 1,000, a 100-point change is a 10% difference. With a market at 7,000, a 100-point change represents a change of less than 1.5 percent. Still, Nasdaq slides of 3% or more have become almost common, making the State Quarters look almost like a stable investment.

There is a parallel between the Salomon rare coin list and the Dow Jones Industrial 30 stocks, but the rare coins over time actually do better as a percentage, and as a gain. There are, of course, flaws that are inherent in any examination of a market basket, and this is true whether stocks are being utilized, or coins. On the very day in 1987 when the stock market crashed—the Dow Industrials dropped hundreds of points—there were other stocks that actually increased in value.

But the trend that emerges is that the coin portfolio substantially outperforms inflation (as evidenced by the Consumer Price Index). Even on a year-to-year basis, there are times when the CPI may change as much as the coins, or more. Since the mid-1970s, however, there has no longer been even a close contest; the rare coins outperform inflation and yield a healthy annual return—more if they are held for a longer rather than shorter period of time.

Not every year is a winner for each investment, whether it is rare coins, gold, silver, farmland, Treasury bills, or any other component of the old Salomon Brothers index. Yet rare coins, over time, have prevailed as an important means of outpacing inflation and outperforming other fixed assets. Over the last 50 years or so, coins on average have substantially outpaced inflation, increased in value at a faster rate than either gold or silver, and generally offered a rate of return that has averaged about 12% each year.

In evaluating the data supplied by Salomon Brothers, it is essential to understand what the market basket selected is not: it cannot, and does not, purport to measure the price gains, or losses, of every coin. Instead, it relies on a market-basket approach, much like the Dow Jones Industrial Average. As such, it is broadly representative of the market as a whole, though individual or specific instances may be to the contrary.

The gains and losses recorded on the previous charts and graphs will differ slightly from the actual percentages and rates of return found in the Salomon Brothers examination because the method of compiling prices for this book differs from the raw auction data used in the compilation of the Salomon Brothers review. But even there, Harvey Stack revealed in an interview some time ago that the compilers did not hesitate to use comparables or similar items when they did not have enough of a database of sales in any given year. In other words, if Indian Head cents were included (which they're not), and a 1906 Indian had been listed, but not many had been sold, it would have been prudent to look at the 1905 Indian cent or the 1907, or both, since they are for all intents and purposes the same plain-vanilla type of coin.

The accompanying chart prepared by me lists the 20 coins that are found in the original Neil S. Berman-Hans Schulman list which was published in 1986, the first time that the Salomon Brothers list was made public.

If the market basket had been compiled in 1938, the last year of the Great Depression, the collection would have cost about $150 to complete; by 1947 (actually about 30 years before it was begun), it would have cost about $430 to build. Considering that lawyers were being paid $31 a week to work on Wall Street that year, the sum was not exactly inconsequential.

By 1955, the market basket had nearly doubled, to $781 in cost. Except for some brief inflation during the Korean War, the Consumer Price Index (CPI) had advanced only modestly in the intervening years. But rare coins increased at an annual rate of almost 14% over the previous year, a trend that would continue for at least the next two decades.

At the very same time that coins were increasing by nearly 14%, U.S. government long-term bonds (15 years and greater terms) yielded a 2.32% rate of return. High-grade municipal bonds, according to the *Statistical Abstract of the United States* and the *Economic Report of the President*, brought 1.98% returns. (The average stock in the Standard & Poors 500 Index had a dividend rate of about 6.3%; the Dow Industrial Average was about 279—a mere shadow of the changes that were to come about in a short time.)

A decade later, in 1968, the identically described coins would have had a value of just about $8,000. In 1978, the total values for all of the coins on the list amounted to about $35,000. That constitutes a 341% gain (or a simple rate of return of about 34% annually). In more than 60 years of toting up these market-basket coins, only nine of those years show a negative growth rate, and at least three of those years essentially were non-growth or loss.

The rate of change for coins over the period of time averages 12.18% using the index. By contrast, high-grade municipal bonds averaged about 5.7% annually during this 50-year period, and U.S. government long-term bonds had an average of 6.5% annually. The Dow's rate of return: a satisfying 8.98% on average, even with 15 years in which there was a negative return.

There was minimal risk with those investments for the return; the 11.47% received for coins is with more risk. Salomon Brothers demonstrated the appeal of rare coins throughout the late 1970s and early 1980s. The annual release of the figures in June of each year led to price comparisons, and investment reviews.

Examining more than a half century of prices yields a result that is not surprising to those who have followed the coin market for any length of time: rare coins are a valid long-term investment vehicle, but have significant short-term volatility. Salomon Brothers regularly tracked the activities in the rare coin market with an annual survey that it released to the public from 1978 until 1990, when coins were dropped from the annual Salomon analysis for fear of litigation. Results of the annual survey, which considered a market basket of type coins of silver dollar, subsidiary, and minor coinage (but no gold coins), were consistently impressive, showing that over long periods of time rare coins had a solid track record that regularly went up in value.

Starting in 1978, Salomon Brothers tracked rare coins, stamps, Chinese ceramics, farmland, bonds, stocks, the Consumer Price Index, Treasury bills, Old Masters paintings, gold, and diamonds. They went to experts in each field and asked for their assistance in compiling representative ways of looking at the market.

The initial showing in 1978 was that stocks had grown 2.8% annually over the prior 10-year period (1968–78), while bonds in the same decade rose 6.1%—the precise change of the Consumer Price Index. (Over the long run, stocks remained a good investment according to the survey and anecdotal evidence.)

By contrast, rare coins in that first survey had shown a consistent 13% annual return, the same as Old Masters—works of art that had not yet exploded to the stratospheric proportions that made the front pages of prestigious daily newspapers in the 1990s. Heading the list then was Chinese ceramics (with a 19.2% return) and gold bullion (with a 16.3% compounded annual rate). Both had been in the headlines before—which rare coins simply had not.

The *New England Economic Review,* a publication of the Federal Reserve Bank of Boston, made the study the focus of an article in May 1979, entitled, "Are Stocks a Bargain?" (It concluded that stocks were well off their historical rate of return and hence were in fact a bargain.)

In comparing rare coins with other indicia of investment vehicles that included farmland, stocks, bonds, stamps, Chinese ceramics, and other tangible assets, Salomon Brothers requested that a model portfolio be formed to act as a market basket. Still, any market basket gives a good general picture of what is transpiring, and how it contrasts over a long period of years. The Dow Jones Industrial Average is one such focal point.

The coin prices that are listed in the chart in this chapter have changed, too—not by date, type, or denomination, but in some instances by grade. The reason has as much to do with the mechanics of reporting as it does with changes in grading terminology. Like the Dow Jones average, which neither represents all publicly held companies, nor even all significant stocks that trade on the exchange, each coin in the portfolio is broadly representative of the marketplace as a whole, and to that extent, its trend-line symbolizes what the market actually does.

Taking the Salomon Brothers survey over a 20-year period of time (the actual survey has gone on for half that time, but the survey has been extended back to prior years using auction and other records), rare coins are demonstrated to be a superior investment vehicle with a phenomenal rate of return that is not approached by any other financial or tangible asset. Does the Salomon Brothers survey precisely parallel how thousands of different coins have gained, or lost, through the years? The answer, obviously, is no. Neither does the Dow Jones Industrial Average, the Nasdaq Composite Index, or any other market-basket approach to the statistics.

No one claims that the Salomon Brothers portfolio is a perfect one, but it constitutes what a serious collector might have accumulated in an era when price appreciation was generally moderate, and gains from a collection were realized over a lifetime.

Investment Opportunities in State Quarters

No one can predict what the future will be. But based on the past, it does appear that the future of rare coins is bright, and that it is still possible to plan your rare coin retirement. State Quarters could be a useful part of that.

Proof issues, particularly Proof-67 and above, have significant possibilities. The uncirculated versions, capable of being acquired from pocket change, are each outlined on their statehood page, together with price trends and an analysis of the overall investment outlook.

Proof coins, in general, are attractive to advanced collectors. Quantitatively, they are limited both in copper-nickel (figure about 2.5 million annually for each coin over the life of the program) and in silver (estimate between 800,000 and 1 million pieces during the life of the program).

Particularly when contrasted with other coins, the relatively modest mintages and overall desirability point to strong possibilities in a secondary market, which is the hallmark of a good investment opportunity in the coin marketplace.

ERROR STATE QUARTERS

Every 10 weeks, the U.S. Mint has to produce a new set of coins, using a new master set of dies for another State Quarter. A year's worth of normal production is compressed into less than 20% of the time. When added to the normal production load for the Mint, the result has been that more than 19 billion coins of all denominations were produced in 1999 alone.

The Mint has averaged between 1.2 billion and 1.7 billion quarters since 1993, and has produced steadily more coins each year throughout the last decade of the 20th century. Production of this was manageable, given the good production staffs at the Philadelphia and Denver mints, but even then, striking errors cropped into the production schematic.

According to error and die-variety expert Alan Herbert, who has been writing about mint errors for more than a quarter century in *Numismatic News*, "I can make the general statement that any of the 460+ classes of minting varieties that have previously been found on the clad quarters will undoubtedly be found on the State quarters." Bill Fivaz, another maven in the error field who served with me on the Board of Governors of the American Numismatic Association, and also devotes considerable energy to the

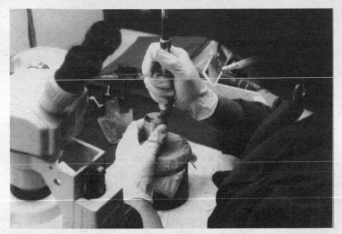

Mint employee at Philadelphia Mint polishing a die.

field of errors and varieties, agrees with Alan Herbert that there will be new error coins to collect, though he disagrees on the terminology.

"I, along with 99% of the other error/variety collectors/ dealers, have a real problem with Alan's use of 'variety' for everything in the P-D-S system. We feel 'variety' is confined to die aberrations, while 'error' is associated with planchet and striking abnormalities."

Alan Herbert's rejoinder: "My personal preference is for the term 'minting varieties,' which includes 'errors,' as well as wear and tear and intentional die use. The big mistake that 99% of the dealers and collectors make is to call anything other than the norm an 'error.' This actually applies to less than a third of the abnormal coins leaving the Mint."

Regardless of the terminology utilized, the reason why many of these errors (or varieties, if you will) can occur is that Mint personnel are used to looking at designs on four or five circulating coins that don't vary in design from year to year (cent through dollar), and the quality control of the human eye gets used to familiar designs, important when a coining press is striking at rates of up to 600 coins per minute.

Bill Fivaz adds that he doubts "that [many] minting varieties (ugh!) will undoubtedly be found on the new quarters." His reason: "I don't feel any significant die varieties will be occurring on the State Quarters because of the new methods used by the Mint. I'd be very surprised to find a doubled die or a repunched mint mark, for example."

Reverse designs that change every 10 weeks, by contrast, are something new to look at—and to figure out. Consequently, it is problematical in the first element of quality control: visual review of the product.

There are a number of different types of general errors that affect all coins, including the State Quarters. The one that brought State Quarters to page one of the daily press turned out to be a rotated die (180-degree rotation) that was erroneously valued at $500 or more.

The Coining Process, or How Coins Are Minted

In order to understand how error coins are produced by the Mint in the first place, it is essential to understand something about the minting and coining process. Coins themselves have been produced since the time of the Lydians around 750 B.C., when crude lumps of electrum were stamped with equally crude dies. By the time of the ancient Greeks, the manufacture of coins, and indeed the minting process, had been elevated to fine art. Kimon, among the earliest of the sculptors of the Greek city-states, hand-cut his dies and created magnificently stylized art in metal.

Originally, dies were all done in intaglio, which is to say that the design was prepared in reverse in the metallic die.

When the die was pressed into a blank planchet (the metal approximately the size of the coin), the design flowed into the contours of the die, in reverse. This method is still used in the year 2000, and indeed, every coin in America's State Coinage series is made from intaglio dies.

The earliest coins evolved from nuggets of electrum, or white gold (an alloy of gold and silver which occurs naturally). Inevitably, these early coins are one-sided only. The reverse invariably has a punch mark left by the tool that was used to force a lump of annealed metal into an obverse die which itself was fixed into an anvil.

By the time of the Greeks, there was a more sophisticated technique that allowed for two-sided coin designs. The lower die, inevitably containing the obverse, was embedded into the anvil. A hammer was utilized by taking the upper or reverse die and placing it upon the planchet (underneath which was the obverse). Several sharp blows into the annealed surface then impressed the design. Inevitably, the reverse which bore the blow wore rapidly and was relatively short-lived.

The basic principle of coin die design from the Lydians and the ancient Greeks survives to the present day, though machinery now does the work once done by hand. Depending upon the skill of the craftsman, the designs could appear sophisticated and constitute exquisite works of art, or could appear to be quite crude. For example, the coins produced in Judea during the Jewish revolt that started in 132 A.D. reveal what one scholar referred to as the product of "die cutters working for the rebel mint, [which] were by no means masters in the tradition of Greek glyptic art. They did not reach even the average level of engraving practice of Hadrianic times, though their typical work is no worse than many contemporary products of the provincial Roman mints . . . Simple Jewish craftsmen, unskilled in the art of engraving, were therefore entrusted with the cutting of the coin dies. They carried out this specialized task with more or less aptitude."

Ancient coins normally have a high relief on thick and relatively heavy flans or planchets. By Medieval times, the Western planchets are inevitably thin and in low relief.

The basic methodology involved the hand-cutting of dies, the cutting of a blank planchet, and the use of a hammer. This continued right up through the Renaissance. The art of the Greeks and the Romans was lost by the time of the fall of Constantinople, and hence Byzantine coinage is often perceived as far more crude. Nonetheless, the technique utilized to produce the coins is identical.

The Renaissance brought a new coining invention, created by none other than the multi-talented Leonardo da Vinci. Da Vinci invented a coin stamp which cut out the blank and thereafter stamped the impression. Whether or not this was ever used cannot be proven, but a century later that point was rendered moot with the invention of the screw press.

The screw press utilizes an elementary principle of physics—the lever. A stationary die, impressed in a blank metal planchet, is forced into the metal by means of a weight and counterbalance, whose pressure is maintained downward, by turning the bar which holds them down a threaded hole that resembles a wood screw. As the pole rotates down the screw, the die sinks into the metal, and after a turn or two of the press, a coin is created.

By the time that the U.S. Mint was authorized in 1792, coinage techniques worldwide had matured to a more sophisticated level. Still, by contemporary standards, they were primitive at best. Precious metal was annealed (the treatment of a planchet through a heating and cooling process that softens it and readies it for striking), and washed. The ingots were then brought to a rolling room which produced strips for small coins, initially at the rate of 7,500 ounces of metal each day. The rolling mill was run by a team of horses which tramped around a stationary pole that revolved and turned the mill. A drawing machine equalized the crudeness of the strips.

Eventually, a planchet cutting press and a milling machine were utilized before the screw coining press did the actual stamping. In 1793, Adam Eckfeldt invented a device for automatically feeding and ejecting the planchets after striking. It consisted "of a very powerful upright screw, on the top of which was affixed a heavy and strong lever worked with great apparent ease by one man at each end, and by which the screw is made to make about one-fourth of a revolution before returning to its former position. At the lower end of the screw, a die is affixed which gives the impression of the obverse, while beneath is the die containing the impression of the reverse."

Well into the 19th century, dies for coinage were still being individually cut by hand into steel which was then hardened by fire. Although master engravers skilled in their craft copied designs faithfully, there are minute but distinct differences in every single die (even of seemingly identical coins) because each version was separately cut into the master model.

Many of these die varieties are widely collected. Others are so insignificant as to not even be generally noted among collectors. Mint records, however, disclose that hundreds of dies were used each year during this period of time—not surprising given that each die was good for only thousands of impressions, rather than millions of them.

Tens of thousands of dies are used by the Mint even today; the Denver Mint alone produces over 140,000 coin dies each year, but with a critical difference from the earlier times: technology has evolved such that nearly every die is alike. Standardization of coin design into truly imperceptible differences between dies was impossible until the invention of the pantograph, epitomized by the *Janvier* reduction-engraving model.

The technique for this originally traces back to the writing machine invented by Thomas Jefferson which copied his correspondence. That machine utilized a device which connected two pens to each other some distance apart. As one pen moved, so did the other, thus copying the movement (and the writing) onto paper. The reduction copying machine is not dissimilar, at least in theory. An engraving tool is positioned on a die while the other end is a fine-tuned tracing device which slowly goes over the surface of a model that is identical in design to the desired end product. As each portion of the design is gone over, it traces itself in reverse, etching into the metal of the die. The Janvier machine, through a series of levers, cog wheels which turn the rounded dies at different rates of speed, and other mechanical devices, is capable of actually reducing at an identical ratio any of the master designs which are created on a copper piece (or sometimes an epoxy piece) called a galvano.

Although this was done in the middle of the 19th century, it is still being done this way as America's State Quarters program is being produced. Even with this technique, master engravers are still required to make fine-line engravings into the die's surface, usually for lettering and other minute details.

There are, altogether, about a dozen different steps that transform an image in the mind's eye of the designer into a coin that can be acquired. The first is a drawing of the design, which is typically (in the case of America's State Quarters) initiated at the state level and shipped to the Mint, where the "concepts" are converted by skilled designers and engravers at the Mint into a coinable design.

From the approved design, a plastilene or modeling clay

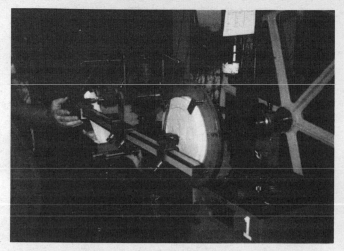

Janvier reducing lathe at the Philadelphia Mint. The machine's concept is a century old and still going strong.

version set on a plaster basin is made. This is a "positive" model that appears to be a larger version of a coin, with fully contoured surfaces. Once the artist or engraver finishes with this, a negative plastilene version is made by pouring plaster over the plastilene.

The resulting model itself becomes a mold so that a plaster positive can be made; this in turn becomes a mold from which a negative plaster is made. The negative plaster model is electroplated, and once that is done, solid backing is added and the model becomes a galvano. The galvano is taken to a reducing machine, usually a Janvier engraving-reducing machine, or a reducing pantograph (portrait lathe) from which a master hub is produced.

A long, straight bar runs along the front of the lathe and is hinged to a fulcrum. A short distance from the fulcrum is a stile, or cutting tool, which (as the device turns to allow the stiles to trace over the design) cuts into the metal that

Annealing furnace at the Philadelphia Mint, where the temperature can approach 2,000 degrees Fahrenheit.

will become the hub. After several times, a final version is prepared. The master hub is then used to produce two master dies. The master dies produce the working hub, a positive, that produces the working die, a negative. Working dies are then made, and these working dies produce coins.

In the 20th century, a variety of new minting machines was invented, including hydraulic coining presses, and even completely automated minting facilities where technicians supervise anywhere from four to a dozen coining presses while overhead conveyor belts effortlessly, and silently, and without human assistance move heat-treated blanks from burnishing mills to the coining press. Thereafter, robots remove the products from the coining press to be counted, bagged, and shipped into circulation.

The typical coining press today—including the kind producing America's State Quarters—produces at a capacity of about 600 coins per minute and perhaps operates more typically at a bit less than a third of that level. Proof coins are produced on hydraulic presses operating at much slower rates, and in a way that allows for the coins to be struck with two blows from the die, rather than the single blow that is typical of circulation strikes.

Common Mint Errors

Errors can occur at almost any time in the coining process, though there are far fewer today than in the past. Die errors, lettering mistakes, doubled dies, and even one date cut over another, are all errors from the past unlikely to occur in the State Quarters program.

What is more likely are striking mistakes, where a coin blank moves off-center and is improperly struck, or is struck twice before it is ejected from the coining press. These have become the truly interesting types that many collectors seek. There are other types, as well.

What's exciting about errors and die varieties is that they are scarce, even rare—and hence valuable—but they are also available by searching your change, or searching through bags of the new State Quarters that can be acquired (at face value) from many banks.

What follows is a listing of general classifications of Mint errors known to have appeared on State Quarters, with a brief explanation of how the error was created and (where there are known prices) a general sense of the value of the mistake.

Alan Herbert devised a planchet (P), die (D), and striking (S) method of cataloging errors, which is easy for serious collectors to remember because it mimics the three main Mints and their mint marks: Philadelphia, Denver, and San Francisco. He starts with planchet varieties such as **(1) improper alloy mixtures**, meaning that the copper-nickel mixture is off from the standard. This can be measured chemically, but more often is seen visually and confirmed by weighing the coin (the weight will differ depending on alloyed composition). This has not been widely seen as of mid-2000, but will likely occur as it does with nearly all coins. Typically, this increases the value of a coin such as a State Quarter 20 to 50 times face value. Error expert Bill Fivaz reports, "I have two Georgia quarters that have improper metal mixture in the clad layers (SG is way off, and they look very dark), so it has occurred on the State Quarters."

Another type is the **damaged or defective planchet (2)**, which is the blank upon which the coin is impressed. Variations on this include planchets whose cladding simply isn't properly produced, metal flaws including gas bubbles trapped in the metal, planchets rolled too thin, and even undersized planchets or those that are elliptical. These have not been widely seen, but an elliptical Massachusetts 2000-P in Choice Brilliant Uncirculated condition recently carried a $400 price tag in Fred Weinberg's price list.

Clipped planchets (3) are yet another type. Although *A Guidebook of United States Coins* suggests that this incomplete coin misses 10–25% percent of the metal, Alan Herbert's viewpoint is that a crescent clip can even show more than a 61% loss of metal. (This occurs when the strip of coin metal fails to move forward between successive strokes on the punch that creates the blank.) Clips come in all sizes and shapes and price ranges. A 1999-D Delaware quarter, 4% clip (i.e., 96% of the design remains with a small thumbnail-size portion clipped away), carried a $75 price tag in a recent Weinberg price list. A Delaware double clip (7% total) saw a $125 asking price. A 20% corner clip on a New Jersey quarter (1999-D) had a $600 price tag. A 15% double clip New Jersey runs $15; a 9% double clip from Georgia is listed at $110; while a triple clip ($125) from Georgia is a $140 coin. A Connecticut double clip (12%) sells for

Production line at the Philadelphia Mint on a day that the Citizens Commemorative Coin Advisory Committee visited. At center, Charles Atherton, a CCCAC member who is also secretary of the Fine Arts Commission.

$115. A double-clipped Massachusetts (22%) carries a $325 price tag.

Lamination flaws or split and broken planchets (4) are yet another major type of error. Foreign substances become trapped in a bad alloy mixture. This includes clad coinage with missing clad layer (fairly scarce) and can be on one side or both. Bill Fivaz, the error expert, notes, " I don't recall ever seeing BOTH clad layers split off . . . it's usually one or the other."

Wrong-stock planchet (5) (a half-dollar thickness, for example, for a quarter, or a quarter where a dime would do) are also possible; as of mid-2000, none had yet been offered for sale (though a Sacagawea dollar with a Susan B. Anthony dollar blank was found). **Extra metal on the planchet ("cud") (6)** is yet another choice. Bill Fivaz defines this as "a piece of the die breaking away, leaving a void, causing the planchet metal to 'ooze' into the cavity, creating an unstruck 'blob' on the coin." Yet another choice is a **blank (7)**, which for the State Quarters, would be indistinguishable from any other clad quarter coin.

Within the production process, there are more types of die varieties than can be easily imagined. Die varieties generally do not produce a unique coin; they produce errors into the hundreds of thousands of pieces for the life of the die (though these may vary by degree or sharpness). Many of the traditional varieties that a true collector will seek in other series to "cherrypick" by examining a design closely and picking out differences are unlikely to occur for the State Quarters. One reason for this is that the production process has changed.

Die-variety specialist Bill Fivaz, who has written (with J.T. Stanton) a truly marvelous book called *The Cherrypickers' Guide to Rare Die Varieties* (3rd ed., 1994), comments that focusing on the letters of "Liberty" and looking for differences might work on Lincoln cents, but it is unlikely to work for the State Quarters. He says, "To my knowledge, no significant die varieties have been reported, and chances are slim to none that there will ever be any since (1) the mint marks are now put on the galvano, eliminating repunched mint marks and/or over-mint marks, and (2) the dies are now produced with a 'single-squeeze' process, ostensibly taking doubled dies, etc., right out of the picture."

If the rush to make dies creates errors in the hubbing process, however, transferring one die from the master could cause varieties—it just either hasn't yet, or it has not been noticed. Time will tell on this one. (The doubling is similar to that on the 1955 doubled-die cent.)

Striking varieties (8) are widely known, and can be expensive. This is where the coin has the die strike it in more than one location, causing multiple images to appear, and inevitably causing the coin to be misshapen in appearance.

One of the most expensive ones to come to light, so far, is a quadruple strike where strikes two, three, and four are about 35% off-center. The Charter Oak coin of Connecticut is the subject, and the price for the coin is $1,100. A 1999-P New Jersey double struck (second strike 80% off-center) carries with it a $650 price tag. Off-center strikes are also widely collected and known for all series of the State Quarters. Depending on the degree a coin is off-center, it can have more or less value. For example, a 98% off-center State Quarter (you can tell from the lettering that it is a State Quarter and not the earlier Washington variety) is a $50 coin. A 10% off-center Massachusetts 2000-D coin is $125. A 25% off-center Massachusetts is $150. A clipped (22%) specimen (also struck 20% off-center) from Massachusetts carries a $325 price tag as a two-error coin. A 20% Connecticut off-center is $200, while a 20% off-center New Jersey is $250. A 25% off-center Pennsylvania is $400.

Most famous, right now, is the rotated reverse die, which some daily periodicals claimed was worth into the thousands of dollars. The easiest way to explain this is that a coin is viewed with its obverse design running from the 6 o'clock position to the 12 o'clock position. On coins, when the obverse is looked at, the lower portion is at 6 o'clock, the upper portion at 12 o'clock. At the very same time, the reverse is oriented differently. If you turn the coin over sideways, right to left, the "top" of the design is at 6 o'clock and the bottom at 12 o'clock. On the other hand, if you pick the coin up at 6 o'clock and flip upward toward 12 o'clock, the reverse now can be seen in a correct rather than inverted view. (By contrast, a medal works exactly the opposite, so that when you rotate it, each side faces upward in the same direction.)

Expert Alan Herbert says of this: "The rotations have been found for all five of the 1999 quarters, from both mints, so there are a lot of them out there, but at this point only a few hundred have been reported in the hobby. Sale prices have run as high as $350, with dealers paying from $25 to $150 for them."

Bill Fivaz doesn't disagree, but he does question the value of the rotated reverses. "The only possible error I can think of right offhand is the overhyped 'rotated reverse' on some of the first five that came out, and I honestly don't know anyone who is buying them, especially at some of the inflated prices I've heard. In my opinion, and it is shared by many errorists, they are a $20–$30 coin, IF you can find someone who wants them."

Alan Herbert does offer a word of caution and urges that if someone wants to buy the mint errors, he or she should proceed cautiously—and with the advice of an expert dealer. "Better issue a stern warning not to buy coins, especially minting varieties on the lay auctions on the Internet. There is one right now asking a minimum bid of $350,000 for a 1943 cent which has been put on a buffing wheel until it is nearly unrecognizable as a coin. The buyer must demand certification, preferably by one of the . . . experts and not some of the third-party grading services, as they are still screwing up listings, mislabeling, and misattributing."

And of course there are other errors, too. Alan Herbert speaks to several of them: "Filled dies are quite common, but no more so than on previous quarters. To have value, they must be on uncirculated-grade (MS-60 or higher) coins. . . ." Visibility under intense magnification is also required, but as Herbert points out, "Many 'finds' have turned out to be either reflection doubling—caused by reflections off the newly minted surface—or machine doubling damage, from the die bouncing on the struck coin." Fred Weinberg, a rare coin dealer (and error coin collector) who also specializes in selling error coins, offers his own interpretation: "In my opinion, to have value, the filled die area must be visible with the naked eye, and cover at least 25–35% of the coin (one side or the other, not combined)."

Regardless, have fun with this method of collecting—and watch and check your pocket change! You could find it truly worthwhile.

Mint Error Prices

Just how worthwhile it is to collect Mint errors can be seen not only from fixed price lists, but also from prices realized at some Teletrade auctions.

Date	State	Type	Condition & Service		Price	Date
1999	DE	Double-struck	ANACS	MS-63	$360	Jun. 99
1999	DE	Off-center	ANACS	MS-63	$220	Jun. 99
1999	GA	On 5¢ planchet	ANACS	MS-63	$320	Dec. 99

Below are examples taken from recent price lists of major error dealers showing just how profitable it can be to check your pocket change for mint errors; condition acts as a multiplicand for these coins. The better the grade, the higher the price:

(1999) States, 90% Off-Center. (ATES OF & top of head) Uniface reverse. Choice BU, $65.00

(1999) States, 85% Off-Center. (STATES OF & top of head) Uniface reverse. Choice BU, $125.00

(1999) States, 95% Off-Center. (ATES shows) Uniface reverse. Choice BU, $50.00

(1999) States, 90% Off-Center. (Planchet damage) Uniface reverse. Choice BU, $50.00

(1999) States, 98% Off-Center. (ATES shows) DSBS. Choice BU, $50.00

(1999) States, 90% Off-Center. (STATES O shows) Uniface reverse. Choice BU, $75.00

1999-P Connecticut, Nice 10% Clip & 5% Off-Center. (Pictured in *Numismatic News* 12/14/99) Choice BU, $275.00

1999-P Connecticut, 10% Double-clipped planchet (2 equal-size clips). Looks 10% each clip. Choice BU, $120.00

1999-P Connecticut, Nice 7% Double-clipped planchet. No reeding opposite bigger clip. Choice BU, $110.00

1999-P Connecticut, Struck 70% Off-Center @ 11:30. PCGS MS-65, $400.00

1999-P Connecticut, Double-Struck. 2nd strike 70% Off-Center. DSBS. Choice BU, $650.00

1999-P Connecticut, Struck 80% Off-Center @ 5:00. PCGS MS-65, $400.00

1999-P Connecticut, Triple-Struck. 2nd & 3rd strikes 40% Off-Center. DSBS. Choice BU, $750.00

1999-P Connecticut, Quadruple (4) Struck. 2nd, 3rd, & 4th strikes are 35% Off-Center & overlapped. UNIQUE. BU, $1,300.00

1999-D Delaware , Struck on a Nickel planchet. Looks Choice BU, PCGS AU-58, $450.00

1999-D Delaware , Struck on a Nickel planchet. PCGS MS-62, $475.00

1999-D Delaware , Struck on a Nickel planchet. PCGS MS-63, $525.00

1999-D Delaware , Struck on a Nickel planchet. PCGS MS-64, $575.00

1999-D Delaware , Struck on a Nickel planchet. PCGS MS-65, $575.00

1999-P Georgia, Double-Struck. 2nd strike 70% Off-Center @ 7:30. Uniface Reverse. PCGS MS-64 , $675.00

1999-P Georgia, Double-Struck. 2nd strike 80% Off-Center @ 7:00. DSBS. PCGS MS-63, $750.00

1999-P Georgia, Double-Struck, both O/C. 1st strike 10% Off-Center @ 12:00; 2nd strike 70% Off-Center @ 6:00. PCGS MS-65, $750.00

1999-P Georgia, Triple-Struck. 2nd & 3rd strike 50% Off-Center @ 2:00. PCGS MS-65, $925.00

1999-P Georgia, Triple-Struck. 2nd & 3rd strikes 65% Off-Center—close overlap, but easily seen. PCGS MS-65, $850.00

1999-P Georgia, Double-Struck. 2nd strike 85% Off-Center @ 9:00. Uniface Reverse. PCGS MS-64, $675.00

1999-P Georgia, 9% Double-clipped planchet (equal sizes). Choice BU, $120.00

1999-P Georgia, Struck 5% Off-Center. Choice BU, $185.00

1999 New Jersey, Double-Struck. 2nd strike is 90% Off-Center @ 11:00. Uniface Reverse. PCGS MS-62, $600.00

1999 New Jersey, Triple-Struck. All 3 Off-Center: 60% @ 1:00; 70% @ 5:00; and 85% @ 11:00. PCGS MS-64, $1,350.00

1999-P New Jersey, 10% Off-Center. BU, $185.00

1999-P New Jersey, 20% Off-Center. Choice BU, $250.00

1999-P New Jersey, Struck 30% Off-Center. (Rim bump and a few scratches on blank portion.) BU, $250.00

1999 Pennsylvania, Struck 90% Off-Center @ 1:00. DSBS. PCGS MS-65, $350.00

1999-P Pennsylvania, Struck 5% Off-Center. Choice BU, $100.00

1999-P Pennsylvania, Struck 20% Off-Center. BU, $275.00

1999-P Pennsylvania, 25% Off-Center. Choice BU, $375.00

How to Select a State's Winning Coin Design and How You Can Design Your State's Coin

How do you create a state's coin design? For the first 10 states, the method was mostly trial and error, and for the first several, it was a rushed process, although the results seem highly satisfactory. For a number of other states, however, a 10-year process seems a long time away, and there has been a minimum of involvement—and little or no guidance from the state officials who eventually will have to make a recommendation to the Mint and the Secretary of the Treasury.

Details of the steps contemplated or taken by states whose design processes are already under way are detailed in the catalog portion of this book. This essay, however, is for state officials and would-be coin designers for states which either have not yet begun, or simply have made only the most preliminary preparations for their state's coin.

As part of the research for this book, I have had the opportunity to contact the governors of all states whose coins are not yet issued and ask how, precisely, they intend to proceed. A response that was typical came from Don Siegelman, now governor of Alabama. Elected in November 1998 for a term expiring in January 2003, the same year that the Alabama coin will enter circulation, Governor Siegelman chose to name what one aide referred to as "a couple of people who will serve on a Commission to select the design for the new State Quarter," as has been done in many other states.

"The exact method of selection has not yet been determined," said Helen Moore, an administrative assistant to the governor. "We have been receiving entries to the Coin Contest for over a year now," Moore said, an experience that has been paralleled in other states that have opened the designing of the reverse of their State Quarter to the population at large, and to schoolchildren in particular.

This strong participation is an important element in the ultimate success of the program in attracting tens of millions of people who want to collect these coins—many of whom have never collected coins before.

Design elements on the first seven coins in circulation as of this writing have some common elements, all of which ought to be considered by any committee deciding what should appear on the reverse side of its State Quarter. There are "strong" designs which work very well, and those that simply replicate prior issues, devoid of originality and lacking in some key characteristics that belong in such a series.

The primer offered here represents my opinions on what makes a good reverse design for the 50-State Quarters program. The observations are based not only on the program as it now exists, but also on past programs for circulating and non-circulating coins that I have witnessed, or participated in, over the course of the last 30 years. The basis for these comments is the underlying root of my own involvement in all phases of the coin field, ranging from design to merchandising and marketing.

Starting in 1973, I served as a consultant to the Canadian Olympic Coin Program, ultimately becoming involved in design suggestions as well as making the case for a gold coin for the 1976 Games. Several programs later, my

CCCAC member Elsie Sterling Howard at the Long Beach Exposition, a coin show she attended to discuss circulating commemorative coins with the general public. Here, she discusses a coin design with a young numismatist.

involvement as a consultant to the Statue of Liberty program helped lead to the creation of the copper-nickel half dollar, the largest-selling U.S. commemorative in history.

As a member of the ANA Board of Governors (then vice president), I worked out an agreement with the James Madison Memorial Foundation and ultimately helped create ANA's "Freedom Pack," which was a numerical edge-marking on about 10,000 half-dollar coins. Later, while I was ANA president, Congress requested that I, and designated others, review all of the designs for the 1995–96 Olympic commemorative coins, which we did at the director of the Mint's office in Washington, D.C.

After my appointment in 1993 as a member of the Citizens Commemorative Coin Advisory Committee (a task I continued with through January 1996), it was routine for me to review design proposals for each of the several leg-

Design template as prepared by the U.S. Mint. This particular design came from the State of Ohio website where it could be downloaded by anyone interested in submitting a design concept.

islative proposals approved by Congress—as well as those which were still in the drawing-board stage. Most recently, I was one of a number of individuals invited to review and comment on the 123 designs submitted for the Sacagawea dollar. I listed the Glenna Goodacre designs and the sweeping eagle vista reverse by Thomas D. Rogers, Jr.—those eventually chosen—among my favorites.

That, in turn, reminded me of an earlier period when I was covering the Bicentennial coin design competition in 1973, when hundreds of designs were turned in for possible use on the reverse of the quarter, half dollar, and dollar coin (with the 1776–1976 double dates).

Drawing on lessons and experiences from each of these instances, and from more than 40 years of collecting coins, tokens, and paper money, here are some hard-and-fast rules that I offer as an opinion on what any governor's design recommendation panel ought to consider, and on what basis it ought to make its recommendation to the governor. None of this leads toward identical designs; indeed,

more questions are asked than answers are provided. However, it offers some general guidelines that go beyond the
Mint's own descriptions, which set forth limitations on substance and style.

For example, the Mint advises: "Suitable subject matter
for design concepts include State landmarks (natural and
man-made), landscapes, historically significant symbols of
State resources or industries," flora, fauna, icons, and even
outlines of the state boundaries.

Not suitable: "State flags and Seals," though some emblems from them are so highly symbolic that they will no
doubt make the final cut. Also, no living person may appear
on the coin, and portraits are discouraged (though obviously, given Caesar Rodney's depiction on the very first
coin, full-length miniatures are permissible).

Following are my comments. If you are a state official,
you can use them to fashion guidelines. If you are an end-
consumer and user of coinage, or a prospective designer,
you can use them to judge how successfully your own
state's coinage is or could be—as well as the coins from the
other 49 states (or 55 states and territories) that there are
(or will be) to collect.

• Coins are for history. Their lifetime is not 25 years, or even
a century. They are for the ages. Let me be specific. Our
image in the year 2000 of what Jesus of Nazareth looks
like comes from Byzantine coins that were struck bearing
his likeness around the year 695 A.D. Our clearest understanding of the ancient Greeks and Romans comes from
their coinage.

• Symbolism on coins can be very powerful and need not
be obvious. Around 49 B.C., Julius Caesar (before Roman
emperors put their portraits on coinage) depicted himself as an elephant crushing Pompey (portrayed as a

snake). The entire Roman world understood what was portrayed—through clever imagery.

• Cheap commercial ploys often work to increase sales. The Alabama 1921 commemorative half dollar, for example, added 2 × 2 in the field and had an 11% increase in sales over the already authorized 59,000 coins. The edge-marking that the James Madison Memorial Foundation and ANA undertook for the Madison (1993) commemorative yielded almost 5% of the uncirculated coins produced.

• Identifiable symbolism is powerful on coinage. People know certain things about their state—and so do nonresidents. New Jersey was a crossroads of the American Revolution with more than 100 battles fought there; what is more natural than Washington crossing the Delaware to call attention to this fact. In 1921, Alabama made a mistake by placing its first governor's portrait along with that of the then-incumbent (Thomas Kilby) on its commemorative half dollar. Some 80 years later, no one seriously recalls either.

• Go with strengths. Georgia peach. South Carolina palmetto. Connecticut's Charter Oak. All have long-standing relationships with their states, some of them formalized, some not. If New Jersey had taken a different route, the Jersey tomato would be an obvious choice. A state should therefore look to a state flower, bird, or tree—or other officially designated item—that has the ability to identify the state and its people.

• Keep the design generally simple. Less is more. The hardest lesson to learn is that what looks great on poster board has to be reduced in size to 24.3 millimeters, or just under an inch around. Certain mottos are required, so there is precious little surface to work with. The Rhode Island tercentenary half dollar of 1936 is one such busy coin. Roger Williams; Indians; corn; large lettering leaving virtually no space—with a reverse showing the Anchor of Hope and no free field—make for an unattractive (and hard-to-strike) coin.

- Make the decision early on whether or not the state's outline should appear on the coin. It works for Pennsylvania, which is a large state, and Massachusetts, which is a smaller one (with an irregular shape). It might not work as easily, however, for Colorado, Wyoming, or the Dakotas. Some states will have them, some will not.

- Where there is an historic context, and former coinage, try to tie it in. That works on two levels. It allows for marketing by many people trying to do the tie-in, but also makes people more aware of the past—and buy the coins of the present. An example: Alabama's state motto changed in 1939; the earlier motto "Here we rest" is on the reverse of the 1921 Alabama half dollar, in the ribbon coming from the eagle's beak (the new motto is "We dare defend our rights"). A decision (as opposed to inaction) should be made as to whether or not to utilize the state motto.

- Once received, proposed designs should be divided into categories, some of which are obvious in advance, others of which will become apparent. For example, in the Bicentennial competition, Independence Hall was a common theme. A grouping of all similar themes with the objective of looking for the best concept makes the job a lot easier. Staff members can and should do this.

  I would not, however, group designs "with" and "without" the state outline, since this is a concept that can be added to virtually any design, or taken away. It may be more interesting to focus on several different ways that a state design can be portrayed: an outline, such as Pennsylvania or Georgia, or a filled-in version such as Massachusetts.

- Choose a topic that can be illustrated. Let's suppose that a state such as Alabama wanted to commemorate its long history, and that it chose to go back 9,000 years to the Russell Cave, site of a national monument. This is one of the richest archaeological deposits in the nation with more than 9,000 years of continuous use. Layers of artifacts were discovered there in the 1950s and it was declared a national monument in 1961. The practical difficulty: illustrating this in metal. By contrast, the Petroglyph national monument in New Mexico could easily show a rock with a rock carving, superimposed over a state whose outline is otherwise essentially square, and make an attractive design in the process.

• Considering the addition of symbols not otherwise incorporated into any design can also be useful. For example, the 2 × 2 of the Alabama centennial commemorative (or the Missouri 2 × 4), lost to history except for numismatists, is evocative. Alabama's numbers are separated by the St. Andrew's cross, taken from the state flag. (The use of flags is otherwise prohibited.)

• Does it have the aesthetic quality you like and want? This is highly subjective, but coins are art: Do you like it, or not? For me, in looking at highly complicated Olympic coinage symbolism, I preferred action figures or classical Greek art to more modernistic styles. (I have to confess I thought that the discreetly nude athletes were evocative of the ancient games, but that was vetoed by everyone concerned.)

• Coins are not medals—they are legal tender. They will be used by people across the country, even as they are collected by people around the world. Avoid high-relief items. Remember that coins are multidimensional, and that paper has just two dimensions. (That's why there is perspective.)

• Don't get caught up in whether an idea is well presented. Mint artisans can translate a simply awful drawing into a beautiful scheme. I recall that when the ANA was designing a commemorative coin that the island nation of Turks & Caicos ultimately produced commemorating the 125th anniversary of the lunar landing, I suggested to artist Don Everhart something evocative of an astronaut standing on the moon, and gave him a stick-figure drawing of an astronaut and an American flag with the ANA logo. His translation into metal was outstanding (Krause Mishler Catalog M-132).

- Don't be afraid to ask for help. There are many people you can turn to. There are amateurs and experts alike who will be happy to help. (Just be selective to be certain that you get useful and accurate advice.) The late Ralph Menconi, a noted sculptor and a member of the Coins and Medals Advisory Panel of the American Revolution Bicentennial Commission, complained that "every congressman is an artist!" What he meant was that they all had artistic ideas, and that it was impossible to make a design by committee. A committee's design of a horse, in other words, frequently resembles a camel.

    Alabama Governor Siegelman's office reached out; in her final sentence, Helen Moore said: "Any suggestions you can make will be greatly appreciated." This chapter is the result.

- Strive for consensus. It is axiomatic that if the committee is representative of the state, and seeks consensus, the result will achieve more popular approval than a design that evolves over a different route.

- Get caught up in the moment. There will be at least 1.2 billion of the coins produced by the Mint, and with luck, the design—and the state—will live on forever.

AMERICA'S NEW STATE QUARTERS

Display of the designs of these philatelic-numismatic combinations from the Washington Mint, Plymouth, Minnesota. This program features a first-day cover postmarked in the capital city of the state with interesting facts about the state and the coin on the envelope's flip side. For more information, www.washingtonmint.com.

STATE QUARTER LISTINGS

Template for Each of the Coin Designs

Each of the states, and each of the coins, utilizes a common template to facilitate finding information that you might consider essential, or merely be interested in. Below is the template with an explanation opposite the template. A significant amount of technical data was obtained from *The Statistical Abstract of the United States,* an official publication of the Department of Commerce. Some of its data differ from encyclopedias, particularly as to the area of a state and how it ranks.

State, Coin Date:	The subject state and the date of coinage as circulated. Coins struck in 1998 but issued in 1999 are listed as 1999
Nickname:	The state's nickname, official or unofficial
Order in Union:	The numerical order (1–50) in which the state entered the Union (and year of entry)
Size:	Square miles (rank out of 50 states)
Population:	Estimated population (pre-2000 census) and rank out of 50 states
State Motto:	Motto if the state has one

State Flower:	Flower if the state has one
State Bird:	Bird if the state has one
State Tree:	Tree if the state has one

Note: Many of these items will find their way onto America's State Quarters.

Selected Noteworthy Places and Events:	Some of the places and events that will be considered by each state's design committee
Web Site:	*http://www.* Address on the World Wide Web
Additional Information:	Useful information that may be considered for the design (if not chosen) or was considered for the design (as it was selected).

Coin Specifications

Obverse Sculptor/Designer:	John Flanagan (1931), revised by William Cousins, assistant engraver, U.S. Mint, 1998. (*Same for all entries.*)
Reverse Designer:	Name of sculptor and drawer (designer) when known.
Obverse Design:	Portrait of George Washington, after Houdon, by John Flanagan, modified by William Cousins (1997). Above bust of Washington: United States of America. Beneath Washington's chin: Liberty, which has appeared on every U.S. coin produced since the Mint Act of April 2, 1792. Beside Washington's hair braid: national motto "In God We Trust." Below neckline: Quarter Dollar. On side of neckline: two initials, JF (John Flanagan), WC (William Cousins). (*Same for all entries.*)
Reverse Design:	Specifies design with certain common elements on every coin. At top: state name; beneath, date entered Union. At bottom: date of issue; beneath, motto "E Pluribus Unum" (Out of many, one), describing how the divided colonies became the United States of America. (*Up to here, same for all entries.*) State design: specified. Designer/Engraver initials.

Mintage Figures:

Proof	initial mintages estimated
Uncirculated "P"	initial mintages approximated
Uncirculated "D"	initial mintages approximated

Selected Specialty

Products Production	*Issue Price*	*Mintage or Sales Limit*
100 coins	$29.95	(Provided to the extent available.)
1,000 coins	$289.95	
First-Day Cover	$19.95	

Design Commentary from Citizens Commemorative Coin Advisory Committee and Fine Arts Commission: Quoting from the CCCAC archives and Fine Arts hearings.

Grading Hints

Obverse: The high points of the coin's obverse are prone to wear; the field off Washington's nose, and the area behind the head curls are prone to contact marks. Wear is most likely to be evident on the hair above Washington's ear and the cheekbones. (*Same for all entries.*)

Reverse: At top: State name; beneath, date entered Union. At bottom, date of issue; beneath, motto "E Pluribus Unum" (Out of many, one), describing how the divided colonies became the United States of America. (*Up to here, same for all entries.*) State design: different on each.

Highest Uncirculated Grade Reported

Below appears data from PCGS Population Report, showing (in the example) that the highest grade received is MS-67, and that the NGC population highest grade is MS-68. Proofs are not listed.

PCGS	NGC	ANACS
MS-67	MS-68	

News or Other Notes

Useful historical data.

Investment Potential

Pricing Information (Typical MS-63 Grade) from Circulation

Single ($.25)		Roll ($10)	
P	D	P	D

The price in May 2000 as a single coin, and as a roll of coins. All uncirculated coins were issued at face value of 25 cents, 40 coins to the roll ($10).

Obverse (same on all State Quarters): Portrait of George Washington, after Houdon, by John Flanagan, modified by William Cousins (1997). Above bust of Washington: United States of America. Beneath Washington's chin: Liberty, which has appeared on every U. S. coin produced since the Mint Act of April 2, 1792. Beside Washington's hair braid: national motto, In God We Trust. Below neckline: Quarter Dollar. On side of neckline: two initials, JF (John Flanagan), WC (William Cousins).

Reverse: At top: State name; beneath, date entered Union. At bottom: date of issue; beneath, motto "E Pluribus Unum" (Out of many, one), describing how the divided colonies became the United States of America. (Up to this point, same on all State Quarters.) State design: Different on each.

DELAWARE

State, Coin Date:	Delaware, 1999
Nickname:	First State
Order in Union:	1 (1787)
Size:	2,396 sq. mi. (49th)
Population:	730,000 (46th)
State Motto:	"Liberty and Independence"
State Flower:	Peach blossom
State Bird:	Blue hen chicken
State Tree:	American holly
Selected Noteworthy Places :	Brandywine Zoo (Wilmington); Holy Trinity (Old Swedes) Church, oldest Protestant church in U.S. in continual use (Wilmington 1698)
Web Site:	http://www.state.de.us
Additional Information:	Named for Lord de la Warr, first governor of Virginia. Since 1899, Delaware has been the corporate home of many of the nation's largest companies, thanks to laws designed to make business operations easier. In 1802, E.I. Du Pont founded a gunpowder mill near Wilmington that has defined the chemical industry. Also known as the "Blue Hen State" for its fighting record in the Revolutionary War. Delaware tercentenary anniversary celebrated 1936 with U.S. Mint commemorative 50-cent coin showing Old Swedes Church and ship *Kalmar Nyckel*.

Coin Specifications

Obverse Sculptor/Designer:	John Flanagan (1931); revised by William Cousins, assistant engraver, U.S. Mint, 1998.
Reverse Designer:	William Cousins, after a design by Eddy Seger.
Obverse Design:	Portrait of George Washington, after Houdon, by John Flanagan, modified by William Cousins (1997). Above bust of Washington: United States of America. Beneath Washington's chin: Liberty, which has appeared on every U.S. coin produced since the Mint Act of April 2, 1792. Beside Washington's hair braid: national motto, "In God We Trust." Below neckline: Quarter Dollar. On

side of neckline: two initials, JF (John Flanagan), WC (William Cousins).

Reverse Design: At top: state name; beneath, date entered Union. At bottom: date of issue; beneath, motto "E Pluribus Unum" (Out of many, one), describing how the divided colonies became the United States of America. State design: "Caesar Rodney," Rodney astride his horse.

Mintage Figures:

Proof	2,500,000 estimated
Uncirculated "P"	373,400,000
Uncirculated "D"	401,424,000

Selected Specialty

Products Production	Issue Price	Mintage or Sales Limit
100 coins	$29.95	}
1,000 coins	$289.95	} limited to 4 million
First-Day Cover	$19.95	200,000

Design Commentary from Citizens Commemorative Coin Advisory Committee and Fine Arts Commission: Citizens Advisory Committee met by conference call on April 9, 1998, with various designs before it. Diehl (chair), Clain-Stefanelli, Sterling Howard, Shockley, Reiver, Bressett, and Atherton participated. Obverse design #1 (common to all series) was accepted. The minutes of 4/9 show the CCCAC "narrowed the choices for the reverse down to four designs," one of which was "#6 Caesar Rodney with a quill pen and the State of Delaware," and another #9 the blue hen. "The Committee suggested the following adjustments for design #6. The state should be removed from the background and the figure of Caesar Rodney and his horse should be moved slightly to the left. The wording 'First State' should be moved to the right (located at about 2:00) with the quill pen above the wording in a penman angle." (Minutes 4/9, p. 1). Fine Arts Commission: CCCAC "has already reviewed some of these and had some input, and they did not feel that this was perhaps the strongest of the designs nor their recommendation"—Fine Arts Commission, 4/16/98, p. 27. Gov. Carper insisted that the words "First State" appear (tr. p. 28), and an early concept included a blue hen. CCCAC's first choice was Caesar Rodney, and the design was redone at its request. The Flanagan observe was "reduced mechanically" (tr. p. 32). Approval of the change in design to allow mottos to be moved was not approved by Congress until May 29 (Pub. Law. 105-176).

Grading Hints

Obverse: The high points of the coin's obverse are prone to wear; the field off Washington's nose, and the area behind the head curls, are prone to contact marks. Wear is most likely to be evident on the hair above Washington's ear and on the cheekbones.

Reverse: Knee, arm, horse's rump; field contact marks.

Highest Uncirculated Grade Reported

PCGS	*NGC*	*ANACS*	Typical
MS-67 (P, D)	MS-66 (P, D)	MS-66 (P)	uncirculated
		MS-65 (D)	grade MS-61

News or Other Notes

It is July 1776, and the weather is hot and humid. In Philadelphia, the delegates to the Continental Congress debate independence and are divided 6–6 on the next step to take. Tiny Delaware is also divided, one delegate favoring independence, the other continuation of the fragile relationship with Great Britain. A third delegate, Caesar Rodney, is 80 miles away in Dover, Delaware. His two-day ride to Philadelphia changed the course of world history, as his decisive vote for American independence carried the day. Gov. Tom Carper authorized a design competition for this coin, and there was hardly a moment of doubt that Rodney would play a role in the coinage.

The first-strike ceremony took place at the Philadelphia Mint on Dec. 7,

1998. Inside the Mint, a separate ceremony was held as Jules Reiver, a member of the Citizens Commemorative Coin Advisory Committee (CCCAC), and I (a former member) were asked by Mint Director Philip Diehl to start other coining presses.

Investment Potential

The Delaware quarter, first of the 50 State coins to be issued, has already had a substantial price appreciation from its initial face-value entry into the marketplace. By 18 months after issue, advertisements in coin periodicals were typically at about $1.75 a coin (P or D mint mark) for a nice uncirculated specimen. The truly scarce portion of the mintage consists of coins in MS-65 or better; most early issues had contact marks in the field, obverse and reverse, which makes finding better-grade uncirculated coins a challenge.

Pricing Information (Typical MS-63 grade) from Circulation

	Single ($.25)		Roll ($10)	
	P	D	P	D
May 2000	$1.75	$1.75	$55	$55

Current fair market value in superior grade (MS-65 and higher) condition. Valuations are courtesy of Dennis Baker and Numismedia, as of May 30, 2000, and are provided exclusively to *The Official Guidebook to America's State Quarters*. Fair Market Value prices listed are for certified coins only (usually PCGS, NGC, or ANACS). Raw coins may bring substantially less. Prices may fluctuate considerably as new issues are brought on the market and certified. As populations increase in a particular grade, coins may be easier to obtain and prices may fall. Where an asterisk appears for a grade, Numismedia has not seen enough trading activity to establish a price at this time. (Valuations ©2000 by Numismedia, Inc. All rights reserved. Used by permission.) A comprehensive listing of fair market value of U.S. coins is found on the web site of Numismedia, http://www.numismedia.com.

	MS-65	MS-66	MS-67
1999 Delaware	20	36	144
1999-D Delaware	24	37	180

Clipped Specimen
(Mint error).

Delaware's tercentenary celebrated by the
U.S. Mint, 1936.

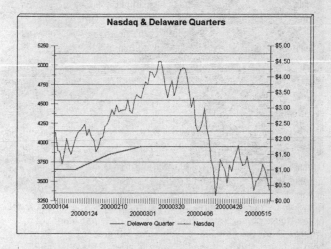

Gov. Tom Carper (Delaware), left; Rep. Michael Castle (R-Del.), chair of the House coinage subcommittee; U.S. Treasurer Mary Ellen Withrow; Mint Director Philip Diehl, and 5th grader Dana Rebeck hold aloft first strikes of the Delaware quarter, December 1998.

PENNSYLVANIA

State, Coin Date:	Commonwealth of Pennsylvania, 1999
Nickname:	Keystone State
Order in Union:	2 (1787)
Size:	46,058 sq. mi. (33rd)
Population:	12.1 million (5th)
State Motto:	"Virtue, Liberty and Independence"
State Flower:	Mountain laurel
State Bird:	Ruffled grouse
State Tree:	Hemlock
Selected Noteworthy Places :	Independence Hall, Betsy Ross House, Liberty Bell, 1st Bank of the United States (all Philadelphia); Pocono Mountains; Valley Forge; Gettysburg; Pennsylvania Dutch country; Carnegie Institute (Pittsburgh)
Web Site:	http://www.state.pa.us
Additional Information:	Named for Admiral William Penn, father of William Penn, founder of the Commonwealth, the scene of America's independence (Independence Hall is located just down the block from the present-day U.S. Mint and the Liberty Bell national historic site). The state was also the site of one of the Civil War's bloodiest battles (Gettysburg), now the location of the national cemetery that Lincoln dedicated in November 1863 with a 267-word speech, and the site of the first commercial U.S. oil well (Titusville, 1859). With a width of about 300 miles, it extends from the East to the start of the Midwest (Ohio), about an eighth of the way across the U.S.

Coin Specifications

Obverse Sculptor/Designer:	John Flanagan, (1931); revised by William Cousins, assistant engraver, U.S. Mint, 1998.
Reverse Designer:	William Cousins.
Obverse Design:	Portrait of George Washington, after Houdon, by John Flanagan, modified by William Cousins (1997). Above

bust of Washington: United States of America. Beneath Washington's chin: Liberty, which has appeared on every U.S. coin produced since the Mint Act of April 2, 1792. Beside Washington's hair braid: national motto, "In God We Trust." Below neckline: Quarter Dollar. On side of neckline: two initials, JF (John Flanagan), WC (William Cousins).

Reverse Design: At top: State name; beneath; date entered Union. At bottom: date of issue; beneath, motto "E Pluribus Unum" (Out of many, one), describing how the divided colonies became the United States of America. State design: outline of the Commonwealth of Pennsylvania, keystone at upper left. State motto at right. At center: allegorical female figure of Commonwealth, depicted from atop the Capitol Dome at Harrisburg.

Mintage Figures:
Proof 2,500,000 estimated
Uncirculated "P" 349,000,000
Uncirculated "D"

Selected Specialty

Products Production	Issue Price	Mintage or Sales Limit
100 coins	$29.95	}
1,000 coins	$289.95	} 4 million combined
First-Day Cover	$19.95	

Design Commentary from Citizens Commemorative Coin Advisory Committee (CCCAC) and Fine Arts Commission: CCCAC met 5/15/98 in Washington (Diehl, Clain-Stefanelli, Shockley, Reiver, Bressett, and Atherton). Minutes (p. 2): "From the submissions of each state the Committee selected designs that they recommended be forwarded to the Commission of Fine Arts. The selections were as follows: Pennsylvania, PA-L, with the keystone, state flower, and bird; PA-I, with an allegorical Liberty, state outline, and the keystone; PA-F rev 1, with the state bird, flower, and words "Virtue, Liberty and Independence," and one with "William Penn and the Lenni Lenape Indians with keystone in background." Fine Arts Commission, 5/21/98 (tr. p. 122). Chairman Carter Brown: "To save time, do we have a consensus that because it is the Keystone State and the keystone is such a fabulous graphic image that if you can live with the one on top, we would prefer it." Other designs included the mountain laurel and the grouse. Brown: "I don't think the grouse is going to mean anything to anybody" (p. 124).

Grading Hints

Obverse: The high points of the coin's obverse are prone to wear; the field off Washington's nose, and the area behind the head curls, are prone to contact marks. Wear is most likely to be evident on the hair above Washington's ear and on the cheekbones.

Reverse: Liberty's arms.

Highest Uncirculated Grade Reported

PCGS MS-66	*NGC*	*ANACS*	Typical
(P) MS-67	MS-64 (P)	MS-66 (P)	uncirculated
(D)	MS-66 (D)	MS-65 (D)	grade MS-63

News or Other Notes

Gov. Tom Ridge authorized a statewide design competition, the winning design of which uses an allegorical figure based upon a 14-foot bronze sculpture that has been atop the Capitol Dome in Harrisburg since 1905. State motto is also utilized in the design. Pennsylvania Quarter released at ceremony in Philadelphia (3/17/99).

Investment Potential

Pennsylvania coins reached $2.25 apiece from either Denver or Philadelphia Mints within a year of issue. The initial demand for the first several coins is extraordinary, in part because there are so many promotions, and products, that have incorporated the coins. The price of the Pennsylvania coins doubled in the first six months of 2000. True enough, with mintages in the millions, these will never be a true rarity; the mintage is less than late-issue 1999 and early-2000 State Quarters. Just by way of comparison, the mintage is similar to the 1973-D and 1974-D Washington quarters—but these are collected by many more Americans. If Mint statistics are correct that 100 million Americans are acquiring this coin, it is a rough coin to obtain, and very tough in MS-67 or above.

Pricing Information (Typical MS-63 grade) from Circulation

	Single ($.25)		Roll ($10)	
	P	D	P	D
May 2000	$2.25	$2.25	$55	$55

A double-strike specimen.

Current fair market value in superior (MS-65 and higher) condition. Valuations are courtesy of Dennis Baker and Numismedia, as of May 30, 2000, and are provided exclusively to *The Official Guidebook to America's State Quarters*. Fair market value prices listed are for certified coins only (usually PCGS, NGC, or ANACS). Raw coins may bring substantially less. Prices may fluctuate considerably as new issues are brought on the market and certified. As populations increase in a particular grade, coins may be easier to obtain and prices may fall. Where an asterisk appears for a grade, Numismedia has not seen enough trading activity to establish a price at this time. (Valuations ©2000 by Numismedia, Inc. All rights reserved. Used by permission.) A comprehensive listing of fair market value of U.S. coins is found on the web site of Numismedia, http://www.numismedia.com.

	MS-65	MS-66	MS-67
1999 Pennsylvania	20	32	—
1999-D Pennsylvania	23	54	—

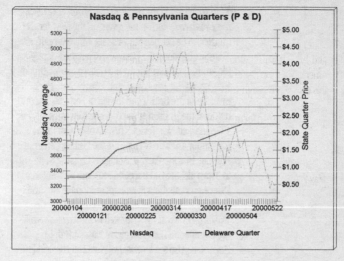

Nasdaq & Pennsylvania Quarters (P & D)

— Nasdaq   — Delaware Quarter

NEW JERSEY

State, Coin Date:	New Jersey, 1999
Nickname:	Garden State
Order in Union:	3 (1787)
Size:	8,215 sq. mi. (46th)
Population:	8.1 million (9th)
State Motto:	"Liberty and Prosperity"
State Flower:	Violet
State Bird:	Eastern goldfinch
State Tree:	Dogwood
Selected Noteworthy Places:	Atlantic City; Grover Cleveland Birthplace; Revolutionary sites (Morristown); Edison laboratory, West Orange; Cape May Historic District; Liberty State Park; more than 125 miles of beaches
Web Site:	http://www.state.nj.us
Additional Information:	New Jersey is the nation's most densely populated state. More than 100 battles during the Revolutionary War were fought in the state, the most famous of which was Washington's rout of the Hessians on Christmas Day

1776 (depicted in the painting *Washington Crossing the Delaware*, and on the reverse of the New Jersey quarter). The Garden State has six different regions: Atlantic City, along the Delaware River, the Shore, Skylands, Southern Shore, and Gateway consisting of Ellis Island, Liberty Island, and Liberty State Park. The invasion of the British and the fall of Fort Lee (on the banks of the Hudson River, opposite New York City) in 1776 marked New Jersey's first involvement in the Revolutionary War. Notable are the Visitors Center at Fort Lee Historic Park, Washington Crossing State Park in Titusville, the Old Barracks Museum in Trenton, Princeton Battlefield State Park in Manalapan, and Rockingham Historic Site in Princeton, where Gen. Washington wrote his "Farewell to the Armies" while the Continental Congress met at Nassau Hall in Princeton. Also see Morristown National Historic Park, our nation's first historic park and the site of Washington's headquarters at Ford Mansion. Borough of Fair Lawn in Bergen County (where I am mayor) has a 16th-century fishing weir of the Lenni Lenape Indians.

Coin Specifications

Obverse Sculptor/Designer: John Flanagan, (1931); revised by William Cousins, assistant engraver, U.S. Mint, 1998.

Reverse Engraver: Alfred Maletsky.

Obverse Design: Portrait of George Washington, after Houdon, by John Flanagan, modified by William Cousins (1997). Above bust of Washington: United States of America. Beneath Washington's chin: Liberty, which has appeared on every U.S. coin produced since the Mint Act of April 2, 1792. Beside Washington's hair braid: national motto, "In God We Trust." Below neckline: Quarter Dollar. On side of neckline: two initials, JF (John Flanagan), WC (William Cousins).

Reverse Design: At top: state name; beneath, date entered Union. At bottom: date of issue; beneath, motto "E Pluribus Unum" (Out of many, one), describing how the divided colonies became the United States of America. State design: "Crossroads of the Revolution," Washington crossing the Delaware, from the 1851 oil painting by Emmanuel Leutze.

Mintage Figures:

Proof	2,500,000 estimated
Uncirculated "P"	363,200,000
Uncirculated "D"	299,028,000

Selected Specialty

Products Production	Issue Price	Mintage or Sales Limit
100 coins	$29.95	
1,000 coins	$289.95	
First-Day Cover	$19.95	

Design Commentary from Citizens Commemorative Coin Advisory Committee (CCCAC) and Fine Arts Commission:

CCCAC met 5/15/98 in Washington (Diehl, Clain-Stefanelli, Shockley, Reiver, Bressett and Atherton) and recommended "NJ-G rev 3 with Washington crossing the Delaware; NH-C rev 1, the horse and rider, the outline of the state without 'Trenton and the star,' and the lighthouse over slightly to the right; NJ-H rev 1, with the lighthouse" and state motto. Fine Arts Hearing 5/21/98: Barnegat lighthouse was termed "vacuous and vapid" by Chairman J. Carter Brown (p. 126); it "could be in any state." The famous painting was the turning point: "Although normally I think it's too much, the silhouette of this is so recognizable" (p. 127).

Grading Hints

Obverse:

The high points of the coin's obverse are prone to wear; the field off Washington's nose, and the area behind the head curls, are prone to contact marks. Wear is most likely to be evident on the hair above Washington's ear and on the cheekbones.

Reverse:　　　　　　　Washington (standing), American flag (pointing toward 1 o'clock), field (upper).

Highest Uncirculated Grade Reported

PCGS	NGC	ANACS	Typical
MS-67 (P, D)	MS-65 (P, D)	MS-66 (P)	uncirculated
		MS-65 (D)	grade MS-63

News or Other Notes

New Jersey Gov. Christine Todd Whitman moved rapidly to have a 15-person committee appointed to work on the design, which the Assembly and Senate promptly approved—astonishing, considering it took years of debate before being able to designate the Jersey tomato as the state fruit or vegetable. Setting the pattern, perhaps, for other states, a number of local numismatists were named to the design committee, whose choice is appropriately representative of New Jersey history. Whitman struck the New Jersey quarter at a ceremony in Philadelphia. It is the first quarter to feature George Washington on both the obverse and reverse (May 3, 1999). Committee members attended the New Jersey first-strike ceremony at the Philadelphia Mint. Among the committee members: Spencer Peck of Oldwick, Garland C. Boothe, Jr., of Westfield, Dr. Clement A. Price from Newark, Gail Greenberg from Moorestown, Eleanor McKelvey from Brigantine, Catherine A. Vaughn from Chatham, Wanda Williams Finnie from Freehold, Melissa J. Cooke of Whippany, William H. Horton, Jr., of Keyport, Glen Beebe of Robbinsville, Thomas DeLuca of Hamilton Square, and Vincent C. Sgro of Jackson.

Investment Potential

New Jersey coins seem to be better struck than some of the earlier counterparts, hence the value is likely to be for upper-level, high-grade specimens only. Nonetheless, as an early addition with modest mintage (relatively speaking to other Washington quarters), this member of the State Quarters Program shows progress. There is a slight scarcity of the D-mint quarter, evidently because of distribution, since "P" and "D" mintages are approximately equal.

Thirty percent off center.   Multi-struck.

Pricing Information (Typical MS-63 grade) from Circulation

	Single ($.25)		Roll ($10)	
	P	D	P	D
May 2000	$.55	$.55	$16	$16

Current fair market value in superior (MS-65 and higher) condition. Valuations are courtesy of Dennis Baker and Numismedia, as of May 30, 2000, and are provided exclusively to *The Official Guidebook to America's State Quarters*. Fair market value prices listed are for certified coins only (usually PCGS, NGC, or ANACS). Raw coins may bring substantially less. Prices may fluctuate considerably as new issues are brought on the market and certified. As populations increase in a particular grade, coins may be easier to obtain and prices may fall. Where an asterisk appears for a grade, Numismedia has not seen enough trading activity to establish a price at this time. (Valuations ©2000 by Numismedia, Inc. All rights reserved. Used by permission.) A comprehensive listing of fair market value of U.S. coins is found on the web site of Numismedia, http://www.numismedia.com.

	MS-65	MS-66	MS-67
1999 New Jersey	23	37	—
1999-D New Jersey	19	37	222

New Jersey numismatist Bill Horton holds the New Jersey quarter at the Philadelphia Mint. The protective glasses are to protect him from injury during the coin striking.

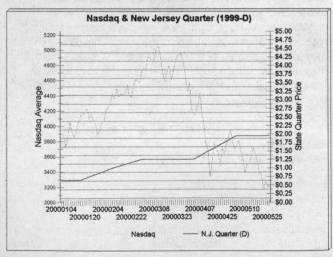

Nasdaq & New Jersey Quarter (1999-D)

GEORGIA

State, Coin Date:	Georgia, 1999
Nickname:	Peach State; Empire State of the South
Order in Union:	4 (1788)
Size:	58,977 sq. mi. (21st)
Population:	7.5 million (10th)
State Motto:	"Wisdom, Justice, Moderation"
State Flower:	Cherokee rose
State Bird:	Brown thrasher
State Tree:	Live oak
Selected Noteworthy Places :	Stone Mountain, Savannah, Atlanta, Chickamauga & Chattanooga National Military Park (oldest and largest military park in the nation; site of the second-bloodiest battle in the Civil War); The Civil War Prison Camp at Andersonville and National POW Museum.
Web Site:	http://www.state.ga.us
Additional Information:	Georgia was named for King George II of England. The name was chosen by James Oglethorpe, Colonial Administrator, in 1732. The U.S. Mint operated a branch mint in Dahlonega, Georgia, from 1838 to 1861. It minted only gold coins. There are 159 counties and 173 cities in Georgia. Margaret Mitchell's classic *Gone With the Wind* defines the view that many of us have of antebellum Georgia. Georgia is actually a state of mountains, and sea, with Atlanta in between, rising like a phoenix from Gen. Sherman's Civil War vendetta. Stone Mountain, Georgia, commemorated on 1925 U.S. Mint legal-tender 50-cent piece.

Coin Specifications

Obverse Sculptor/Designer:	John Flanagan, (1931); revised by William Cousins, assistant engraver, U.S. Mint, 1998.
Reverse Designer:	T. James Farrell (TJF).
Obverse Design:	Portrait of George Washington, after Houdon, by John Flanagan, modified by William Cousins (1997). Above

bust of Washington: United States of America. Beneath Washington's chin: Liberty, which has appeared on every U.S. coin produced since the Mint Act of April 2, 1792. Beside Washington's hair braid: national motto, "In God We Trust." Below neckline: Quarter Dollar. On side of neckline: two initials, JF (John Flanagan), WC (William Cousins).

Reverse Design: At top: state name; beneath, date entered Union. At bottom: date of issue; beneath, motto "E Pluribus Unum" (Out of many, one), describing how the divided colonies became the United States of America. State design: outline of state of Georgia, peach, motto above. TJF designer initials at right.

Mintage Figures:

Proof	2,500,000 estimated
Uncirculated "P"	451,188,000
Uncirculated "D"	488,744,000

Selected Specialty Products Production

	Issue Price	Mintage or Sales Limit
First-Day Cover	$19.95	
100 Coins	$29.95	
1000 Coins	$289.95	

Design Commentary from Citizens Commemorative Coin Advisory Committee (CCCAC) and Fine Arts Commission:

CCCAC meeting of 5/15/98 looked at recommending a choice of four: GA-E rev 1, with the outline of the state, book and hands with scroll, and the sunburst, taking out the four stars and peach; GA-H rev 1 with the outline of the state, peach and flowers, and state motto; GA-G with the state outline and a peach and the words "Wisdom, Justice, Moderation," taking out the four stars; GA-E rev 1 with the state bird and flower over the outline of the state. Fine Arts Commission met (5/21/98); recommendations included "the state silhouette with the slogan Hope, with symbols of recreation and education"; the second is the state bird . . . and the Cherokee rose, and the state map."

The map outline with integration of the peach was preferred.

Grading Hints

Obverse:

The high points of the coin's obverse are prone to wear; the field off Washington's nose, and the area behind the head curls, are prone to contact marks. Wear is most likely to be evident on the hair above Washington's ear and on the cheekbones.

Reverse:

Rounded inside curve of peach.

Highest Uncirculated Grade Reported

PCGS	NGC	ANACS	Typical
MS-68 (P)	MS-65 (P)	MS-65 (P)	Uncirculated
MS-67 (D)	MS-64 (D)	MS-65 (D)	Grade MS-63

News or Other Notes

The Georgia quarter, the fourth State Quarter, was unveiled at a press conference in Atlanta, Georgia. At the event, U.S. Treasurer Mary Ellen Withrow, Georgia Gov. Roy Barnes, and others handed out this peach of a coin (July 19, 1999). Mint Director Philip Diehl was quoted as saying that he did not think that the use of the state outline was "a strong design element," but overall the design frames this quite nicely.

Investment Potential

In the first year after its issue, the price of the Georgia coin moved toward nearly a dollar (95 cents being quoted in May 2000), representing a substantial return to those who held coins acquired from circulation. Mintage is relatively low (about on par with 1973-D or 1974-D Washington quarters). The coin's design seems to ensure the better-grade specimens were found, but by the same token it becomes essential to have the coin to complete the first year of the series, as well as the America's State coinage collection. Overall, high potential for the future.

Pricing Information (Typical MS-63 grade) from Circulation

	Single ($.25)		Roll ($10)	
	P	D	P	D
May 2000	$.95	$.95	$20	$20

Multiple clips.

Current fair market value in superior (MS-65 and higher) condition. Valuations are courtesy of Dennis Baker and Numismedia, as of May 30, 2000, and are provided exclusively to *The Official Guidebook to America's State Quarters*. Fair market value prices listed are for certified coins only (usually PCGS, NGC, or ANACS). Raw coins may bring substantially less. Prices may fluctuate considerably as new issues are brought on the market and certified. As populations increase in a particular grade, coins may be easier to obtain and prices may fall. Where an asterisk appears for a grade, Numismedia has not seen enough trading activity to establish a price at this time. (Valuations ©2000 by Numismedia, Inc. All rights reserved. Used by permission.) A comprehensive listing of fair market value of U.S. coins is found on the web site of Numismedia, http://www.numismedia.com.

	MS-65	MS-66	MS-67
1999 Georgia	19	42	300
1999-D Georgia	23	54	—

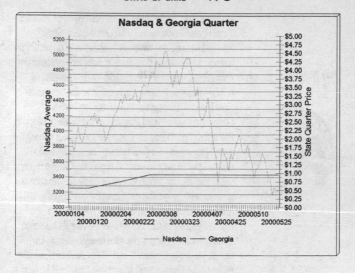

Nasdaq & Georgia Quarter

— Nasdaq — Georgia

CONNECTICUT

State, Coin Date:	Connecticut, 1999
Nickname:	Constitution State
Order in Union:	5 (1788)
Size:	5,544 sq. mi. (48th)
Population:	3.3 million (28th)
State Motto:	"Qui transtulit sustinet" (He who transplanted still sustains)
State Flower:	Mountain laurel
State Bird:	American robin
State Tree:	White oak
Selected Noteworthy Places:	Mystic Seaport; Nautilus Memorial, Groton; Gillette Castle, Hadlyme; Valley Railroad, Essex; New-Gate Prison, East Granby; Branford Trolley Museum, East Haven; home of Mark Twain and Harriet Beecher Stowe, Hartford
Web Site:	http://www.state.ct.us
Additional Information:	Origin of the name Connecticut: Quinnehtukqut—

Mohegan for "Long River Place" or "Beside the Long Tidal River." Nickname: "The Constitution State," adopted by the Legislature in 1959. From Connecticut's history: 1639—first constitution adopted, establishing representative government; 1656—first municipal public library in America, a bequest to the "towne of New Haven." During the American Revolution, Connecticut Gen. Israel Putnam at the battle of Bunker Hill cried: "Don't fire until you see the whites of their eyes!" Patriot-spy Nathan Hale, as he was about to be hanged by the British, said: "I regret that I have but one life to lose for my country." Connecticut has no county government; below the state are 169 municipalities. The Charter Oak depicted on the coin (downed in a lightning strike in the 1850s) hid the Royal Charter to maintain Connecticut's colonial independence. On Oct. 9, 1662, the General Court of Connecticut formally received the Charter won from King Charles II by Gov. John Winthrop, Jr., who had crossed the Atlantic for the purpose. Some 25 years later, with the succession of James II to the throne, Sir Edmund Andros, His Majesty's agent, followed up failure of various strategies by arriving in Hartford with an armed force to seize the Charter. After hours of debate, with the Charter on the table between the opposing parties, the candlelit room suddenly went dark. Moments later when the candles were relighted, the Charter was gone. Capt. Joseph Wadsworth is credited with having removed and secreted the Charter in the majestic oak on the Wyllys estate. The tree finally fell during a great storm on Aug. 21, 1856. Connecticut's tercentenary (1935) was honored with a U.S. Mint commemorative 50-cent piece which also depicted the Charter Oak.

Coin Specifications

Obverse Sculptor/Designer: John Flanagan, (1931); revised by William Cousins, assistant engraver, U.S. Mint, 1998.

Reverse Designer: T. James Ferrell (TJF).

Obverse Design: Portrait of George Washington, after Houdon, by John Flanagan, modified by William Cousins (1997). Above bust of Washington: United States of America. Beneath Washington's chin: Liberty, which has appeared on every U.S. coin produced since the Mint Act of April 2, 1792. Beside Washington's hair braid: national motto, "In God We Trust." Below neckline: Quarter Dollar. On side of neckline: two initials, JF (John Flanagan), WC (William Cousins).

Reverse Design: At top: state name; beneath, date entered Union. At bottom: date of issue; beneath, motto "E Pluribus Unum" (Out of many, one), describing how the divided colonies became the United States of America. State design: Charter Oak Tree ("The Charter Oak"), designer initials TJF.

Mintage Figures:

Proof	2,500,000 estimated
Uncirculated "P"	688,744,000
Uncirculated "D"	657,880,000

Selected Specialty

Products Production	*Issue Price*	*Mintage or Sales Limit*
100 coin bag P or D	$35.50	
1,000 coin bag P or D	$300.00	
First-Day Cover	$19.95	

Design Commentary from Citizens Commemorative Coin Advisory Committee (CCCAC) and Fine Arts Commission: CCCAC met 5/15/98 in Washington (Diehl, Clain-Stefanelli, Shockley, Reiver, Bressett and Atherton) and recommended CT-A rev 1, with the Charter Oak and a brick wall; CT-B with the Charter Oak and a scroll; CR-D with the Charter Oak but with the scroll removed. Fine Arts Hearing (5/21/98) has the Mint report: "Connecticut sent in one design concept, which was the Charter Oak, and they were quite adamant about that. It was the only thing they wanted" (p. 128).

Chairman Carter Brown "loved" two of the versions submitted.

Grading Hints

Obverse: The high points of the coin's obverse are prone to wear; the field off Washington's nose, and the area behind the head curls, are prone to contact marks. Wear is most likely to be evident on the hair above Washington's ear and on the cheekbones.

Reverse: Off-center main branch (thicker branches) from 6 o'clock to 12 o'clock will take and show contact marks.

Highest Uncirculated Grade Reported

PCGS	NGC	ANACS	Typical
MS-67 (P, D)	MS-66 (D)	MS-65 (P)	uncirculated
	MS-64 (P)	MS-65 (D)	grade MS-63

News or Other Notes

Connecticut's "Charter Oak" quarter, the fifth and final quarter of 1999, was unveiled at a ceremony in Philadelphia. (Oct. 7, 1999). The most artistic of the first year's designs, the Charter Oak previously appeared on the 1935 Connecticut tricentennial coin, authorized by Congress by the Act of June 21, 1934. See Ganz, *The Official Guide to U.S. Commemorative Coins*, p. 175 (1999).

Investment Potential

Mintages of the Connecticut coin were increased by the Mint to about 650,000,000 or more per mint. Similar perhaps to the 1982-D quarter in terms of quantity, this coin has been scooped up because it is so pretty. It has made a jewelry connection, removing more from the marketplace. Priced around 55 cents (or a doubling since issued), this one has particularly good potential even with the higher mintage.

Pricing Information (Typical MS-63 grade) from Circulation

	Single ($.25)		Roll ($10)	
	P	D	P	D
May 2000	$.55	$.55	$17	$17

A double strike.

Current fair market value in superior (MS-65 and higher) condition. Valuations are courtesy of Dennis Baker and Numismedia, as of May 30, 2000, and are provided exclusively to *The Official Guidebook to America's State Quarters*. Fair market value prices listed are for certified coins only (usually PCGS, NGC, or ANACS). Raw coins may bring substantially less. Prices may fluctuate considerably as new issues are brought on the market and certified. As populations increase in a particular grade, coins may be easier to obtain and prices may fall. Where an asterisk appears for a grade, Numismedia has not seen enough trading activity to establish a price at this time. (Valuations ©2000 by Numismedia, Inc. All rights reserved. Used by permission.) A comprehensive listing of fair market value of U.S. coins is found on the web site of Numismedia, http://www.numismedia.com.

	MS-65	MS-66	MS-67
1999 Connecticut	26	35	—
1999-D Connecticut	16	24	162

Connecticut half-dollar commemorative (1935) also featured the Charter Oak.

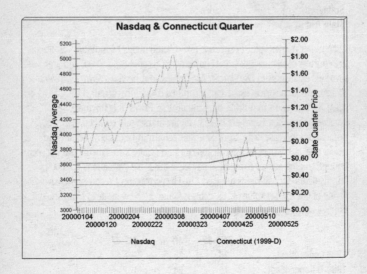

MASSACHUSETTS

State, Coin Date:	Commonwealth of Massachusetts, 2000
Nickname:	Bay State
Order in Union:	6 (1788)
Size:	9,241 sq. mi. (45th)
Population:	6.2 million (13th)
State Motto:	"By the sword we seek peace, but peace only under liberty" (translated from the Latin)
State Flower:	Mayflower
State Bird:	Chickadee
State Tree:	American elm
Selected Noteworthy Places:	Plymouth Rock; Cape Cod; Boston's Freedom Trail; Boston Museum of Fine Arts; Old Sturbridge Village; Walden Pond; USS Constitution (Old Ironsides); Kennedy presidential library; Minuteman National Park, Shaker Village
Web Site:	http://www.state.ma.us
Additional Information:	The state dog is the Boston terrier, the state beverage is cranberry juice, and the state fish is the cod. No wonder that historic symbol, "The Minuteman," is depicted on the Massachusetts quarter. Pilgrims landed at Plymouth in 1620, the first Thanksgiving was celebrated in 1621. The American Revolution began at Lexington and Concord in 1775. Boston's Freedom Trail remains a magnificent walking tour, with Mother Goose's Grave, the Old North Church, Paul Revere's residence, and many sites in between (great for a children's visit). Deborah Samson fought in the War of Independence under the name of Robert Shurtleff with courage, determination, and outstanding service, and rendered a unique contribution as a woman to American independence. Her masquerade remained undiscovered until she was wounded in battle. Another note: Johnny Appleseed was designated the official folk hero of the Commonwealth on Aug. 2, 1996. The Boston cream pie, created in the 19th century, was

chosen as the official state dessert on Dec. 12, 1996. A civics class from Norton High School sponsored the bill. The pie beat out other candidates, including the toll house cookie and Indian pudding. The chocolate chip cookie was designated the official cookie of the Commonwealth on July 9, 1997. A third-grade class from Somerset proposed the bill to honor the cookie invented in 1930 at the Toll House Restaurant in Whitman. Lexington-Concord 1775 battle is commemorated with a Minuteman statue rendering on U.S. Mint commemorative 50-cent piece (1925); Crispus Attucks, first person killed in American Revolution, is honored on a 1998 $1 coin.

Coin Specifications

Obverse Sculptor/Designer: John Flanagan, (1931); revised by William Cousins, assistant engraver, U.S. Mint, 1998.

Reverse Designer: Thomas D. Rogers, Sr. (TDR).

Obverse Design: Portrait of George Washington, after Houdon, by John Flanagan, modified by William Cousins (1997). Above bust of Washington: United States of America. Beneath Washington's chin: Liberty, which has appeared on every U.S. coin produced since the Mint Act of April 2, 1792. Beside Washington's hair braid: national motto, "In God We Trust." Below neckline: Quarter Dollar. On side of neckline: two initials, JF (John Flanagan), WC (William Cousins).

Reverse Design: At top: state name; beneath, date entered Union. At bottom: date of issue; beneath, motto "E Pluribus Unum" (Out of many, one), describing how the divided colonies became the United States of America. State design: map of Commonwealth of Massachusetts, "The Bay State," statue of the Minuteman, after the statue by Daniel Chester French at Lexington-Concord. See the Lexington-Concord sesquicentennial half dollar of 1925, Ganz, *The Official Guide to U.S. Commemorative Coins,* p. 159 (1999), for details.

Mintage Figures:

Proof	2,500,000 estimated
Uncirculated "P"	629.8 million
Uncirculated "D"	535.18 million

Selected Specialty

Products Production	Issue Price	Mintage or Sales Limit
100 coin bag	$35.50	}
1,000 coin bag	$300.00	} 10 million combined
First-Day Cover	$19.95	75,000

Design Commentary from Citizens Commemorative Coin Advisory Committee (CCCAC) and Fine Arts Commission: CCCAC meeting 1/5/99 at Washington (Clain-Stefanelli, Howard, Shockley, Bressett, Reiver and Atherton). Official minutes: "The Committee's preference was the *US[S] Constitution* depicted on MA-B. There was concern in suggesting two coins with ships within the same year. However they felt this was a very strong coin. They also selected the Minuteman with the state outline in MA-A, the lighthouse in MA-C, and "The Sacred Cod" in MA-D. Fine Arts Hearing (1/21/99) has Chairman Carter Brown wishing to "bag the fish" (the sacred cod) (tr. p. 124), then adding: "That Minuteman is such a great soldier."

Grading Hints

Obverse: The high points of the coin's obverse are prone to wear; the field off Washington's nose, and the area behind the head curls, are prone to contact marks. Wear is most likely to be evident on the hair above Washington's ear and on the cheekbones.

Reverse: Minuteman rifle, head.

Highest Uncirculated Grade Reported

PCGS	NGC	ANACS	Typical
MS-67 (P)	MS-67 (P)	MS-67 (P)	uncirculated
MS-67 (D)	MS-68 (D)		grade MS-63

News or Other Notes

The U.S. Mint offered a Massachusetts First-Day Commemorative Coin Cover. This limited edition cover (75,000 announced maximum) features two Massachusetts quarters from the first day of mintage—Dec. 20, 1999. Each cover includes quarters from both the Philadelphia and Denver Mints on a handsome display card with the 33-cent Flag-Over-City postage stamp. The postmark of January 3, 2000, Boston, Massachusetts, marks the day the Massachusetts quarters were first released to the Federal Reserve Bank and to the public. The mintage figures of 450 million (P and D, each) have not dimmed the popularity of the issue, in part because it is both historic and beautiful. The use of the Florentine finish for the state outline is particularly striking.

Investment Potential

First of the year 2000 issue coins has a relatively high mintage (about the same as the 1982-D Washington quarter), but it seems that many of the coins are being withdrawn from circulation, a good sign when supply and demand dictate price. This one could be the key to the series for this year, as Delaware is to 1999. Higher grade material from circulation is available, meaning that the Mint has perhaps finally worked out production problems that plagued Year One.

Pricing Information (Typical MS-63 grade) from Circulation

	Single ($.25)		Roll ($10)	
	P	D	P	D
May 2000	$.55	$.55	$16	$16

Some rejected designs.

Current fair market value in superior (MS-65 and higher) condition. Valuations are courtesy of Dennis Baker and Numismedia, as of May 30, 2000, and are provided exclusively to *The Official Guidebook to America's State Quarters*. Fair market value prices listed are for certified coins only (usually PCGS, NGC, or ANACS). Raw coins may bring substantially less. Prices may fluctuate considerably as new issues are brought on the market and certified. As populations increase in a particular grade, coins may be easier to obtain and prices may fall. Where an asterisk appears for a grade, Numismedia has not seen enough trading activity to establish a price at this time. (Valuations ©2000 by Numismedia, Inc. All rights reserved. Used by permission.) A comprehensive listing of fair market value of U.S. coins is found on the web site of Numismedia, http://www.numismedia.com.

	MS-65	MS-66	MS-67
2000 Massachusetts	17	25	66
2000-D Massachusetts	16	24	53

In 1925, Lexington and Concord's sesquicentennial was celebrated with the use of the Minuteman statue by Daniel Chester French.

Chrispus Attucks, first person in the American Revolution, Battle of Lexington & Concord, on 1998 commemorative.

Massachusetts quarter concept designers pose with the selected Minuteman design and enjoy their newfound celebrity, as they answer questions at an impromptu press conference following the ceremony. The winning design concept was submitted by two elementary school students—a seventh grader at Belmont Day School and a sixth grader at St. Bernard's elementary school.

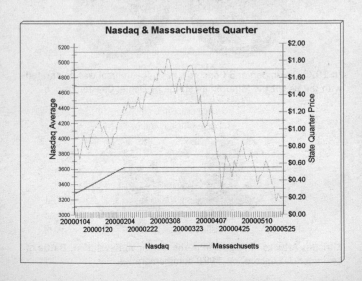

MARYLAND

State, Coin Date:	Maryland, 2000
Nickname:	Old Line State
Order in Union:	7 (1788)
Size:	12,297 sq. mi. (42nd)
Population:	5.1 million (19th)
State Motto:	"Manly deeds, womanly words" (from the Latin)
State Flower:	Black-eyed Susan
State Bird:	Baltimore oriole
State Tree:	White oak
Selected Noteworthy Places:	State House (oldest in continuous use in U.S.), U.S. Naval Academy (Annapolis); C&O Canal National Historic Park; Baltimore's Inner Harbor, including Camden Yards; Fort McHenry; Antietam battlefield
Web Site:	http://www.state.md.us
Additional Information:	Made up from a land grant to Lord Baltimore (1632), Baltimore was the site of the attack on Fort McHenry during the War of 1812, giving rise to the *Star Spangled Banner.* The name "Old Line" came from Maryland's reliability to Washington during the Revolutionary War. Through its new quarter, the seventh state honors the Maryland State House. A distinctive building dating back to 1772, it features the country's largest wooden dome built without nails. Besides housing Maryland's colonial legislature, from 1783–84, the Maryland State House served as the nation's first peacetime capital. The Treaty of Paris was ratified here, officially ending the Revolutionary War. A treasure preserved, the State House continues as the country's oldest state capital building still in legislative use. Leaf clusters from the official state tree, the white oak, and the nickname "The Old Line State" complete the selected design. Maryland is nicknamed the Old Line State in honor of its "troops of the line" that saved Gen. Washington and his troops during the Battle of Long Island (August 1776) by holding firm. These troops won praise from Washington, as commander-

in-chief of the Continental Army during the Revolutionary War. Maryland's tercentenary (1934) was honored with a U.S. Mint 50-cent piece honoring Lord Baltimore.

Coin Specifications

Obverse Sculptor/Designer:	John Flanagan, (1931); revised by William Cousins, assistant engraver, U.S. Mint, 1998.
Reverse Designer:	William J. Krawczewicz.
Obverse Design:	Portrait of George Washington, after Houdon, by John Flanagan, modified by William Cousins (1997). Above bust of Washington: United States of America. Beneath Washington's chin: Liberty, which has appeared on every U.S. coin produced since the Mint Act of April 2, 1792. Beside Washington's hair braid: national motto, "In God We Trust." Below neckline: Quarter Dollar. On side of neckline: two initials, JF (John Flanagan), WC (William Cousins).
Reverse design:	At top: state name; beneath, date entered Union. At bottom: date of issue; beneath, motto "E Pluribus Unum" (Out of many, one), describing how the divided colonies became the United States of America. State design: Old State House Capitol Dome. Maryland State House surrounded by white oak leaf clusters and the nickname "The Old Line State" complete the design.

Mintage Figures:

Proof	2,500,000 estimated
Uncirculated "P"	684.48 million
Uncirculated "D"	556.526 million

Selected Specialty Products Production	*Issue Price*	*Mintage or Sales Limit*
100 coin bag P or D	$35.50	} (P 43,250 bags; D 48,200 bags) }

Selected Specialty Products Production	Issue Price	Mintage or Sales Limit
1,000 coin bag P or D	$300.00 (P 1,725 bags; D 1,970 bags)	} 7 million combined

Design Commentary from Citizens Commemorative Coin Advisory Committee (CCCAC) and Fine Arts Commission:

CCCAC meeting 1/5/99 at Washington (Clain-Stefanelli, Howard, Shockley, Bressett, Reiver and Atherton). Minutes: "The Committee strongly endorsed the Ark and the Dove depicted on MD-C. They also liked the depiction of Fort McHenry on MD-H and the State House in MD-E." Fine Arts Hearing (1/21/99): The group appeared to prefer the Star-Spangled Banner version (tr. p. 120–21) and thought building designs "lacked perspective" (p. 122).

Grading Hints

Obverse: The high points of the coin's obverse are prone to wear; the field off Washington's nose, and the area behind the head curls, are prone to contact marks. Wear is most likely to be evident on the hair above Washington's ear and on the cheekbones.

Reverse: Middle rim on dome, top ball of dome, flag, fields.

Highest Uncirculated Grade Reported

PCGS	NGC	ANACS	Typical
		MS-65 (P)	uncirculated grade MS-63

News or Other Notes

On Wednesday, Oct. 14, 1998, Gov. Parris Glendening presented five State Quarter design concepts to the U.S. Mint. These designs were the result of a statewide design contest. From the 280 submissions, five were chosen by a committee appointed for this purpose. The semifinal designs included: Maryland State House Dome by William Krawczewicz; an Outline of the State of Maryland, also by William Krawczewicz; The Ark and the Dove, also by William Krawczewicz; Maryland State House by Frank O'Rourke; and Fort McHenry & The Star Spangled Banner, John F. Fieseler/Francis Scott Key Memorial Foundation, Inc. and Donald Curtis

Gov. Parris N. Glendening favored the State House Dome and chose that design on April 29, 1999, over five others recommended by the Maryland Commemorative Coin Committee. He established this commission specifically to evaluate quarter design submissions. The winning designer is a graphic artist at the White House and lives in Maryland; he was also designer for the common reverse of the 1996 Atlanta Olympic Games $5 gold piece and the 1995 Atlanta $1 common reverse for the Olympics.

Effective April 17, 2000, 9 a.m. Eastern Time, the U.S. Mint began selling the Maryland First-Day Commemorative Coin Cover. This limited-edition cover—only 75,000 to be produced—features two Maryland quarters from the first day of mintage, Feb. 28, 2000. Each cover includes quarters from both the Philadelphia and Denver Mints on a handsome display card with the 33-cent Flag-Over-City postage stamp. The postmark of March 13, 2000, Annapolis, Maryland, marks the day Maryland quarters were first released to the Federal Reserve Bank and to the public.

Investment Potential

Brisk trading of the Maryland coins began at once, and dealers were selling them for more than double face value less than six weeks after issuance. About 600 million from both P and D mints were anticipated. Design is less than stellar (the Fort McHenry was a favorite of the coin design committee). The coin's surface features appear to mar easily and hence better-grade material may simply be broadly unavailable. Sales of other products requiring all of the coins continues unabated, taking some available from the marketplace, causing price rises and shortages.

Pricing Information (Typical MS-63 grade) from Circulation

	Single ($.25)		Roll ($10)	
	P	D	P	D
May 2000	$.55	$.55	$16	$16

Current fair market value in superior (MS-65 and higher) condition. Valuations are courtesy of Dennis Baker and Numismedia, as of May 30, 2000, and are provided exclusively to *The Official Guidebook to America's State Quarters*. Fair market value prices listed are for certified coins only (usually PCGS, NGC, or ANACS). Raw coins may bring substantially less. Prices may fluctuate considerably as new issues are brought on the market and certified. As populations increase in a particular grade, coins may be easier to obtain and prices may fall. Where an asterisk appears for a grade, Numismedia has not seen enough trading activity to establish a price at this time. (Valuations ©2000 by Numismedia, Inc. All rights reserved. Used by permission.) A comprehensive listing of fair market value of U.S. coins is found on the web site of Numismedia, http://www.numismedia.com.

	MS-65	MS-66	MS-67
2000 Maryland	24	60	180
2000-D Maryland	—	—	—

Maryland's 300th anniversary was celebrated by the U.S. Mint in 1934 with these portraits of Lord Baltimore and the state seal.

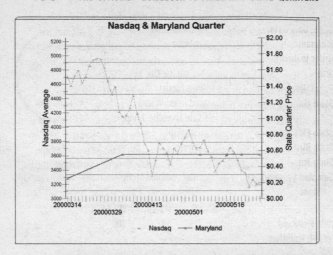

With Governor Glendening's help, and with U.S. Treasurer Mary Ellen Withrow watching, a Maryland fifth grader places the new quarter into the official 50 States Map. Quarters are minted in the order that states ratified the Constitution, making Maryland's the seventh quarter released on March 13, 2000.

SOUTH CAROLINA

State, Coin Date:	South Carolina, 2000
Nickname:	Palmetto State
Order in Union:	8 (1788)
Size:	31,189 sq. mi. (40th)
Population:	3.8 million (26th)
State Motto:	"Prepared in mind and deed; while I breathe, I hope"
State Flower:	Yellow jessamine
State Bird:	Carolina wren
State Tree:	Palmetto
Selected Noteworthy Places:	Fort Sumter National Monument and Charles Pinckney National Historic Site; Patriots Point Naval Museum, Charleston Harbor; Charleston Museum (oldest in U.S., 1773); Hilton Head Island; Revolutionary War battle sites; State Museum
Web Site:	http://www.state.sc.us
Additional Information:	At Fort Sumter, the Civil War began in 1861; in 2000, the legislature finally voted to remove the Confederate battle flag from atop the State Capitol. The palmetto was adopted as the "Official State Tree of the State of South Carolina" by Joint Resolution No. 63, approved March 17, 1939. The South Carolina palmetto is classified by the U.S. Department of Agriculture as "Inodes Palmetto" (also called Sabal Palmetto) and commonly known as the "Cabbage Palmetto." It has long been closely associated with the history of South Carolina, and is represented on the State Flag as well as on the State Seal, where it is symbolical of the defeat of the British fleet by the fort, built of palmetto logs, on Sullivan's Island. Beginning in 1998, the South Carolina Department of Parks, Recreation, and Tourism accepted quarter design suggestions. Design contributions came to the Mint from them, from schoolchildren and the South Carolina Numismatic Society. From these contributions emerged five semifinalist design concepts. The Citizens Commemorative Coin Advisory Committee (CCCAC) and the Fine Arts Commission narrowed these five

semifinalist design concepts down to three choices. Gov. Jim Hodges then made his final decision, indicating that the palmetto tree represents South Carolina's strength; the Carolina wren's song symbolizes the hospitality of the state's people, with the wren perched upon the state flower, the yellow jessamine.

Coin Specifications

Obverse Sculptor/Designer: John Flanagan, (1931); revised by William Cousins, assistant engraver, U.S. Mint, 1998.

Reverse Designer: Thomas D. Rodgers.

Obverse Design: Portrait of George Washington, after Houdon, by John Flanagan, modified by William Cousins (1997). Above bust of Washington: United States of America. Beneath Washington's chin: Liberty, which has appeared on every U.S. coin produced since the Mint Act of April 2, 1792. Beside Washington's hair braid: national motto, "In God We Trust." Below neckline: Quarter Dollar. On side of neckline: two initials, JF (John Flanagan), WC (William Cousins).

Reverse Design: At top: state name; beneath, date entered Union. At bottom: date of issue; beneath, motto "E Pluribus Unum" (Out of many, one), describing how the divided colonies became the United States of America. State design: map outlining state; "The Palmetto State" inside map; state tree and state bird perched on the state flower.

Mintage Figures:
Proof
Uncirculated "P" 741.73 million
Uncirculated "D" 565.92 million

Selected Specialty Products Production	*Issue Price*	*Mintage or Sales Limit*
100 coin bag P or D		} (P 49,660 bags; D 52,225 bags) }
1,000 coin bag P or D		} (P 1,540 bags; D 1,790 bags) }

Design Commentary from Citizens Commemorative Coin Advisory Committee (CCCAC) and Fine Arts Commission:

CCCAC meeting 1/5/99 at Washington (Clain-Stefanelli, Howard, Shockley, Bressett, Reiver and Atherton). "The Committee liked the design SC-B depicting Fort Moultrie with changes. For a clearer design, they suggested removing the larger ship ... They liked the State House in SC-C as well as the state bird and flower (SC-C and SC-E). For design SC-E they suggested removing the top of the branch and placing the bird to the left away from the state." Fine Arts Hearing (1/21/99), Comm'r. Barbaralee Diamonstein-Spielvogel: "I think we have to go with Palmetto State ..." (tr. p. 124). There was also some concern about design element placement (pp. 126–27) which Brown said should best be left to the governor. The Commission did like one design that the CCCAC rejected, and the Mint therefore discounted (p. 128). One committee member wanted Charlestown landing.

Grading Hints

Obverse: The high points of the coin's obverse are prone to wear; the field off Washington's nose, and the area behind the head curls, are prone to contact marks. Wear is most likely to be evident on the hair above Washington's ear and on the cheekbones.

Reverse: Top of palmetto tree; wren's beak.

Highest Uncirculated Grade Reported (*To be announced*)

PCGS	NGC	ANACS

News or Other Notes

Spanish and French explorers arriving in the late 1500s found a land inhabited by many small tribes of Native Americans, the largest of which were the Cherokees and the Catawbas. Early European attempts at settlement failed, but in 1670 a permanent English settlement was established on the coast near present-day

Charleston. The colony, named Carolina after King Charles I, was divided in 1710 into South Carolina and North Carolina. By the time of the American Revolution, South Carolina was one of the richest colonies in America. Its merchants and planters formed a strong governing class, contributing many leaders to the fight for independence. More Revolutionary War battles and skirmishes were fought in South Carolina than any other state. With the invention of the cotton gin, cotton became a major crop, particularly in the upcountry. A new capital city, Columbia, was founded in the center of the state. The Civil War began here, when Confederate troops fired on Fort Sumter in Charleston Harbor on April 12, 1861.

Investment Potential

The South Carolina coin looks promising, since out of the starting gate it had a retail price that was double face value. Not many IPOs can say as much. Of course, coins are not like stocks; they can't be split because they rise too high in value. Even if mintage was increased by 500 million, with 100 million Americans or more collecting them, these coins are headed for scarcity and were hard to obtain in a superior state of preservation.

Pricing Information (Typical MS-63 grade) from Circulation
(To be announced)

Columbia, South Carolina, sesquicentennial 50-cent piece struck (1936) by U.S. Mint with palmetto tree reverse.

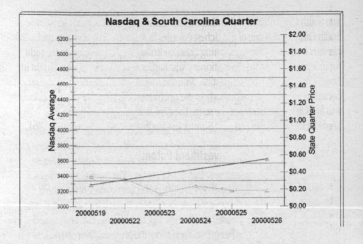

NEW HAMPSHIRE

State, Coin Date:	New Hampshire, 2000
Nickname:	Granite State
Order in Union:	9 (1788)
Size:	9,283 sq. mi. (44th)
Population:	1.2 million (42nd)
State Motto:	"Live free or die"
State Flower:	Purple lilac
State Bird:	Purple finch
State Tree:	White birch
Selected Noteworthy Places:	Kearsarge Indian Museum; Revolutionary-era forts on tiny New Castle Island; Frye's Measure Mill, America's only remaining water-powered measure mill; and Belknap Mill, the oldest unaltered textile mill in America. Home of President Franklin Pierce; Robert Frost; Augustus Saint-Gaudens National Historic Site
Web Site:	http://www.state.nh.us
Additional Information:	"The Old Man of the Mountain" is a rock formation

found on Mount Cannon in northern New Hampshire. Composed of five layers of Conway red granite, it appears to show a distinct profile of an elderly man gazing eastward. Today, the formation, measuring over 40 feet high with a lateral distance of 25 feet, is held in place by cables and turnbuckles to prevent further slipping and possible destruction. The New Hampshire quarter design began when Gov. Jeanne Shaheen established a Commemorative Quarter Committee with representatives from the Department of Cultural Affairs, arts educators, numismatists, historical societies, the Senate and House, and New Hampshire citizens. The committee opened a competition to all New Hampshire residents to submit design concepts for the New Hampshire quarter and even created a web site to report on the selection process and other information about the program. Over 300 designs and ideas were submitted to the Governor's Commemorative Coin Committee for deliberation and selection. The designs were grouped by subject matter (e.g., Old Man, State Symbols, etc.) and the Committee started the long process of selection. Three meetings were required to select the final five concepts, which were then sent to the U.S. Mint, with backup imagery and documentation, for transformation into finished artwork:

THE OLD MAN OF THE MOUNTAIN with nine stars indicating New Hampshire's rank as the Ninth State, the enabling vote for the Constitution of the United States, and the inscription "The Granite State."

THE OLD MAN OF THE MOUNTAIN with an eagle soaring beneath it, with "The Granite State."

ROBERT FROST IMAGERY based on his poem *The Road Not Taken,* including a forest scene with white birches (state tree) and a forked road.

A COVERED BRIDGE with mountain/forest scenery, emblematic of the natural beauty of New Hampshire.

A TOWN MEETING HOUSE indicating New Hampshire's unique political structure of town government.

Coin Specifications

Obverse Sculptor/Designer:	John Flanagan, (1931); revised by William Cousins, assistant engraver, U.S. Mint, 1998.
Reverse Designer:	William Cousins.
Obverse Design:	Portrait of George Washington, after Houdon, by John Flanagan, modified by William Cousins (1997). Above bust of Washington: United States of America. Beneath Washington's chin: Liberty, which has appeared on every U.S. coin produced since the Mint Act of April 2, 1792. Beside Washington's hair braid: national motto, "In God We Trust." Below neckline: Quarter Dollar. On side of neckline: two initials, JF (John Flanagan), WC (William Cousins).
Reverse Design:	At top: state name; beneath, date entered Union. At bottom: date of issue; beneath, motto "E Pluribus Unum" (Out of many, one), describing how the divided colonies became the United States of America. State design: "Old Man of the Mountain," a natural rock formation; state motto "Live Free or Die" in field; nine stars representing the ninth state admitted to the Union, WC (William Cousins).

Mintage Figures: *To be announced.*
Proof
Uncirculated "P"
Uncirculated "D"

Selected Specialty

Product Production	*Issue Price*	*Mintage or Sales Limit*
100 coin bag	*$35.50*	
1,000 coin bag	*$300.00*	

Design Commentary from Citizens Commemorative Coin Advisory Committee (CCCAC) and Fine Arts Commission:	Hearing (1/21/99), Chairman J. Carter Brown: "I agree that the 'Live Free or Die' is such a wonderful motto that I think that maybe we could make some recommendation that that is a plus." Comm'r. Barbaralee Diamonstein-Spielvogel: "I think the meeting house is quite nice. This covered bridge . . . is somewhat lessened" (tr. p. 114).

Grading Hints

Obverse:	The high points of the coin's obverse are prone to wear; the field off Washington's nose, and the area behind the head curls, are prone to contact marks. Wear is most likely to be evident on the hair above Washington's ear and on the cheekbones.
Reverse:	Nose of Old Man of the Mountain.

Highest Uncirculated Grade Reported (*To be announced*)

PCGS   **NGC**   **ANACS**

News or Other Notes

First to declare its independence and adopt its own constitution, New Hampshire was the ninth and deciding state in accepting the national Constitution as that of a republic, never to be known under any other form of government. New Hampshire's John Langdon was the first acting vice president of the United States, and was president of the Senate when Washington was elected first president. The first American public library was established at Peterborough. The world-recognized "Concord Coach" was made here, as was America's first cog-railroad to Mount Washington dating from 1869. New Hampshire has 1,300 lakes or ponds and 40,000 miles of rivers and streams which provide year-round fishing and recreation in scenic surroundings, as well as power for the state's many industries. Portsmouth, the only seaport, has an historic past and a prosperous present with its large navy yard. Q. David Bowers and Kenneth Bressett are reported to be the driving force behind the "Old Man" design. Interview, David Sundman, August 2000.

Investment Potential (*Coins struck 8/00*)

Pricing Information (Typical MS-63 grade) from Circulation
(*To be announced*)

VIRGINIA

State, Coin Date:	Commonwealth of Virginia, 2000
Nickname:	Old Dominion
Order in Union:	10 (1788)
Size:	42,326 sq. mi. (36th)
Population:	6.8 million (12th)
State Motto:	"Sic semper tyrannis" (Thus always to tyrants)
State Flower:	Dogwood
State Bird:	Cardinal
State Tree:	Dogwood
Selected Noteworthy Places:	Colonial Williamsburg is an important reminder today. Mount Vernon is the ancestral home of George Washington. Appomattox Courthouse National Historic Park; Arlington National Cemetery; Monticello; Charlottesville (University of Virginia)
Web Site:	http://www.state.va.us
Additional Information:	The state motto of Virginia was proclaimed by John Wilkes Booth as he shot President Abraham Lincoln. Jamestown was the first permanent settlement in North America (1607). State is named for Queen Elizabeth I (the Virgin Queen). The Virginia quarter, the tenth coin released under the 50 State Quarters program, honors our nation's oldest colony, Jamestown, which turns 400 years old in 2007. The selected design features the three ships *Susan Constant, Godspeed,* and *Discovery.* These ships brought the first English settlers

to Jamestown. On April 10, 1606, King James I of England chartered the Virginia Company to encourage colonization in the New World. The first expedition, consisting of the three ships depicted on the quarter, embarked from London on Dec. 20, 1606. On May 12, 1607, they landed on a small island along the James River nearly 60 miles from the mouth of the Chesapeake Bay. It was here the original settlers (104 men and boys) established the first permanent English settlement called Jamestown, in honor of King James I.

Coin Specifications

Obverse Sculptor/Designer: John Flanagan, (1931); revised by William Cousins, assistant engraver, U.S. Mint, 1998.

Reverse Designer: Edgar M. Stevens IV

Obverse Design: Portrait of George Washington, after Houdon, by John Flanagan, modified by William Cousins (1997). Above bust of Washington: United States of America. Beneath Washington's chin: Liberty, which has appeared on every U.S. coin produced since the Mint Act of April 2, 1792. Beside Washington's hair braid: national motto, "In God We Trust." Below neckline: Quarter Dollar. On side of neckline: two initials, JF (John Flanagan), WC (William Cousins).

Reverse Design: At top: state name; beneath, date entered Union. At bottom: date of issue; beneath, motto "E Pluribus Unum" (Out of many, one), describing how the divided colonies became the United States of America. State design: three ships, *Susan Constant, Godspeed,* and *Discovery* which brought the first English settlers to Jamestown; "1607–2007," "quadricentennial" anniversary of Jamestown. EMS in light water.

Mintage Figures: *TO BE ANNOUNCED.*
Proof
Uncirculated "P"
Uncirculated "D"

Selected Specialty Product Production	*Issue Price*	*Mintage or Sales Limit*

Design Commentary from Citizens Commemorative Coin Advisory Committee (CCCAC) and Fine Arts Commission

Hearing (1/21/99) saw commissioners having no difficulty in choosing either Mount Vernon (two versions) or Colonial Williamsburg (tr. p. 123). Virginia's governor went in a different direction.

Grading Hints

Obverse:
The high points of the coin's obverse are prone to wear; the field off Washington's nose, and the area behind the head curls, are prone to contact marks. Wear is most likely to be evident on the hair above Washington's ear and on the cheekbones.

Reverse:
Ship's center sail.

Highest Uncirculated Grade Reported (*To be announced*)

PCGS	*NGC*	*ANACS*

News or Other Notes

The selection of the design for Virginia's new quarter began when Gov. James Gilmore III selected State Treasurer Susan F. Dewey to serve as liaison to the U.S. Mint for the 50 State Quarters program. Ideas were solicited from colleges, universities, museums, and state agencies. Public comment was overwhelming, with thousands of responses received. Representatives from the Library of Virginia, the Department of Historic Resources, the Virginia Tourism Corporation, and the Department of General Services assisted the state treasurer in selecting design concepts for the Virginia quarter. The citizens of Virginia were encouraged to provide their comments. Gov. Gilmore then forwarded his final design concept recommendation, the Jamestown Quadricentennial, to the Secretary of the Treasury, who gave final approval.

Investment Potential (*COINS NOT YET STRUCK*)

Pricing Information (Typical MS-63 grade) from Circulation
(*TO BE ANNOUNCED*)

Mount Vernon, from the 1982 Washington bisesquicentennial half dollar.

NEW YORK

State, Coin Date:	New York, 2001
Nickname:	The Empire State
Order in Union:	11 (1788)
Size:	53,989 sq. mi. (27th)
Population:	18.2 million (3rd)
State Motto:	"Excelsior" (Ever upward)
State Flower:	Rose
State Bird:	Bluebird
State Tree:	Sugar maple
Selected Noteworthy Places:	Empire State Building, World Trade Center, Statue of Liberty (all New York City); Lake Placid Olympic Site (1932, 1980); Niagara Falls; Cooperstown Baseball Hall of Fame; Mansions of Hudson Valley (Hyde Park); Montauk Lighthouse; Sagamore Hill; U.S. Military

	Academy at West Point; Metropolitan Museum of Art (New York City); United Nations
Web Site:	http://www.state.ny.us
Additional Information:	"New York has been an integral part of the fabric of our nation," Gov. George Pataki said. "We'd like as many people as possible to participate." Thousands of schoolchildren did, with overlays of the New York City skyline, the Statue of Liberty superimposed on a state map with the phrase "Gateway to Freedom," and others. New York submitted five to the Commission of Fine Arts on March 6, 2000. The commission accepted the Statue of Liberty design and one with colonial troops celebrating their victory at Saratoga.

New York State–related commemorative 50-cent coins include: Hudson sesquicentennial (1935), Albany bisesquicentennial (1936), Long Island tercentenary (1936), and New Rochelle bisesquicentennial (1938).

Coin Specifications

Obverse Sculptor/Designer:	John Flanagan, (1931); revised by William Cousins, assistant engraver, U.S. Mint, 1998.
Reverse Designer:	*To be announced.*
Obverse Design:	Portrait of George Washington, after Houdon, by John Flanagan, modified by William Cousins (1997). Above bust of Washington: United States of America. Beneath Washington's chin: Liberty, which has appeared on every U.S. coin produced since the Mint Act of April 2, 1792. Beside Washington's hair braid: national motto, "In God We Trust." Below neckline: Quarter Dollar. On side of neckline: two initials, JF (John Flanagan), WC (William Cousins).
Reverse Design:	At top: state name; beneath, date entered Union. At bottom: date of issue; beneath, motto "E Pluribus Unum" (Out of many, one), describing how the divided colonies became the United States of America. State Design: Statue of Liberty superimposed on outline map of state.

Mintage Figures:	*TO BE ANNOUNCED.*
Proof	
Uncirculated "P"	
Uncirculated "D"	

Selected Specialty		
Products Production	*Issue Price*	*Mintage or Sales Limit*

Design Commentary from Citizens Commemorative Coin Advisory Committee (CCCAC) and Fine Arts Commission: On 2/17/2000, the Fine Arts Commission panned designs showing the first U.S. Capitol in New York City and the Hudson ship *Half Moon*, but approved either a map of New York with the Statue of Liberty superimposed or a Colonial scene of the victory at Saratoga. Fine Arts members preferred the map and Statue of Liberty.

Grading Hints

Obverse: The high points of the coin's obverse are prone to wear; the field off Washington's nose, and the area behind the head curls, are prone to contact marks. Wear is most likely to be evident on the hair above Washington's ear and on the cheekbones.

Reverse: *DESIGN NOT FINALIZED.*

Highest Uncirculated Grade Reported (*TO BE ANNOUNCED*)

PCGS	NGC	ANACS

News or Other Notes

Saratoga was one of the major battles of the Revolutionary War, taking place Sept. 19–Oct. 17, 1777. Gen. Horatio Gates was the American commander; Gen. John Burgoyne headed up the British forces, which lost 7,000 men to the

Americans' mere 150 casualties. The surrender of Burgoyne led directly to the French entry into the War for Independence. The New York coin faces the classic battle that has plagued New York State politics for years: whether to give credence to upstate interests (Saratoga) or allow domination by New York City (Statue of Liberty) designs. Gov. Pataki, himself from Peekskill (upstate), eventually recommended the Statue of Liberty design to the Treasury Secretary. For the coin program, students submitted drawings, flooding Pataki's office with hundreds of sketches of state symbols, New York City landmarks, and even one donkey pulling a boat up the Erie Canal in the hope that their images would end up on the back of the new State Quarter.

A rejected design.

Albany, New York, commemorative.

Investment Potential (*COINS NOT YET STRUCK*)

Pricing Information (Typical MS-63 grade) from Circulation
(*TO BE ANNOUNCED*)

NORTH CAROLINA

State, Coin Date:	North Carolina, 2001
Nickname:	Tarheel State
Order in Union:	12 (1789)
Size:	52,672 sq. mi. (29th)
Population:	7.6 million (11th)
State Motto:	"Esse quam videri" (To be, rather than to seem)
State Flower:	Dogwood
State Bird:	Cardinal
State Tree:	Pine
Selected Noteworthy Places:	Kitty Hawk (site of Wright Brothers' first flight); Biltmore Estate, Asheville; Lighthouse at Cape Hatteras; Chimney Rock Park; Great Smokey Mountains; Battleship *North Carolina* (Wilmington); Sandburg home; Mint museum, Charlotte
Web Site:	http://www.state.nc.us
Additional Information:	Roanoke Island ("lost" colony) honored with 1937 U.S. Mint commemorative 50-cent coin honoring 350th anniversary depicting Sir Walter Raleigh and Virginia Dare. North Carolina's governor recommended a design honoring the first flight efforts of Wilbur and Orville Wright (the Wright Brothers) in 1903. Special commemoration of this is already planned by the U.S. Mint with non-circulating legal-tender coins in 2003. The concept design viewed by the Fine Arts Commission (2/17/00) shows the open-air plane above the dunes of Kitty Hawk, where the Wright Brothers (of Ohio) first flew. The design is after a famous photo taken with a camera set by Orville Wright on Dec. 17, 1903, with Orville piloting, Wilbur alongside the wings.

Coin Specifications

Obverse Sculptor/Designer:	John Flanagan, (1931); revised by William Cousins, assistant engraver, U.S. Mint, 1998.
Reverse Designer:	*TO BE ANNOUNCED.*
Obverse Design:	Portrait of George Washington, after Houdon, by John Flanagan, modified by William Cousins (1997). Above

bust of Washington: United States of America. Beneath Washington's chin: Liberty, which has appeared on every U.S. coin produced since the Mint Act of April 2, 1792. Beside Washington's hair braid: national motto, "In God We Trust." Below neckline: Quarter Dollar. On side of neckline: two initials, JF (John Flanagan), WC (William Cousins).

Reverse Design: At top: state name; beneath, date entered Union. At bottom: date of issue; beneath, motto "E Pluribus Unum" (Out of many, one), describing how the divided colonies became the United States of America. State design: Wilbur and Orville Wright at Kitty Hawk, December 1903, Orville piloting, Wilbur off the wing.

Mintage Figures: TO BE ANNOUNCED.
Proof
Uncirculated "P"
Uncirculated "D"

Selected Specialty
Products Production *Issue Price* *Mintage or Sales Limit*

Design Commentary The Fine Arts Commission (2/17/00) declined to
from Citizens approve two different drawings showing Cape Hatteras
Commemorative Coin and the Cape's famous lighthouse, one with a pelican in
Advisory Committee flight. Definitely preferred the "first flight" theme. This
(CCCAC) and Fine Arts will also be the subject of other non-circulating
Commission: commemorative coins in 2003.

Grading Hints

Obverse: The high points of the coin's obverse are prone to wear; the field off Washington's nose, and the area behind the head curls, are prone to contact marks. Wear is most likely to be evident on the hair above Washington's ear and on the cheekbones.
Reverse: Wingspan; Wilbur Wright left arm.

Highest Uncirculated Grade Reported (*To be announced*)

PCGS   **NGC**   **ANACS**

News or Other Notes (*To be announced*)

Investment Potential (*Coins not yet struck*)

Pricing Information (Typical MS-63 grade) from Circulation
(*to be announced*)

Roanoke Commemorative half dollar.

RHODE ISLAND

State, Coin Date:	State of Rhode Island and Providence Plantations, 2001
Nickname:	Little Rhody (the Ocean State)
Order in Union:	13 (1790)
Size:	1,231 sq. mi. (50th)
Population:	989,000 (43rd)
State Motto:	Hope
State Flower:	Violet
State Bird:	Rhode Island red
State Tree:	Red maple
Selected Noteworthy Places:	Touro Synagogue (1763) is the oldest in the U.S.; Roger Williams National Memorial in Providence, Samuel Slater's Mill in Pawtucket, the Gen. Nathaniel Greene Homestead in Coventry, and Block Island; Newport mansions; Gilbert Stuart birthplace; Tennis Hall of Fame
Web Site:	http://www.state.ri.us
Additional Information:	Rhode Island support for freedom of religion, conscience, and action, started by Roger Williams, who was exiled by the Massachusetts Bay Colony Puritans in 1636 and was the founder of the present state capital, Providence. Williams was followed by other religious exiles who founded Pocasset, now Portsmouth, in 1638, and Newport in 1639. Tourism is one of Rhode Island's largest industries. Providence tercentenary (Roger Williams' founding) was commemorated in 1936 by a U.S. Mint–issued 50-cent piece.

Coin Specifications

Obverse Sculptor/Designer:	John Flanagan, (1931); revised by William Cousins, assistant engraver, U.S. Mint, 1998.
Reverse Designer:	*To be announced.*
Obverse Design:	Portrait of George Washington, after Houdon, by John Flanagan, modified by William Cousins (1997). Above

bust of Washington: United States of America. Beneath Washington's chin: Liberty, which has appeared on every U.S. coin produced since the Mint Act of April 2, 1792. Beside Washington's hair braid: national motto, "In God We Trust." Below neckline: Quarter Dollar. On side of neckline: two initials, JF (John Flanagan), WC (William Cousins).

Reverse Design: At top: state name; beneath, date entered Union. At bottom: date of issue; beneath, motto "E Pluribus Unum" (Out of many, one), describing how the divided colonies became the United States of America. State design: founding of Rhode Island by Roger Williams, boat, Native Americans.

Mintage Figures: TO BE ANNOUNCED.
Proof
Uncirculated "P"
Uncirculated "D"

Selected Specialty
Products Production   *Issue Price*   *Mintage or Sales Limit*

Design Commentary   Fine Arts Commission met 2/17/00 and approved a
from Citizens   rendering of Roger Williams walking ashore with an
Commemorative Coin   Indian chieftain, while a boat in the background awaits.
Advisory Committee   Rejects: Williams along a rock-strewn shoreline with
(CCCAC) and Fine Arts   the word "hope," a sailboat in open water with the
Commission: inscription "Ocean State," and a portrait of Gilbert
Stuart with 13 stars.

Grading Hints

Obverse: The high points of the coin's obverse are prone to wear; the field off Washington's nose, and the area behind the head curls, are prone to contact marks. Wear is most likely to be evident on the hair above Washington's ear and on the cheekbones.

Reverse: Williams' hand, face, Native American headdress.

Highest Uncirculated Grade Reported (*To be announced*)

PCGS   NGC   ANACS

News or Other Notes

Executive Order 99-4 was signed April 7, 1999, by Gov. Lincoln Almond directing
that the Rhode Island Council on the Arts organize a "Coin Concept Advisory
Panel" whose membership included the president of the Rhode Island School of
Design, the chairman of the Rhode Island Historical Preservation & Heritage
Commission, a Rhode Island numismatist, "and Sen. John Chafee or designee in
recognition of his original introduction of the Act in the United States Senate."
The aim was "to give highest consideration to concepts which promote Rhode
Island's rich heritage and recognize Rhode Island's historical significance among
the original thirteen colonies." Randall Rosenbaum, executive director of the
Rhode Island State Council on the Arts, advises that "We solicited and received
several hundred coin concepts from Rhode Island citizens."

Investment Potential (*Coins not yet struck*)

Pricing Information (Typical MS-63 grade) from Circulation
(*To be announced*)

Rhode Island, 1936 commemorative coin.

VERMONT

State, Coin Date:	Vermont, 2001
Nickname:	Green Mountain State
Order in Union:	14 (1791)
Size:	9,615 sq. mi. (43rd)
Population:	591,000 (49th)
State Motto:	"Freedom and unity"
State Flower:	Red clover
State Bird:	Hermit thrush
State Tree:	Sugar maple
Selected Noteworthy Places:	Maple Grove Maple Museum; President Calvin Coolidge homestead; Rock of Ages Quarry; Bennington Battleground Monument
Web Site:	http://www.state.vt.us
Additional Information:	Explored and claimed for France by Champlain in 1609, the first English settlers moved into Vermont in 1724 and built Fort Dummer on the site of present-day Brattleboro. England gained control of the area in 1763 after the French and Indian Wars. The Green Mountain Boys, led by Ethan Allen, won fame by capturing Fort Ticonderoga from the British on May 10, 1775, in the early days of the Revolutionary War. In 1777, Vermont adopted its first constitution, abolishing slavery and providing for universal male suffrage without property qualifications. In 1791, Vermont became the 14th state to join the Union. Vermont leads the nation in the production of monument granite, marble, and maple syrup. Tourism is a major industry not only for the ski

areas but also for fall "color," quite unlike any other place in the world. A Vermont sesquicentennial coin was issued in 1927 by the U.S. Mint with a bust of Ira Allen, founder of Vermont.

Coin Specifications

Obverse Sculptor/Designer: John Flanagan, (1931); revised by William Cousins, assistant engraver, U.S. Mint, 1998.

Reverse Designer: *TO BE ANNOUNCED.*

Obverse Design: Portrait of George Washington, after Houdon, by John Flanagan, modified by William Cousins (1997). Above bust of Washington: United States of America. Beneath Washington's chin: Liberty, which has appeared on every U.S. coin produced since the Mint Act of April 2, 1792. Beside Washington's hair braid: national motto, "In God We Trust." Below neckline: Quarter Dollar. On side of neckline: two initials, JF (John Flanagan), WC (William Cousins).

Reverse Design: At top: state name; beneath, date entered Union. At bottom: date of issue; beneath, motto "E Pluribus Unum" (Out of many, one), describing how the divided colonies became the United States of America. State design:

Mintage Figures: *TO BE ANNOUNCED.*
Proof
Uncirculated "P"
Uncirculated "D"

Selected Specialty
Products Production   *Issue Price*   *Mintage or Sales Limit*

Design Commentary from Citizens Commemorative Coin Advisory Committee (CCCAC) and Fine Arts Commission:	Appeared 2/17/00 before Fine Arts Commission, which accepted two designs: a single snowflake with the state motto on either side, and homage to the state's maple sugar industry with a single farmer tapping into three trees (also with the state motto). Multiple snowflakes and a ski bobcat were rejects.

Grading Hints

Obverse:	The high points of the coin's obverse are prone to wear; the field off Washington's nose, and the area behind the head curls, are prone to contact marks. Wear is most likely to be evident on the hair above Washington's ear and on the cheekbones.
Reverse:	*DESIGN NOT FINALIZED.*

Highest Uncirculated Grade Reported

PCGS	NGC	ANACS

News or Other Notes

As a result of Executive Order 02-99, the Vermont Arts Council oversaw the solicitation of design concepts for the reverse ("tails" side) of a new quarter to be developed by the U.S. Mint for circulation in 2001). The deadline for submission was May 14, 1999, and the unveiling of concepts approved by the governor was scheduled for June 16, 1999. Several people independently suggested that the profile of Camel's Hump should be the main feature of the design. Others suggested a variety of views of the White River along Route 107. Still others suggested a variety of views of Holstein cows. In the end, the State Coin Selection Committee (designated in the Executive Order) was permitted to decide to combine any or all of these elements into a single concept, and forward that on to the governor for his review. The executive order governing reads:

STATE OF VERMONT
Executive Department
EXECUTIVE ORDER

WHEREAS, the United States Congress approved and the President signed Public Law 105-124, the "Fifty States Commemorate Coin Program Act" (the "Act") to "honor the unique Federal republic of 50 states that comprise the United States", and "to promote the diffusion of knowledge among the youth of the United States about the individual states, their history and geography, and the rich diversity of the national heritage"; and

WHEREAS, five state quarter dollars were issued every year beginning in 1999 in the order in which the States ratified the Constitution or were admitted into the Union; and

WHEREAS, Vermont was the 14th state to ratify the Constitution of the United States on January 10, 1791; and

WHEREAS, Vermont was among the third group of five states which coins will commemorate for release in 2001; and

WHEREAS, under the Act, the Gov. of the State of Vermont is responsible for establishing a selection process and submitting coin concepts which are emblematic of the State of Vermont to the Citizens Commemorative Coin Advisory Committee (CCCAC) and the Fine Arts Commission of the United States for consideration, with final approval by the Secretary of the Treasury.

NOW, THEREFORE, I, HOWARD DEAN, by the authority vested in me as Gov. of the State of Vermont do hereby declare and order that:

- Vermont residents are hereby encouraged to submit design concepts for consideration.
- The Vermont Arts Council is hereby assigned the responsibility for submitting coin concepts to the Gov.
- The Vermont Arts Council shall solicit and receive coin concepts from Vermont residents for consideration.
- The Vermont Arts Council shall organize a Coin Concept Advisory panel to be chaired by a representative of the Vermont Arts Council, and to consist of the following individuals or their designee:

the State Archivist, the Director of the Vermont Historical Society, the Director of the Vermont Crafts Council, the Director of the Vermont Department of Historical Preservation, the Vermont State Treasurer, the Vermont State Curator, the Vermont Department of Tourism and Marketing, the Director of the Vermont Museum and Gallery Alliance, and a private citizen.

The Coin Concept Advisory panel shall review such coin design concepts and recommend five concepts for submission to the Gov. During this process, the panel shall:

- Give highest consideration to concepts which promote Vermont's rich heritage and recognize Vermont's historical significance among the thirteen original colonies; and

- Abide by the federal design concept standards provided for in the Act, which are outlined in Attachment A to this Order; and
- Abide by the state design concept standards provided for in the Act, which are outlined in Attachment B to this Order; and
- Meet no later than June 11, 1999, to review the coin design concepts submitted to it; and
- Consult with Vermont historians, Vermont coin experts, and Vermont residents in its review of the coin design concepts; and
- Recommend five coin design concepts to the Gov. no later than June 16, 1999.

Investment Potential (*COINS NOT YET STRUCK*)

Pricing Information (Typical MS-63 grade) from Circulation
(*TO BE ANNOUNCED*)

1927 Vermont commemorative half dollar.   A proposed design.

KENTUCKY

State, Coin Date:	Commonwealth of Kentucky, 2001
Nickname:	Bluegrass State
Order in Union:	15 (1792)
Size:	40,411 sq. mi. (37th)
Population:	3.9 million (25th)
State Motto:	"United we stand; divided we fall"
State Flower:	Goldenrod
State Bird:	Cardinal
State Tree:	Tulip poplar
Selected Noteworthy Places:	Run for the Roses (Kentucky Derby), May of each year (2000 was 126th running); My Old Kentucky Home State Park, Bardstown, Kentucky; Bluegrass Railroad Museum, Versailles; Lincoln birthplace
Web Site:	http://www.state.ky.us
Additional Information:	"My Old Kentucky Home" must have been part of a farm, for in 1997, Kentucky had the fourth-largest number of farms in the nation. Kentucky's 88,000 farms averaged 159 acres. Tourism and travel is Kentucky's third-largest revenue-producing industry. The title comes from a song by Stephen Foster, written in January 1853. The lyrics are not politically correct in the 21st century.

Coin Specifications

Obverse Sculptor/Designer:	John Flanagan, (1931); revised by William Cousins, assistant engraver, U.S. Mint, 1998.
Reverse Designer:	*TO BE ANNOUNCED.*
Obverse Design:	Portrait of George Washington, after Houdon, by John Flanagan, modified by William Cousins (1997). Above bust of Washington: United States of America. Beneath Washington's chin: Liberty, which has appeared on every U.S. coin produced since the Mint Act of April 2, 1792. Beside Washington's hair braid: national motto, "In God We Trust." Below neckline: Quarter Dollar. On side of neckline: two initials, JF (John Flanagan), WC

(William Cousins).

Reverse Design: At top: state name; beneath, date entered Union. At bottom: date of issue; beneath, motto "E Pluribus Unum" (Out of many, one), describing how the divided colonies became the United States of America. State design: "My Old Kentucky Home," thoroughbred in front of fence.

Mintage Figures:
Proof
Uncirculated "P"
Uncirculated "D"

To be announced.

Selected Specialty		
Products Production	**Issue Price**	**Mintage or Sales Limit**

Design Commentary from Citizens Commemorative Coin Advisory Committee (CCCAC) and Fine Arts Commission: Gov. Paul Patton prefers a thoroughbred race horse standing in front of a farm house ("My Old Kentucky Home"). Also approved: Daniel Boone with his dog, crouching position. Rejected: Boone at the Cumberland Gap; Lincoln's birthplace.

Grading Hints

Obverse: The high points of the coin's obverse are prone to wear; the field off Washington's nose, and the area behind the head curls, are prone to contact marks. Wear is most likely to be evident on the hair above Washington's ear and on the cheekbones.

Reverse: Horse's hindquarter; head of horse.

Highest Uncirculated Grade Reported (*To be announced*)

PCGS	NGC	ANACS

News or Other Notes

The Kentucky Quarter Project Committee, headed by Kentucky First Lady Judi Patton, received nearly 1,800 design concepts from people across the state. The committee then narrowed the submissions to a smaller pool, from which Gov. and Mrs. Patton chose 12 finalists for the public to vote on. The original design concepts (as drawn by the citizens of Kentucky) differed substantially from the revisions made by the engraving staff of the Mint, which took the concepts and made them coinable. Kentuckians liked My Old Kentucky Home, a horse and jockey, Abraham Lincoln's birthplace, and Daniel Boone for the back of the quarter. They were submitted to the U.S. Mint on June 21, 1999. A total of 12 entries were placed on display in the Capitol front lobby and on the Internet for the public to vote on Tuesday through Thursday, June 15–17. The Capitol ballot box received 509 votes, and 57,994 votes were cast through the web site. The top seven designs can be seen on the Internet at http://www.state.ky.us/agencies/gov/quarter.htm.

The concept designers were:

Tommy Turner, Judge Executive of Larue County
Entry: America's First Frontier, Birthplace of Lincoln

Benjamin Blair, University of Kentucky student from Campbellsville
Entry: My Old Kentucky Home with plank fences in front, horses grazing

John Ward, engineering designer from Mount Sterling (2 entries)
Entry: Thoroughbred running with jockey aboard
Entry: My Old Kentucky Home

Charlotte Cash, art teacher at Cumberland County High School
Entry: Daniel Boone with long rifle, dog under tree

Ronald J. Inabinet, graphic designer from Union
Entry: Horse behind plank fence in field, house in background

Brian Orms, graphic artist from Louisville
Entry: My Old Kentucky Home

Investment Potential (*COINS NOT YET STRUCK*)

Pricing Information (Typical MS-63 grade) from Circulation
(*TO BE ANNOUNCED*)

Kentucky semi-finalists.

Daniel Boone commemorative in the 1930s.

TENNESSEE

State, Coin Date:	Tennessee, 2002
Nickname:	Volunteer State
Order in Union:	16 (1796)
Size:	42,146 sq. mi. (36th)
Population:	5.5 million (17th)
State Motto:	"Agriculture and commerce"
State Flower:	Iris
State Bird:	Mockingbird
State Tree:	Tulip poplar
Selected Noteworthy Places:	Great Smokey Mountains National Park; Andrew Johnson National Historic Site; The Hermitage (Andrew Jackson), Nashville; Shiloh, Chickamauga, and Chattanooga National Military Parks; Grand Ol' Opry; Opryland; Dollywood theme park; Graceland (home of Elvis)
Web Site:	http://www.state.tn.us
Additional Information:	Gov. Don Sundquist announced March 27, 2000, a statewide contest for students, artisans, and citizens to choose the Tennessee quarter. "I am excited about the designs that Tennesseans will come up with in representing the Volunteer State," Sundquist said. "There are many creative and talented people who will make us proud." The Tennessee Coin Commission, appointed by Sundquist, will oversee the project. Commission members include:

- Chairman Gary Burhop, Memphis
- Pat Tigrett, Memphis
- Lewis Donelson, Memphis

- Margaret Britton Vaughn, Bell Buckle
- Sidney Brown, Clarksville
- John Thornton, Chattanooga
- Wilma Dykeman, Newport

Coin Specifications

Obverse Sculptor/Designer: John Flanagan, (1931); revised by William Cousins, assistant engraver, U.S. Mint, 1998.

Reverse Designer: *To be announced.*

Obverse Design: Portrait of George Washington, after Houdon, by John Flanagan, modified by William Cousins (1997). Above bust of Washington: United States of America. Beneath Washington's chin: Liberty, which has appeared on every U.S. coin produced since the Mint Act of April 2, 1792. Beside Washington's hair braid: national motto, "In God We Trust." Below neckline: Quarter Dollar. On side of neckline: two initials, JF (John Flanagan), WC (William Cousins).

Reverse Design: At top: state name; beneath, date entered Union. At bottom: date of issue; beneath, motto "E Pluribus Unum" (Out of many, one), describing how the divided colonies became the United States of America. State Design: *To be announced.*

Mintage Figures: *To be announced.*
Proof
Uncirculated "P"
Uncirculated "D"

Selected Specialty Products Production	*Issue Price*	*Mintage or Sales Limit*

Design Commentary from Citizens Commemorative Coin Advisory Committee (CCCAC) and Fine Arts Commission: *Hearing results to be announced.*

Grading Hints

Obverse: The high points of the coin's obverse are prone to wear; the field off Washington's nose, and the area behind the head curls, are prone to contact marks. Wear is most likely to be evident on the hair above Washington's ear and on the cheekbones.

Reverse: *DESIGN NOT FINALIZED.*

Highest Uncirculated Grade Reported (*To BE ANNOUNCED*)

PCGS   **NGC**   **ANACS**

News or Other Notes (*To BE ANNOUNCED*)

Investment Potential (*COINS NOT YET STRUCK*)

Pricing Information (Typical MS-63 grade) from Circulation
(*To BE ANNOUNCED*)

OHIO

State, Coin Date:	Ohio, 2002
Nickname:	Buckeye State
Order in Union:	17 (1803)
Size:	44,828 sq. mi. (34th)
Population:	11.2 million (7th)
State Motto:	"With God, all things are possible"
State Flower:	Scarlet carnation
State Bird:	Cardinal
State Tree:	Buckeye
Selected Noteworthy Places:	Birthplace, homes, and memorials to U.S. presidents: William H. Harrison, Grant, Garfield, Hayes, Benjamin Harrison, McKinley, Taft, and Harding; Air Force Museum (Dayton); Pro Football Hall of Fame; Mound City Group National Monuments (prehistoric)
Web Site:	http://www.state.oh.us
Additional Information:	The Cleveland–Great Lakes Expo (1936) was commemorated on a U.S. 50-cent piece; the McKinley Memorial, Niles, Ohio, on a gold dollar (1916–17). Ohio's bicentennial is celebrated in 2003, and it has made the quarter's appearance a part of the celebration. The Ohio Bicentennial Commission accepted quarter designs to be reviewed by an 11-member Ohio Commemorative Quarter Program Committee announced by Gov. Bob Taft. The deadline for submissions was May 25, 2000. The committee selected several representative designs that were displayed on the state web site from June 20–22, 2000. Visitors were able to point and click to register their opinions on their favorite designs. The top three to five designs will then be sent to a graphic artist for fine tuning before making their final journey to the U.S. Mint in Washington, D.C. The Mint's Citizens Commemorative Coin Advisory Committee (CCCAC) will review the drawings and recommend candidate designs to the U.S. Fine Arts Commission. The designs will then head to the Secretary of the Treasury for

review and approval. Once the Ohio Commemorative Quarter Program Committee and Gov. Taft approve the final design, it will head to Philadelphia for the minting process.

The Ohio Bicentennial Commission
Ohio Quarter Program
State House, Room 021 N.
Columbus, OH 43215

Members of the Ohio Commemorative Quarter Program Committee are:

- Tom Noe, president, Vintage Coins, Toledo (chair)
- Bill Kamb, Ruscilli Construction, president, Columbus Numismatic Society
- Beth Deisher, editor, *Coin World* newspaper, Bellefontaine
- Randell McShepard, executive director, City Year Cleveland
- Sen. Robert Latta (R-Bowling Green)
- Sen. Anthony Latell (D-Girard)
- Rep. Priscilla Mead (R-Upper Arlington)
- Rep. Bob Gooding (R-Waldo)
- George Zimmermann, chairman, Ohio Bicentennial Commission
- Steve George, executive director, Ohio Bicentennial Commission
- Dr. Gary Ness, director, Ohio Historical Society

Coin Specifications

Obverse Sculptor/Designer:	John Flanagan, (1931); revised by William Cousins, assistant engraver, U.S. Mint, 1998.
Reverse Designer:	*TO BE ANNOUNCED.*
Obverse Design:	Portrait of George Washington, after Houdon, by John Flanagan, modified by William Cousins (1997). Above bust of Washington: United States of America. Beneath Washington's chin: Liberty, which has appeared on

every U.S. coin produced since the Mint Act of April 2, 1792. Beside Washington's hair braid: national motto, "In God We Trust." Below neckline: Quarter Dollar. On side of neckline: two initials, JF (John Flanagan), WC (William Cousins).

Reverse Design: At top: state name; beneath, date entered Union. At bottom: date of issue; beneath, motto "E Pluribus Unum" (Out of many, one), describing how the divided colonies became the United States of America. State design: *To BE ANNOUNCED.*

Mintage Figures: *To BE ANNOUNCED.*
Proof
Uncirculated "P"
Uncirculated "D"

Selected Specialty Products Production	*Issue Price*	*Mintage or Sales Limit*

Design Commentary *HEARING RESULTS TO BE ANNOUNCED.*
from Citizens
Commemorative Coin
Advisory Committee
(CCCAC) and Fine Arts
Commission:

Grading Hints

Obverse: The high points of the coin's obverse are prone to wear; the field off Washington's nose, and the area behind the head curls, are prone to contact marks. Wear is most likely to be evident on the hair above Washington's ear and on the cheekbones.

Reverse: *DESIGN NOT FINALIZED.*

Highest Uncirculated Grade Reported (*To be announced*)

PCGS   NGC   ANACS

News or Other Notes

The design committee picked 10 design ideas from among nearly 7,300 suggestions. Concepts selected feature landmarks familiar to Ohioans, including aviation and invention symbols, the Lake Erie shore, an outline of the state, and the Serpent Mound. The 11-member committee of the Ohio Bicentennial Commission selected the ideas, which were developed into designs by artists at Ohio State, Kent State, and Bowling Green State universities. "No particular designs were chosen," said Brian Newbacher, the commission spokesman. "They just wanted enough concepts to capture a broad spectrum of ideas." The top three to five designs were to be sent to the U.S. Mint by June 30, 2000. Gov. Bob Taft and the 11-member Ohio Commemorative Quarter Program Committee were to select the design to be used.

Ten design concepts made the semifinals: An outline of the state with Lake Erie, aviation, and invention symbols, including Thomas Edison's lightbulb (Edison was born in 1847 in Milan); an outline of the state with the state bird, the cardinal, and buckeye leaves; the State House with aviation symbols; Marblehead's 1822 lighthouse and the Lake Erie shore; a celebration of the spirit of invention that would honor Edison and state contributions to air and space travel; pioneers of flight, showing the lunar landing, John Glenn's *Friendship* 7 space capsule circling the Earth, and the Wright Brothers' airplane; Johnny Appleseed; Serpent Mound superimposed on a relief map of Ohio (the quarter-mile-long mound in Adams County was built by the Adnea people between 800 B.C. and 100 A.D.; it was a favorite of schoolchildren who submitted designs); the Underground Railroad; transportation, in a design that includes canal boats, riverboats, and the National Road, which was cut through Ohio in the 1830s.

Investment Potential (*COINS NOT YET STRUCK*)

Pricing Information (Typical MS-63 grade) from Circulation
(*TO BE ANNOUNCED*)

1936 Cleveland commemorative half dollar.

1936 Cincinnati commemorative half dollar.

McKinley commemorative gold dollar (Niles, Ohio), 1916.

Ohio's semi-final designs.

LOUISIANA

State, Coin Date:	Louisiana, 2002
Nickname:	Pelican State
Order in Union:	18 (1812)
Size:	49,651 sq. mi. (31st)
Population:	4.4 million (22nd)
State Motto:	"Union, justice, confidence"
State Flower:	Magnolia
State Bird:	Eastern brown pelican
State Tree:	Cypress
Selected Noteworthy Places:	New Orleans French Quarter, Mardi Gras, Battle of New Orleans site; Garden District, New Orleans; U.S. Mint; Longfellow-Evangeline State Memorial Park; culture and cuisine of Spanish, French, Cajun. Tourist info number: 1-800-33-GUMBO
Web Site:	http://www.state.la.us
Additional Information:	The Louisiana Purchase was commemorated on a gold dollar (1903) coin; the Lewis and Clark expedition was commemorated on a 1904-05 gold dollar and by the Sacagawea dollar regular circulating coin first issued in 2000. The design was assisted pursuant to **Executive Order 99-36, and EXECUTIVE ORDER NO. MJF 99-40,** of Aug. 18, 1999, the text of which requires:

SECTION 1: The Louisiana Commemorative Coin Advisory Commission (hereafter "Commission") is established within the executive department, Office of the Gov.

SECTION 2: The duties of the Commission shall include, but are not limited to, the following:

A. Identifying a minimum of three (3) designs, design concepts, and/or themes emblematic of the state of Louisiana that are appropriate for coinability, have broad appeal to the citizens of Louisiana, are informative about the state of Louisiana, and are considered enduring representations or symbols of the state of Louisiana;

B. Preparing and/or obtaining supporting documentation that is necessary and/or appropriate for each design, design concept, and/or theme, including background materials, photographs, sketches, and/or depictions;
C. Obtaining full releases for all designs, design concepts, and/or themes, that are covered by a copyright, trademark, or any other type of privacy or publicity right; and
D. Submitting the designs, design concepts, and/or themes for the Louisiana commemorative coin and all related materials and/or releases to the Gov. no later than April 1, 2000.

AMEND EXECUTIVE ORDER NO. MJF 99-36 LOUISIANA COMMEMORATIVE COIN ADVISORY COMMISSION

WHEREAS, Executive Order No. MJF 99-36, signed on July 30, 1999, established the Louisiana Commemorative Coin Advisory Commission; and
WHEREAS, it is necessary to amend Executive Order No. MJF 99-36 in order to add additional members to the Commission;
NOW THEREFORE, I, M.J. "MIKE" FOSTER, JR., Gov. of the state of Louisiana, by virtue of the authority vested by the Constitution and the laws of the state of Louisiana, do hereby order and direct as follows:
SECTION 1: Section 4 of Executive Order No. MJF 99-36 is amended to provide as follows:
The Commission shall be composed of a maximum of eighteen (18) members appointed by, and serving at the pleasure of, the Gov. The membership of the Commission shall be selected as follows:
A. The Gov., or the Gov.'s designee;
B. The state treasurer, or the state treasurer's designee;

C. A collector of Louisiana currency printed subsequent
to Louisiana's admittance into the Union in 1812;
D. A collector of coins minted at the New Orleans Mint;
and
E. A minimum of seven (7) and a maximum of
fourteen (14) citizens of the state of Louisiana
knowledgeable about rare coins and/or the geography,
flora, fauna, history, political development, and/or
natural heritage of the state of Louisiana selected from
the seven (7) congressional districts of Louisiana.
SECTION 2: All other sections and subsections of
Executive Order No. MJF 99-36 shall remain in full
force and effect.
Section 3: The provisions of this Order are effective
upon signature and shall remain in effect until
amended, modified, terminated, or rescinded by the
Gov., or terminated by operation of law.

Coin Specifications

Obverse Sculptor/Designer:	John Flanagan, (1931); revised by William Cousins, assistant engraver, U.S. Mint, 1998.
Reverse Designer:	*TO BE ANNOUNCED.*
Obverse Design:	Portrait of George Washington, after Houdon, by John Flanagan, modified by William Cousins (1997). Above bust of Washington: United States of America. Beneath Washington's chin: Liberty, which has appeared on every U.S. coin produced since the Mint Act of April 2, 1792. Beside Washington's hair braid: national motto, "In God We Trust." Below neckline: Quarter Dollar. On side of neckline: two initials, JF (John Flanagan), WC (William Cousins).
Reverse Design:	At top: state name; beneath, date entered Union. At bottom: date of issue; beneath, motto "E Pluribus Unum" (Out of many, one), describing how the divided colonies became the United States of America. State design: *TO BE ANNOUNCED.*

Mintage Figures: *TO BE ANNOUNCED.*
Proof
Uncirculated "P"
Uncirculated "D"

Selected Specialty
Products Production   *Issue Price*   *Mintage or Sales Limit*

Design Commentary   *HEARING RESULTS TO BE ANNOUNCED.*
  from Citizens
  Commemorative Coin
  Advisory Committee
  (CCCAC) and Fine Arts
  Commission:

Grading Hints

Obverse: The high points of the coin's obverse are prone to wear; the field off Washington's nose, and the area behind the head curls, are prone to contact marks. Wear is most likely to be evident on the hair above Washington's ear and on the cheekbones.

Reverse: *DESIGN NOT FINALIZED.*

Highest Uncirculated Grade Reported (*To BE ANNOUNCED*)

PCGS   *NGC*   *ANACS*

News or Other Notes

LOUISIANA COMMEMORATIVE COIN ADVISORY COMMISSION OFFICIAL RULES To participate in the design and/or design theme search by submitting an entry, the submission must be on an approved entry form. In addition, the design and/or design theme entry must meet all of the following criteria:

- The design and/or design theme must be designed and submitted by a Louisiana resident and/or a school located in the state of Louisiana;
- The name, address, and telephone number of the resident or school must be written on the back of the entry form; no designer's name or identifying mark may appear on the front of the entry form;
- The design and/or design theme submission must be received by the Commission on or before February 11, 2000;
- The design and/or design theme must be suitable for coinability, that is the coin can be made by the minting process used by the U.S. Mint;
- The design and/or design theme must be attractive and appealing to the citizens of the state of Louisiana;
- The design and/or design theme must contain at least (1) enduring symbol, representation, and/or emblem of the state of Louisiana which will inform and/or impart facts or information to a viewer about the state of Louisiana;
- The design and/or design theme must be educational, and easily understood by both the youth of the state of Louisiana and the youth of other states;
- The design and/or design theme must promote and instill a feeling of pride in the citizens of the state of Louisiana;
- The design and/or design theme must not be likely to offend any person of normal sensibilities;
- The design and/or design theme must not promote an industry, business, or activity to the detriment of any other industry, business, or activity;
- The design and/or design theme must not contain the head and shoulders portrait or bust of any person living or dead, or portrait of any living person;
- The design and/or design theme must not contain the State Flag or the State Seal of the state of Louisiana;
- The design and/or design theme must not contain an inscription, but it may contain a title; and
- The design and/or design theme must not contain a logo or depiction of any specific commercial, private, educational, civic, religious, sport, or other organization whose membership or ownership is not universal.

No payment, compensation, consideration, award, reward or other recognition in any form or manner is expressly or impliedly offered by the state of Louisiana or the Commission by this request for design and/or design theme entries and/or submissions, or by any other act or actions related to the search for selection of a design for Louisiana's commemorative quarter. All entries and/or submissions received by the Gov., the Office of the Gov., and/or the Commission shall automatically become the sole property of the state of Louisiana, Office of the Gov., including all intellectual property rights (such as copyrights or trademarks, etc.) and the reproduction and/or alteration rights associated with or derived from any such submission. No previously copyrighted or published designs or design themes may be submitted. As owner of each entry and/or submission, the state of Louisiana through the Office of the Gov., the Gov., and/or the Commission, shall have the unfettered right and discretion to use, alter, modify, reproduce, duplicate, mint, mold, display, destroy and/or copy any submission in any manner and for any purpose. Accordingly, the state of Louisiana through the Office of the Gov., the Gov., and/or the Commission, may at any time assign, transfer, and/or license any or all of its intellectual property rights and reproduction and/or alteration rights in any such entry and/or submission received to third parties, including, but not limited to, the United States Department of Treasury. The state of Louisiana through the Office of the Gov., the Gov., and/or the Commission, reserves the right to accept, reject, or refuse, in whole or in part, any design, design concept, or design theme that is submitted. Submission and/or entries shall not be accepted from any individual who is not a legal resident of the state of Louisiana. No submission or entry shall be returned. Submissions and/or entries are limited to one per resident and to one per school. Submissions and/or entries must be made on an approved entry form. Entry forms may be obtained through the Office of the Gov.'s web site, http://www.gov.state.la.us; the state of Louisiana's web site, http:www.state.la.us/docs/whatsnew.htm; and/or by writing to the Office of the Gov., attention: Louisiana Coin Advisory Commission, PO Box 94004, Baton Rouge, LA 70804.

Twenty-nine semi-finalists were narrowed down to 10 finalists for submission to the Gov. by April 1, 2000. He was to select five for submission to the U.S. Mint in July 2000.

Investment Potential (*COINS NOT YET STRUCK*)

Pricing Information (Typical MS-63 grade) from Circulation
(TO BE ANNOUNCED)

Louisiana semi-finalists.

INDIANA

State, Coin Date:	Indiana, 2002
Nickname:	Hoosier State
Order in Union:	19 (1816)
Size:	36,420 sq. mi. (38th)
Population:	5.9 million (14th)
State Motto:	"The Crossroads of America"
State Flower:	Peony
State Bird:	Cardinal
State Tree:	Tulip tree
Selected Noteworthy Places:	Lincoln log cabin historic site; Tippecanoe Battlefield Memorial Park; Benjamin Harrison home; Indianapolis 500 raceway; Notre Dame; National Collegiate Football Hall of Fame
Web Site:	http://www.state.in.us
Additional Information:	"Designs for Indiana's quarter were reviewed by a selection committee impaneled by the Indiana Arts Commission. The committee will make recommendations to the Gov. regarding preliminary designs. The Gov. will select no fewer than three, and no more than five preliminary designs to be submitted to the U.S. Mint. . . . Creators of successful designs surrender all rights to images used in production, marketing, promotions, and other activities related to the Indiana Commemorative Quarter and the U.S. Mint's 50-State Quarters Program. Artists must provide proof of design originality." Entries had to be postmarked no later than Dec. 10, 1999, for use with a year 2002 date. When Indiana First Lady Judy O'Bannon announced the call for design concepts for Indiana's Commemorative Quarter, few could have anticipated the submission of more than 3,700 design ideas. Impressive as that response was, it has been eclipsed by the public's opportunity to weigh in with their opinions on which design best represents Indiana. Between Feb. 7–25, 2000, people could register votes for their favorite design themes by visiting the

Indiana Arts Commission (IAC) web site. They could also vote by ballots printed in several newspapers throughout the state. "When online voting concluded, nearly 155,000 votes had been registered," said IAC Executive Director Dorothy L. Ilgen. "[A]lmost 2,100 ballots were submitted by the postmark deadline." From more than 3,700 entries, the Indiana Quarter Design Committee selected 17 semi-final design themes as most emblematic of Indiana and best meeting guidelines established by the U.S. Mint. "Crossroads of America" theme was prominent, as were historic and tour sites. See http://www.state/in.us/iac/html/StateQuarter/semi.html, according to Rex A. Van Zant of the Indiana Fine Arts Commission, for the recommended seven designs the governor must review. From these he had to select between three and five to send to the Mint by June 23, 2000.

Coin Specifications

Obverse Sculptor/Designer: John Flanagan, (1931); revised by William Cousins, assistant engraver, U.S. Mint, 1998.

Reverse Designer: *To be announced.*

Obverse Design: Portrait of George Washington, after Houdon, by John Flanagan, modified by William Cousins (1997). Above bust of Washington: United States of America. Beneath Washington's chin: Liberty, which has appeared on every U.S. coin produced since the Mint Act of April 2, 1792. Beside Washington's hair braid: national motto, "In God We Trust." Below neckline: Quarter Dollar. On side of neckline: two initials, JF (John Flanagan), WC (William Cousins).

Reverse Design: At top: state name; beneath, date entered Union. At bottom: date of issue; beneath, motto "E Pluribus Unum" (Out of many, one), describing how the divided colonies became the United States of America. State design:

Mintage Figures: *TO BE ANNOUNCED.*
Proof
Uncirculated "P"
Uncirculated "D"

Selected Specialty
Products Production   *Issue Price*   *Mintage or Sales Limit*

Design Commentary   *HEARING RESULTS TO BE ANNOUNCED.*
  from Citizens
  Commemorative Coin
  Advisory Committee
  (CCCAC) and Fine Arts
  Commission:

Grading Hints

Obverse: The high points of the coin's obverse are prone to wear;
                      the field off Washington's nose, and the area behind the
                      head curls, are prone to contact marks. Wear is most
                      likely to be evident on the hair above Washington's ear
                      and on the cheekbones.
Reverse: *DESIGN NOT FINALIZED.*

Highest Uncirculated Grade Reported (*TO BE ANNOUNCED*)

	PCGS	NGC	ANACS

News or Other Notes

Josh Harvey, a high school student from Centerville, Indiana, is credited as having designed a coin with a sports theme. Also in the finals: the state outline with a cardinal, 19 stars, and the "Crossroads of America" logo, by Joan Butler of Rushville; the state outline beside the torch and stars from the state flag, by Seth

Fulkerson of Evansville; and a portrait of Chief Little Turtle, submitted by Zac Shuck of Kokomo. *Coin World* quoted Gov. Frank O'Bannon as stating that "the images that people most identify with Indiana" are on these coins.

Investment Potential (*Coins not yet struck*)

Pricing Information (Typical MS-63 grade) from Circulation
(*To be announced*)

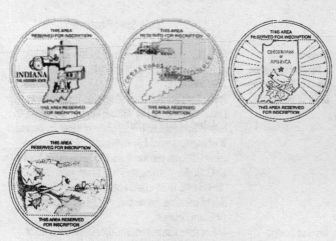

Indiana semi-finalists.

MISSISSIPPI

State, Coin Date:	Mississippi, 2002
Nickname:	Magnolia State
Order in Union:	20 (1817)
Size:	48,286 sq. mi. (32nd)
Population:	2.8 million (31st)
State Motto:	"Virtute et armis" (By virtue and arms)
State Flower:	Magnolia
State Bird:	Mockingbird
State Tree:	Magnolia
Selected Noteworthy Places:	Seafood Industry Museum, Biloxi; Tupelo and Vicksburg national battlefields and military park; Antebellum homes; Mississippi coast
Web Site:	http://www.state.ms.us
Additional Information:	*To be announced.*

Coin Specifications

Obverse Sculptor/Designer:	John Flanagan, (1931); revised by William Cousins, assistant engraver, U.S. Mint, 1998.
Reverse Designer:	*To be announced.*
Obverse Design:	Portrait of George Washington, after Houdon, by John Flanagan, modified by William Cousins (1997). Above bust of Washington: United States of America. Beneath Washington's chin: Liberty, which has appeared on every U.S. coin produced since the Mint Act of April 2, 1792. Beside Washington's hair braid: national motto, "In God We Trust." Below neckline: Quarter Dollar. On side of neckline: two initials, JF (John Flanagan), WC (William Cousins).
Reverse Design:	At top: state name; beneath, date entered Union. At bottom: date of issue; beneath, motto "E Pluribus Unum" (Out of many, one), describing how the divided colonies became the United States of America. State design: *To be announced.*

Mintage Figures: *TO BE ANNOUNCED.*
Proof
Uncirculated "P"
Uncirculated "D"

Selected Specialty
Products Production   *Issue Price*   *Mintage or Sales Limit*

Design Commentary   *HEARING RESULTS TO BE ANNOUNCED.*
  from Citizens
  Commemorative Coin
  Advisory Committee
  (CCCAC) and Fine Arts
  Commission:

Grading Hints

Obverse: The high points of the coin's obverse are prone to wear; the field off Washington's nose, and the area behind the head curls, are prone to contact marks. Wear is most likely to be evident on the hair above Washington's ear and on the cheekbones.

Reverse: *DESIGN NOT FINALIZED.*

Highest Uncirculated Grade Reported (*TO BE ANNOUNCED*)

PCGS   NGC   ANACS

News or Other Notes (*TO BE ANNOUNCED*)

Investment Potential (*COINS NOT YET STRUCK*)

Pricing Information (Typical MS-63 grade) from Circulation
(*TO BE ANNOUNCED*)

ILLINOIS

State, Coin Date:	Illinois, 2003
Nickname:	Land of Lincoln (The Prairie State)
Order in Union:	21 (1818)
Size:	57,918 sq. mi. (25th)
Population:	12.1 million (5th)
State Motto:	"State sovereignty, national union"
State Flower:	Violet
State Bird:	Cardinal
State Tree:	Oak
Selected Noteworthy Places:	Chicago; Chicago museums; Lincoln home, office at Springfield; Frank Lloyd Wright historic district, Oak Park
Web Site:	http://www.state.il.us
Additional Information:	The U.S. Mint struck a commemorative half dollar in 1918 on the occasion of the centennial of the statehood of Illinois.

Coin Specifications

Obverse Sculptor/Designer:	John Flanagan, (1931); revised by William Cousins, assistant engraver, U.S. Mint, 1998.
Reverse Designer:	*TO BE ANNOUNCED.*
Obverse Design:	Portrait of George Washington, after Houdon, by John Flanagan, modified by William Cousins (1997). Above bust of Washington: United States of America. Beneath Washington's chin: Liberty, which has appeared on every U.S. coin produced since the Mint Act of April 2, 1792. Beside Washington's hair braid: national motto, "In God We Trust." Below neckline: Quarter Dollar. On side of neckline: two initials, JF (John Flanagan), WC (William Cousins).
Reverse Design:	At top: state name; beneath, date entered Union. At bottom: date of issue; beneath, motto "E Pluribus Unum" (Out of many, one), describing how the divided colonies became the United States of America. State design: *TO BE ANNOUNCED.*

Mintage Figures: Proof Uncirculated "P" Uncirculated "D"	*TO BE ANNOUNCED*

Selected Specialty Products Production	*Issue Price*	*Mintage or Sales Limit*

Design Commentary from Citizens Commemorative Coin Advisory Committee (CCCAC) and Fine Arts Commission:	*HEARING RESULTS TO BE ANNOUNCED.*

Grading Hints

Obverse: The high points of the coin's obverse are prone to wear; the field off Washington's nose, and the area behind the head curls, are prone to contact marks. Wear is most likely to be evident on the hair above Washington's ear and on the cheekbones.

Reverse: *DESIGN NOT FINALIZED.*

Highest Uncirculated Grade Reported (*To be announced*)

PCGS   *NGC*   *ANACS*

News or Other Notes (*To be announced*)

Investment Potential (*Coins not yet struck*)

Pricing Information (Typical MS-63 grade) from Circulation
(*To be announced*)

Illinois centennial commemorated by the U.S. Mint, 1918.

ALABAMA

State, Coin Date:	Alabama, 2003
Nickname:	Yellowhammer State
Order in Union:	22 (1819)
Size:	52,237 sq. mi. (30th)
Population:	4.4 million (23rd)
State Motto:	"We dare defend our rights"
State Flower:	Camellia
State Bird:	Yellowhammer
State Tree:	Southern pine
Selected Noteworthy Places:	Alabama Space & Rocket Center, first White House of the Confederacy; Tuskegee Institute and Carter Museum; Helen Keller Birthplace; Russell Cave National Monument
Web Site:	http://www.state.al.us
Additional Information:	The U.S. Mint was authorized in 1920 to strike a half dollar to commemorate the 1919 centennial of Alabama (the coin is dated 1921). Unlike the State Quarters coin, it bore the portraits of the first and then-current Alabama governor, the first time a living person appeared on U.S. coinage. The motto appearing, "Here we rest," was the state motto through 1939. Since then, as above. Gov. Don Spiegelman's office advised on 5/9/00: "We have been receiving entries to the Coin Contest for over a year now." It also advised that "The Gov. has indicated a couple of people who will serve on a commission to select the design for the new State Quarter, however the exact method of selection has not yet been determined."

Grading Hints

Obverse:	The high points of the coin's obverse are prone to wear; the field off Washington's nose, and the area behind the head curls, are prone to contact marks. Wear is most likely to be evident on the hair above Washington's ear and on the cheekbones.
Reverse:	*DESIGN NOT FINALIZED.*

Highest Uncirculated Grade Reported (*To be announced*)

PCGS   **NGC**   **ANACS**

News or Other Notes (*To be announced*)

Investment Potential (*Coins not yet struck*)

Pricing Information (Typical MS-63 grade) from Circulation
(*To be announced*)

Alabama, 1921.

MAINE

State, Coin Date:	Maine, 2003
Nickname:	Pine Tree State
Order in Union:	23 (1820)
Size:	33,741 sq. mi. (39th)
Population:	1.2 million (39th)
State Motto:	"Dirigo" (I direct)
State Flower:	White pine cone and tassel
State Bird:	Chickadee
State Tree:	Eastern white pine
Selected Noteworthy Places:	Acadia National Park, Campobello International Island; Maritime Museum; Bush summer White House at Kennebunkport
Web Site:	http://www.state.me.us
Additional Information:	Maine's centennial (1920) saw issuance of a commemorative 50-cent piece bearing the Seal of the state with pine tree at center. Maine Legislature resolved to "Direct the Governor to establish a Commission to Recommend to the Governor Candidate Designs for the Maine State Quarter to be Submitted to the United States Mint."
	Presented by: Senator Small of Sagadahoc. Co-sponsored by: Reps. Etnier of Harpswell, Mayo of Bath. Public Hearing: 03/17/99. Majority (OTP-AM) Accepted 05/04/99. Amended by: CA S-135. seven public members. The amendment also adds a fiscal note to the resolve. Final disposition: Finally passed, Signed 05/13/99, Resolve Laws, Chapter 26.

Coin Specifications

Obverse Sculptor/Designer:	John Flanagan, (1931); revised by William Cousins, assistant engraver, U.S. Mint, 1998.
Reverse Designer:	*TO BE ANNOUNCED.*
Obverse Design:	Portrait of George Washington, after Houdon, by John Flanagan, modified by William Cousins (1997). Above bust of Washington: United States of America. Beneath

Washington's chin: Liberty, which has appeared on every U.S. coin produced since the Mint Act of April 2, 1792. Beside Washington's hair braid: national motto, "In God We Trust." Below neckline: Quarter Dollar. On side of neckline: two initials, JF (John Flanagan), WC (William Cousins).

Reverse Design: At top: state name; beneath, date entered Union. At bottom: date of issue; beneath, motto "E Pluribus Unum" (Out of many, one), describing how the divided colonies became the United States of America. State Design: *TO BE ANNOUNCED.*

Mintage Figures: *TO BE ANNOUNCED.*
Proof
Uncirculated "P"
Uncirculated "D"

Selected Specialty Products Productions	*Issue Price*	*Mintage or Sales Limit*

Design Commentary *HEARING RESULTS TO BE ANNOUNCED.*
  from Citizens
  Commemorative Coin
  Advisory Committee
  (CCCAC) and Fine Arts
  Commission:

Grading Hints

Obverse: The high points of the coin's obverse are prone to wear; the field off Washington's nose, and the area behind the head curls, are prone to contact marks. Wear is most likely to be evident on the hair above Washington's ear and on the cheekbones.

Reverse: *DESIGN NOT FINALIZED.*

Highest Uncirculated Grade Reported (*To Be Announced*)

PCGS   NGC   ANACS

News or Other Notes

There was some controversy in Maine over the creation of a commission to assist in the process of determining coin designs. The state legislature began to authorize it legislatively, and the original proposal for a commission established by the governor was amended to recommend that candidate designs for the Maine State Quarter be reviewed by a panel composed of seven public members. The amendment also adds a fiscal note to the resolve (the cost to be absorbed by the governor's office). Rep. Randy Bumps (R-China, Maine) voted against; in an e-mail 5/9/00 to the author, he discussed the controversy:

> I serve as the Ranking Minority Member on this Committee. Sen. Mary Small had submitted the bill, and acknowledged in her public testimony that the legislation was intended to prompt the Gov. in his responsibility to recommend a design for the quarter. Apparently, Gov. King had not seemed entirely responsive to Senator Small and others interested in the design of the quarter.
>
> My review of the federal law allowing for the design of these quarters placed the responsibility for recommending a design squarely with the Gov. of each state. Furthermore, Maine's deadline was still quite distant at the time the Committee considered the legislation. As a result, I would have preferred that the bill's sponsor and proponents work more closely with the Gov. to advocate for the establishment of a working group of interested parties to develop a recommended design. Each committee or commission as suggested (and ultimately approved) requires staff, funding, and legislative oversight that is available in short supply in a part-time legislature like exists in Maine. When taken in the context of all the other proposed study groups, commissions, and committees, I had hoped that Sen. Small and other interested parties could renew their efforts to work with Gov. King in the absence of a legislative mandate. As you know, that minority opinion did not prevail. I hope this helps to explain the nature of my dissent. I certainly support the creation of a design for the "Maine quarter." I also believe the involvement of all those interested in the design is very appropriate.

Investment Potential (*Coins not yet struck*)

Pricing Information (Typical MS-63 grade) from Circulation
(*To be announced*)

Maine's centennial commemorated, 1920.

MISSOURI

State, Coin Date:	Missouri, 2003
Nickname:	The Show Me State
Order in Union:	24 (1821)
Size:	69,709 sq. mi. (21st)
Population:	5.5 million (16th)
State Motto:	"The welfare of the people shall be supreme law" (from the Latin)
State Flower:	Hawthorne
State Bird:	Bluebird
State Tree:	Dogwood
Selected Noteworthy Places :	Gateway Arch, St. Louis; Truman Library; Mark Twain area, Hannibal; Pony Express Museum, St. Joseph;

	Churchill Memorial, Fulton
Web Site:	http://www.state.mo.us
Additional Information:	The U.S. Mint struck a Missouri centennial (1921) 50-cent coin celebrating frontier heritage of the "Show Me" state.

Coin Specifications

Obverse Sculptor/Designer:	John Flanagan, (1931); revised by William Cousins, assistant engraver, U.S. Mint, 1998.
Reverse Designer:	*TO BE ANNOUNCED.*
Obverse Design:	Portrait of George Washington, after Houdon, by John Flanagan, modified by William Cousins (1997). Above bust of Washington: United States of America. Beneath Washington's chin: Liberty, which has appeared on every U.S. coin produced since the Mint Act of April 2, 1792. Besides Washington's hair braid: national motto, "In God We Trust." Below neckline: Quarter Dollar. On side of neckline: two initials, JF (John Flanagan), WC (William Cousins).
Reverse Design:	At top: state name; beneath, date entered Union. At bottom: date of issue; beneath, motto "E Pluribus Unum" (Out of many, one), describing how the divided colonies became the United States of America. State design: *TO BE ANNOUNCED.*

Mintage Figures:	*TO BE ANNOUNCED.*
Proof	
Uncirculated "P"	
Uncirculated "D"	

Selected Specialty Products Production	*Issue Price*	*Mintage or Sales Limit*

Design Commentary from Citizens Commemorative Coin Advisory Committee (CCCAC) and Fine Arts Commission: *HEARING RESULTS TO BE ANNOUNCED.*

Grading Hints

Obverse: The high points of the coin's obverse are prone to wear; the field off Washington's nose, and the area behind the head curls, are prone to contact marks. Wear is more likely to be evident on the hair above Washington's ear on the cheekbones.

Reverse: *DESIGN NOT FINALIZED.*

Highest Uncirculated Grade Reported (*To BE ANNOUNCED*)

PCGS	NGC	ANACS

News or Other Notes (*To BE ANNOUNCED*)

Investment Potential (*COINS NOT YET STRUCK*)

Pricing Information (Typical MS-63 grade) from Circulation
(*To be announced*)

Missouri centennial half dollar, 1921.

ARKANSAS

State, Coin Date:	Arkansas, 2003
Nickname:	The Razorback State
Order in Union:	25 (1836)
Size:	53,182 sq. mi. (28th)
Population:	2.6 million (33rd)
State Motto:	"The people rule" (from the Latin)
State Flower:	Apple blossom
State Bird:	Mockingbird
State Tree:	Pine
Selected Noteworthy Places :	Hot Springs National Park, Crater of Diamonds, Arkansas Post (founded on Arkansas River, 1686, French historic monument
Web Site:	http://www.state.ar.us
Additional Information:	Arkansas centennial 50-cent coins were struck (1935–39) by the U.S. Mint with two varieties, one with Sen. Joseph Robinson's portrait, the other more traditional.

Four stars of Arkansas signal sovereignty of France (until 1782); Spain; United States (1836), Confederacy (1861–65) on reverse of coin.

Coin Specifications

Obverse Sculptor/Designer: John Flanagan, (1931); revised by William Cousins, assistant engraver, U.S. Mint, 1998.

Reverse Designer: *To be announced.*

Obverse Design: Portrait of George Washington, after Houdon, by John Flanagan, modified by William Cousins (1997). Above bust of Washington: United States of America. Beneath Washington's chin: Liberty, which has appeared on every U.S. coin produced since the Mint Act of April 2, 1792. Beside Washington's hair braid: national motto, "In God We Trust." Below neckline: Quarter Dollar. On side of neckline: two initials, JF (John Flanagan), WC (William Cousins).

Reverse Design: At top: state name; beneath, date entered Union. At bottom: date of issue; beneath, motto "E Pluribus Unum" (Out of many, one), describing how the divided colonies became the United States of America. State design: *To be announced.*

Mintage Figures: *To be announced.*
Proof
Uncirculated "P"
Uncirculated "D"

Selected Specialty Products Production   *Issue Price*   *Mintage or Sales Limit*

Design Commentary from Citizens Commemorative Coin Advisory Committee (CCCAC) and Fine Arts Commission: *Hearing results to be announced.*

Grading Hints

Obverse: The high points of the coin's obverse are prone to wear; the field off Washington's nose, and the area behind the head curls, are prone to contact marks. Wear is most likely to be evident on the hair above Washington's ear and on the cheekbones.

Reverse: *DESIGN NOT FINALIZED.*

Highest Uncirculated Grade Reported (*To be announced*)

PCGS   *NGC*   *ANACS*

News or Other Notes (*To be announced*)

Investment Potential (*Coins not yet struck*)

Pricing Information (Typical MS-63 grade) from Circulation
(*To be announced*)

Arkansas commemorative, 1936.

MICHIGAN

State, Coin Date:	Michigan, 2004
Nickname:	The Wolverine State (Great Lakes State)
Order in Union:	26 (1837)
Size:	96,705 sq. mi. (11th)
Population:	9.8 million (8th)
State Motto:	"If you seek a pleasant peninsula, look about you" (from the Latin)
State Flower:	Apple blossom
State Bird:	Robin
State Tree:	White pine
Selected Noteworthy Places:	Henry Ford Museum; Dossin Great Lakes Museum; Mackinac Island; Cereal City U.S.A. (Kellogg at Battle Creek); Motown Historic Museum, Detroit
Web Site:	http://www.migov.state.mi.us
Additional Information:	*To BE ANNOUNCED.*

Coin Specifications

Obverse Sculptor/Designer:	John Flanagan, (1931); revised by William Cousins, assistant engraver, U.S. Mint, 1998.
Reverse Designer:	*To BE ANNOUNCED.*
Obverse Design:	Portrait of George Washington, after Houdon, by John Flanagan, modified by William Cousins (1997). Above bust of Washington: United States of America. Beneath

Washington's chin: Liberty, which has appeared on every U.S. coin produced since the Mint Act of April 2, 1792. Beside Washington's hair braid: national motto, "In God We Trust." Below neckline: Quarter Dollar. On side of neckline: two initials, JF (John Flanagan), WC (William Cousins).

Reverse Design: At top: state name; beneath, date entered Union. At bottom: date of issue; beneath, motto "E Pluribus Unum" (Out of many, one), describing how the divided colonies became the United States of America. State design: *To be announced.*

Mintage Figures: *To be announced.*
Proof
Uncirculated "P"
Uncirculated "D"

Selected Specialty
Products Production *Issue Price* *Mintage or Sales Limit*

Design Commentary *Hearing results to be announced.*
from Citizens
Commemorative Coin
Advisory Committee
(CCCAC) and Fine Arts
Commission:

Grading Hints

Obverse: The high points of the coin's obverse are prone to wear; the field off Washington's nose, and the area behind the head curls, are prone to contact marks. Wear is most likely to be evident on the hair above Washington's ear and on the cheekbones.

Reverse: *Design not finalized.*

Highest Uncirculated Grade Reported (*TO BE ANNOUNCED*)

PCGS   **NGC**   **ANACS**

News or Other Notes (*TO BE ANNOUNCED*)

Investment Potential (*COINS NOT YET STRUCK*)

FLORIDA

State, Coin Date:	Florida, 2004
Nickname:	Sunshine State
Order in Union:	27 (1845)
Size:	59,928 sq. mi. (23rd)
Population:	15 million (4th)
State Motto:	"In God We Trust"
State Flower:	Orange blossom
State Bird:	Mockingbird
State Tree:	Sabal palmetto palm
Selected Noteworthy Places :	St. Augustine (1565), Walt Disney World (Magic Kingdom), Kennedy Space Center, Ringling Circus Museum, Everglades National Park
Web Site:	http://www.state.fl.us
Additional Information:	*To be announced.*

Coin Specifications

Obverse Sculptor/Designer:	John Flanagan, (1931); revised by William Cousins, assistant engraver, U.S. Mint, 1998.
Reverse Designer:	*To be announced.*
Obverse Design:	Portrait of George Washington, after Houdon, by John Flanagan, modified by William Cousins (1997). Above bust of Washington: United States of America. Beneath Washington's chin: Liberty, which has appeared on every U.S. coin produced since the Mint Act of April 2, 1792. Beside Washington's hair braid: national motto, "In God We Trust." Below neckline: Quarter Dollar. On side of neckline: two initials, JF (John Flanagan), WC (William Cousins).
Reverse Design:	At top: state name; beneath, date entered Union. At bottom: date of issue; beneath, motto "E Pluribus Unum" (Out of many, one), describing how the divided colonies became the United States of America. State design: *To be announced.*

Mintage Figures: TO BE ANNOUNCED.
Proof
Uncirculated "P"
Uncirculated "D"

Selected Specialty
Products Production   *Issue Price*   *Mintage or Sales Limit*

Design Commentary   *HEARING RESULTS TO BE ANNOUNCED.*
  from Citizens
  Commemorative Coin
  Advisory Committee
  (CCCAC) and Fine Arts
  Commission:

Grading Hints

Obverse: The high points of the coin's obverse are prone to wear;
                         the field off Washington's nose, and the area behind the
                         head curls, are prone to contact marks. Wear is most
                         likely to be evident on the hair above Washington's ear
                         and on the cheekbones.
Reverse: *DESIGN NOT FINALIZED.*

Highest Uncirculated Grade Reported (*TO BE ANNOUNCED*)

PCGS   *NGC*   *ANACS*

News or Other Notes (*TO BE ANNOUNCED*)

Investment Potential (*COINS NOT YET STUCK*)

Pricing Information (Typical MS-63 grade) from Circulation
(*TO BE ANNOUNCED*)

TEXAS

State, Coin Date:	Texas, 2004
Nickname:	Lone Star State
Order in Union:	28 (1845)
Size:	267,277 sq. mi. (2nd)
Population:	19.8 million (2nd)
State Motto:	"Friendship"
State Flower:	Bluebonnet
State Bird:	Mockingbird
State Tree:	Pecan
Selected Noteworthy Places:	Texas was once a nation, winning independence from Mexico in 1836 to become the Republic of Texas. All told, the flags of six nations have flown over the Lone Star State (Spain, France, Mexico, Republic of Texas, U.S., Confederacy); Alamo, Johnson Space Center, Houston
Web Site:	http://www.state.tx.us
Additional Information:	The Lone Star State's centennial (1934) was honored with a 50-cent commemorative coin struck 1934–38.

Coin Specifications

Obverse Sculptor/Designer: John Flanagan, (1931); revised by William Cousins, assistant engraver, U.S. Mint, 1998.

Reverse Designer: *TO BE ANNOUNCED.*

Obverse Design: Portrait of George Washington, after Houdon, by John Flanagan, modified by William Cousins (1997). Above bust of Washington: United States of America. Beneath Washington's chin: Liberty, which has appeared on every U.S. coin produced since the Mint Act of April 2, 1792. Beside Washington's hair braid: national motto, "In God We Trust." Below neckline: Quarter Dollar. On side of neckline: two initials, JF (John Flanagan), WC (William Cousins).

Reverse Design: At top: state name; beneath, date entered Union. At bottom: date of issue; beneath, motto "E Pluribus Unum" (Out of many, one), describing how the divided colonies became the United States of America. State design: *TO BE ANNOUNCED.*

Mintage Figures: *TO BE ANNOUNCED.*
Proof
Uncirculated "P"
Uncirculated "D"

Selected Specialty Products Production   *Issue Price*   *Mintage or Sales Limit*

Design Commentary from Citizens Commemorative Coin Advisory Committee (CCCAC) and Fine Arts Commission: *HEARING RESULTS TO BE ANNOUNCED.*

Grading Hints

Obverse: The high points of the coin's obverse are prone to wear; the field off Washington's nose, and the area behind the head curls, are prone to contact marks. Wear is most likely to be evident on the hair above Washington's ear and on the cheekbones.

Reverse: *DESIGN NOT FINALIZED.*

Highest Uncirculated Grade Reported (*TO BE ANNOUNCED*)

PCGS   **NGC**   **ANACS**

News or Other Notes (*TO BE ANNOUNCED*)

Investment Potential (*COINS NOT YET STRUCK*)

Pricing Information (Typical MS-63 grade) from Circulation
(*TO BE ANNOUNCED*)

Texas centennial, U.S. Mint, 1936.

IOWA

State, Coin Date:	Iowa, 2004
Nickname:	Hawkeye State
Order in Union:	29 (1846)
Size:	56,276 sq. mi. (26th)
Population:	2.9 million (30th)
State Motto:	"Our liberties we prize and our rights we will maintain"
State Flower:	Wild rose
State Bird:	Eastern goldfinch
State Tree:	Oak
Selected Noteworthy Places:	Effigy Mounds National Monument, Harpers Ferry; Hoover birthplace and national historic site; old Iowa Territory (from Minnesota and North Dakota south) and Mississippi and Missouri rivers; Grant Wood paintings, Davenport Municipal Art Gallery
Web Site:	http://www.state.ia.us
Additional Information:	The Iowa centennial was commemorated (1946) with a 50-cent U.S. Mint–issued commemorative. *American Gothic,* by Grant Wood, was depicted on the reverse of the 1980 American Arts gold medallion struck by the U.S. Mint, precursor to bullion coinage.

Coin Specifications

Obverse Sculptor/Designer:	John Flanagan, (1931); revised by William Cousins, assistant engraver, U.S. Mint, 1998.
Reverse Designer:	*TO BE ANNOUNCED.*

Obverse Design: Portrait of George Washington, after Houdon, by John Flanagan, modified by William Cousins (1997). Above bust of Washington: United States of America. Beneath Washington's chin: Liberty, which has appeared on every U.S. coin produced since the Mint Act of April 2, 1792. Beside Washington's hair braid: national motto, "In God We Trust." Below neckline: Quarter Dollar. On side of neckline: two initials, JF (John Flanagan), WC (William Cousins).

Reverse Design: At top: state name; beneath, date entered Union. At bottom: date of issue; beneath, motto "E Pluribus Unum" (Out of many, one), describing how the divided colonies became the United States of America. State design: *TO BE ANNOUNCED.*

Mintage Figures: *TO BE ANNOUNCED.*
Proof
Uncirculated "P"
Uncirculated "D"

Selected Specialty
Products Production   *Issue Price*   *Mintage or Sales Limit*

Design Commentary   *HEARING RESULTS TO BE ANNOUNCED.*
  from Citizens
  Commemorative Coin
  Advisory Committee
  (CCCAC) and Fine Arts
  Commission:

Grading Hints

Obverse: The high points of the coin's obverse are prone to wear; the field off Washington's nose, and the area behind the head curls, are prone to contact marks. Wear is most likely to be evident on the hair above Washington's ear and on the cheekbones.

Reverse: *DESIGN NOT FINALIZED.*

Highest Uncirculated Grade Reported (*To be announced*)

PCGS   **NGC**   **ANACS**

News or Other Notes (*To be announced*)

Investment Potential (*Coins not yet struck*)

Pricing Information (Typical MS-63 grade) from Circulation
(*To be announced*)

Iowa 1946 Centennial commemorative.

WISCONSIN

State, Coin Date:	Wisconsin, 2004
Nickname:	America's Dairyland (The Badger State)
Order in Union:	30 (1848)
Size:	65,499 sq. mi. (22nd)
Population:	5.3 million (18th)
State Motto:	"Forward"
State Flower:	Wood violet
State Bird:	Robin
State Tree:	Sugar maple
Selected Noteworthy Places:	Wisconsin Dells; Old Wade House and Carriage Museum; Circus World Museum; Green Bay Packers; America's Dairyland
Web Site:	http://www.state.wi.us
Additional Information:	Wisconsin territorial centennial commemorated (1936) with U.S. Mint 50-cent piece using Seal of territory, badger.

Coin Specifications

Obverse Sculptor/Designer:	John Flanagan, (1931); revised by William Cousins, assistant engraver, U.S. Mint, 1998.
Reverse Designer:	*To be announced.*
Obverse Design:	Portrait of George Washington, after Houdon, by John Flanagan, modified by William Cousins (1997). Above bust of Washington: United States of America. Beneath Washington's chin: Liberty, which has appeared on every U.S. coin produced since the Mint Act of April 2, 1792. Beside Washington's hair braid: national motto, "In God We Trust." Below neckline: Quarter Dollar. On side of neckline: two initials, JF (John Flanagan), WC (William Cousins).
Reverse Design:	At top: state name; beneath, date entered Union. At bottom: date of issue; beneath, motto "E Pluribus Unum" (Out of many, one), describing how the divided colonies became the United States of America. State design: *To be announced.*

Mintage Figures: *To be announced.*
Proof
Uncirculated "P"
Uncirculated "D"

Selected Specialty
Products Production   *Issue Price*   *Mintage or Sales Limit*

Design Commentary   *Hearing results to be announced.*
  from Citizens
  Commemorative Coin
  Advisory Committee
  (CCCAC) and Fine Arts
  Commission:

Grading Hints

Obverse: The high points of the coin's obverse are prone to wear;
the field off Washington's nose, and the area behind the
head curls, are prone to contact marks. Wear is most
likely to be evident on the hair above Washington's ear
and on the cheekbones.

Reverse: *Design not finalized.*

Highest Uncirculated Grade Reported (*To be announced*)

PCGS   *NGC*   *ANACS*

News or Other Notes (*To be announced*)

Investment Potential (*Coins not yet struck*)

Pricing Information (Typical MS-63 grade) from Circulation
(*To be announced*)

Wisconsin, 1936.

CALIFORNIA

State, Coin Date:	California, 2005
Nickname:	The Golden State
Order in Union:	31 (1850)
Size:	158,869 sq. mi. (3rd)
Population:	33 million (1st)
State Motto:	"Eureka" (I have found it)
State Flower:	Golden poppy
State Bird:	California valley quail
State Tree:	California redwood
Selected Noteworthy Places:	Disneyland; Rose Bowl; Redwood forests; Napa Valley viniculture; Hollywood; San Francisco; Death Valley National Monument; gold fields at Sutter's Mill
Web Site:	http://www.state.ca.us
Additional Information:	California's diamond jubilee (75th anniversary of statehood) was commemorated in 1925 by a U.S. Mint–issued 50-cent coin showing a grizzly bear and a miner panning for gold.

Coin Specifications

Obverse Sculptor/Designer:	John Flanagan, (1931); revised by William Cousins, assistant engraver, U.S. Mint, 1998.
Reverse Designer:	*TO BE ANNOUNCED.*
Obverse Design:	Portrait of George Washington, after Houdon, by John Flanagan, modified by William Cousins (1997). Above bust of Washington: United States of America. Beneath Washington's chin: Liberty, which has appeared on every U.S. coin produced since the Mint Act of April 2, 1792. Beside Washington's hair braid: national motto, "In God We Trust." Below neckline: Quarter Dollar. On side of neckline: two initials, JF (John Flanagan), WC (William Cousins).
Reverse Design:	At top: state name; beneath, date entered Union. At bottom: date of issue; beneath, motto "E Pluribus Unum" (Out of many, one), describing how the divided colonies became the United States of America. State design: *TO BE ANNOUNCED.*

Mintage Figures:	*TO BE ANNOUNCED.*
Proof	
Uncirculated "P"	
Uncirculated "D"	

Selected Specialty		
Products Production	*Issue Price*	*Mintage or Sales Limit*

Design Commentary	*HEARING RESULTS TO BE ANNOUNCED.*
from Citizens	
Commemorative Coin	
Advisory Committee	
(CCCAC) and Fine Arts	
Commission:	

Grading Hints

Obverse:	The high points of the coin's obverse are prone to wear; the field off Washington's nose, and the area behind the head curls, are prone to contact marks. Wear is most likely to be evident on the hair above Washington's ear and on the cheekbones.
Reverse:	*DESIGN NOT FINALIZED.*

Highest Uncirculated Grade Reported

PCGS	*NGC*	*ANACS*

News or Other Notes (*TO BE ANNOUNCED*)

Investment Potential (*COINS NOT YET STRUCK*)

Pricing Information (Typical MS-63 grade) from Circulation
(*TO BE ANNOUNCED*)

California 75th anniversary of statehood, 1925.

MINNESOTA

State, Coin Date:	Minnesota, 2005
Nickname:	Gopher State (North Star State)
Order in Union:	32 (1858)
Size:	86,943 sq. mi. (12th)
Population:	4.8 million (20th)
State Motto:	"L'Etoile du Nord" (The Star of the North)
State Flower:	Pink-and-white lady's slipper
State Bird:	Common loon
State Tree:	Red pine
Selected Noteworthy Places:	Minnehaha Falls; north shore of Lake Superior; Mayo Clinic; Fort Snelling
Web Site:	http://www.state.mn.us
Additional Information:	*To be announced.*

Coin Specifications

Obverse Sculptor/Designer:	John Flanagan, (1931); revised by William Cousins, assistant engraver, U.S. Mint, 1998.
Reverse Designer:	*To be announced.*
Obverse Design:	Portrait of George Washington, after Houdon, by John Flanagan, modified by William Cousins (1997). Above bust of Washington: United States of America. Beneath Washington's chin: Liberty, which has appeared on every U.S. coin produced since the Mint Act of April 2, 1792. Beside Washington's hair braid: national motto, "In God We Trust." Below neckline: Quarter Dollar. On side of neckline: two initials, JF (John Flanagan), WC (William Cousins).
Reverse Design:	At top: state name: beneath, date entered Union. At bottom: date of issue; beneath, motto "E Pluribus Unum" (Out of many, one), describing how the divided colonies became the United States of America. State design: *To be announced.*

Mintage Figures: To be announced.
Proof
Uncirculated "P"
Uncirculated "D"

Selected Specialty
Products Production   *Issue Price*   *Mintage of Sales Limit*

Design Commentary   HEARING RESULTS TO BE ANNOUNCED.
  from Citizens
  Commemorative Coin
  Advisory Committee
  (CCCAC) and Fine Arts
  Commission:

Grading Hints

Obverse: The high points of the coin's obverse are prone to wear;
                      the field off Washington's nose, and the area behind the
                      head curls, are prone to contact marks. Wear is most
                      likely to be evident on the hair above Washington's ear
                      and on the cheekbones.

Reverse: DESIGN NOT FINALIZED.

Highest Uncirculated Grade Reported (To be announced)

PCGS   *NGC*   *ANACS*

News or Other Notes (To be announced)

Investment Potential (*COINS NOT YET STRUCK*)

Pricing Information (Typical MS-63 grade) from Circulation
(*TO BE ANNOUNCED*)

OREGON

State, Coin Date:	Oregon, 2005
Nickname:	Beaver State
Order in Union:	33 (1859)
Size:	97,132 sq. mi. (10th)
Population:	3.3 million (28th)
State Motto:	"She flies with her own wings"
State Flower:	Oregon grape
State Bird:	Western meadowlark
State Tree:	Douglas fir
Selected Noteworthy Places:	Bonneville Dam, Columbia River; John Day Fossil Beds National Monument; Crater Lake National Park
Web Site:	http://www.state.or.us
Additional Information:	The Oregon Trail was commemorated on a U.S. 50-cent piece (1926–39). Conestoga wagon trip of 2,000 miles.

Coin Specifications

Obverse Sculptor/Designer:	John Flanagan, (1931); revised by William Cousins, assistant engraver, U.S. Mint, 1998.
Reverse Designer:	*TO BE ANNOUNCED.*

Obverse design: Portrait of George Washington, after Houdon, by John Flanagan, modified by William Cousins (1997). Above bust of Washington: United States of America. Beneath Washington's chin: Liberty, which has appeared on every U.S. coin produced since the Mint Act of April 2, 1792. Beside Washington's hair braid: national motto, "In God We Trust." Below neckline: Quarter Dollar. On side of neckline: two initials, JF (John Flanagan), WC (William Cousins).

Reverse design: At top: state name; beneath, date entered Union. At bottom: date of issue; beneath, motto "E Pluribus Unum" (Out of many, one), describing how the divided colonies became the United States of America. State design: *TO BE ANNOUNCED.*

Mintage Figures: *TO BE ANNOUNCED.*
Proof
Uncirculated "P"
Uncirculated "D"

Selected Specialty
Products Production   *Issue Price*   *Mintage or Sales Limit*

Design Commentary   *HEARING RESULTS TO BE ANNOUNCED.*
  from Citizens
  Commemorative Coin
  Advisory Committee
  (CCCAC) and Fine Arts
  Commission:

Grading Hints

Obverse: The high points of the coin's obverse are prone to wear; the field off Washington's nose, and the area behind the head curls, are prone to contact marks. Wear is most likely to be evident on the hair above Washington's ear and on the cheekbones.

Reverse: *DESIGN NOT FINALIZED.*

Highest Uncirculated Grade Reported

PCGS   NGC   ANACS

News or Other Notes (*To be announced*)

Investment Potential (*Coins not yet struck*)

Pricing Information (Typical MS-63 grade) from Circulation
(*To be announced*)

Oregon trail commemoratives, struck 1926–1939, by U.S. Mint.

KANSAS

State, Coin Date:	Kansas, 2005
Nickname:	Sunflower State
Order in Union:	34 (1861)
Size:	82,282 sq. mi. (15th)
Population:	2.7 million (32nd)
State Motto:	"Ad astra per aspera" (To the stars through difficulties)
State Flower:	Native sunflower
State Bird:	Western meadowlark
State Tree:	Cottonwood
Selected Noteworthy Places:	Eisenhower Center, Abilene; Dodge City—Boot Hill; John Brown's Cabin; Agriculture Hall of Fame
Web Site:	http://www.state.ks.us
Additional Information:	"I feel it is important for the citizens of Kansas to be involved in the selection process for the coin . . . Kansas will not be represented on the quarter until 2005, and efforts to collect suggestions are unlikely to be received prior to 2003, per the Treasury's recommendations. To ensure proposed designs receive full consideration in this process, I suggest constituents contact the Office of the Gov. closer to this date for information about the selection procedures."—Bill Graves, Gov. (May 26, 2000).

Coin Specifications

Obverse Sculptor/Designer:	John Flanagan, (1931); revised by William Cousins, assistant engraver, U.S. Mint, 1998.
Reverse Designer:	*TO BE ANNOUNCED.*
Obverse Design:	Portrait of George Washington, after Houdon, by John Flanagan, modified by William Cousins (1997). Above bust of Washington: United States of America. Beneath Washington's chin: Liberty, which has appeared on every U.S. coin produced since the Mint Act of April 2, 1792. Beside Washington's hair braid: national motto, "In God We Trust." Below neckline: Quarter Dollar. On side of neckline: two initials, JF (John Flanagan), WC (William Cousins).

Reverse Design: At top: state name; beneath, date entered Union. At bottom: date of issue; beneath, motto "E Pluribus Unum" (Out of many, one), describing how the divided colonies became the United States of America. State design: *TO BE ANNOUNCED.*

Mintage Figures: *TO BE ANNOUNCED.*
Proof
Uncirculated "P"
Uncirculated "D"

Selected Specialty
Products Production   *Issue Price*   *Mintage or Sales Limit*

Design Commentary   *HEARING RESULTS TO BE ANNOUNCED.*
  from Citizens
  Commemorative Coin
  Advisory Committee
  (CCCAC) and Fine Arts
  Commission:

Grading Hints

Obverse: The high points of the coin's obverse are prone to wear; the field off Washington's nose, and the area behind the head curls, are prone to contact marks. Wear is most likely to be evident on the hair above Washington's ear and on the cheekbones.

Reverse: *DESIGN NOT FINALIZED.*

Highest Uncirculated Grade Reported (*TO BE ANNOUNCED*)

PCGS   *NGC*   *ANACS*

News or Other Notes (*To be announced*)

Investment Potential (*Coins not yet struck*)

Pricing Information (Typical MS-63 grade) from Circulation
(*To be announced*)

WEST VIRGINIA

State, Coin Date:	West Virginia, 2005
Nickname:	Mountain State
Order in Union:	35 (1863)
Size:	24,231 sq. mi. (41st)
Population:	1.8 million (35th)
State Motto:	"Montani semper liberi" (Mountaineers are always free)
State Flower:	Big rhododendron
State Bird:	Cardinal
State Tree:	Sugar maple
Selected Noteworthy Places:	Harper's Ferry National Historic Park; exhibition coal mine, Beckley; mountains and forests
Web Site:	http://www.state.wv.us
Additional Information:	Gov. Tiffey wrote me May 22, 2000: "In response to your 5/19 e-mail, West Virginia remains interested in this important historical program. As the 35th state in the Union, West Virginia will not have its quarter distributed for several more years as production occurs in the order of states admitted to the Union of states. Thank you for your interest. E.P. Tiffey."

Coin Specifications

Obverse Sculptor/Designer:	John Flanagan, (1931); revised by William Cousins, assistant engraver, U.S. Mint, 1998.
Reverse Designer:	*To be announced.*
Obverse Design:	Portrait of George Washington, after Houdon, by John Flanagan, modified by William Cousins (1997). Above bust of Washington: United States of America. Beneath Washington's chin: Liberty, which has appeared on every U.S. coin produced since the Mint Act of April 2, 1792. Beside Washington's hair braid: national motto, "In God We Trust." Below neckline: Quarter Dollar. On side of neckline: two initials, JF (John Flanagan), WC (William Cousins).
Reverse Design:	At top: state name; beneath, date entered Union. At

bottom: date of issue; beneath, motto "E Pluribus Unum" (Out of many, one), describing how the divided colonies became the United States of America. State design: *To be announced.*

Mintage Figures: Proof Uncirculated "P" Uncirculated "D"	*To be announced.*

Selected Specialty Products Production	*Issue Price*	*Mintage or Sales Limit*
Design Commentary from Citizens Commemorative Coin Advisory Committee (CCCAC) and Fine Arts Commission:	*To be announced.*	

Grading Hints

Obverse:	The high points of the coin's obverse are prone to wear; the field off Washington's nose, and the area behind the head curls, are prone to contact marks. Wear is most likely to be evident on the hair above Washington's ear and on the cheekbones.
Reverse:	*Design not finalized.*

Highest Uncirculated Grade Reported (*To be announced*)

PCGS	NGC	ANACS

News or Other Notes (*To be announced*)

Investment Potential (*Coins not yet struck*)

Pricing Information (Typical MS-63 grade) from Circulation
(*To be announced*)

NEVADA

State, Coin Date:	Nevada, 2006
Nickname:	Silver State
Order in Union:	36 (1864)
Size:	110,567 sq. mi. (7th)
Population:	1.8 million (36th)
State Motto:	"All for our country"
State Flower:	Sagebrush
State Bird:	Mountain bluebird
State Tree:	Single-leaf piñon and bristle-cone pine
Selected Noteworthy Places:	Death Valley National Monument; Lehman Caves National Monument; Las Vegas "Strip"; Carson City and Bonanza silver mines; Hoover Dam
Web Site:	http://www.state.nv.us

Additional Information: The Nevada State Treasurer's Office has been designated as the contact for the U.S. Treasury staff in implementing Nevada's commemorative coin. "Presently, we are determining the best process to select a design which best depicts the heritage of Nevada. I hope this information is helpful, and good luck with your research and your book."—C.J. Smith, assistant to Treasurer Krolicki

Coin Specifications

Obverse Sculptor/Designer: John Flanagan, (1931); revised by William Cousins, assistant engraver, U.S. Mint, 1998.

Reverse Designer: *TO BE ANNOUNCED.*

Obverse Design: Portrait of George Washington, after Houdon, by John Flanagan, modified by William Cousins (1997). Above bust of Washington: United States of America. Beneath Washington's chin: Liberty, which has appeared on every U.S. coin produced since the Mint Act of April 2, 1792. Beside Washington's hair braid: national motto, "In God We Trust." Below neckline: Quarter Dollar. On side of neckline: two initials, JF (John Flanagan), WC (William Cousins).

Reverse Design: At top: state name; beneath, date entered Union. At bottom: date of issue; beneath, motto "E Pluribus Unum" (Out of many, one), describing how the divided colonies became the United States of America. State design: *TO BE ANNOUNCED.*

Mintage Figures: *TO BE ANNOUNCED.*
Proof
Uncirculated "P"
Uncirculated "D"

*Selected Specialty
Products Production*   *Issue Price*   .   *Mintage or Sales Limit*

Design Commentary from Citizens Commemorative Coin Advisory Committee (CCCAC) and Fine Arts Commission:

HEARING RESULTS TO BE ANNOUNCED.

Grading Hints

Obverse:

The high points of the coin's obverse are prone to wear; the field off Washington's nose, and the area behind the head curls, are prone to contact marks. Wear is most likely to be evident on the hair above Washington's ear and on the cheekbones.

Reverse:

DESIGN NOT FINALIZED.

Highest Uncirculated Grade Reported (*To BE ANNOUNCED*)

PCGS   *NGC*   *ANACS*

News or Other Notes (*To BE ANNOUNCED*)

Investment Potential (*Coins NOT YET STRUCK*)

Pricing Information (Typical MS-63 grade) from Circulation
(TO BE ANNOUNCED)

NEBRASKA

State, Coin Date:	Nebraska, 2006
Nickname:	Cornhusker State
Order in Union:	37 (1867)
Size:	77,358 sq. mi. (16th)
Population:	1.7 million (38th)
State Motto:	"Equality before the law"
State Flower:	Goldenrod
State Bird:	Western meadowlark
State Tree:	Cottonwood
Selected Noteworthy Places:	Strategic Air Command Museum, Ashland; Oregon Trail landmarks; agate fossil beds; Chimney Rock Historic Site; Buffalo Bill Ranch Historic Park
Web Site:	http://www.state.ne.us
Additional Information:	TO BE ANNOUNCED.

Coin Specifications

Obverse Sculptor/Designer:	John Flanagan, (1931); revised by William Cousins, assistant engraver, U.S. Mint, 1998.
Reverse Designer:	TO BE ANNOUNCED.
Obverse Design:	Portrait of George Washington, after Houdon, by John Flanagan, modified by William Cousins (1997). Above bust of Washington: United States of America. Beneath Washington's chin: Liberty, which has appeared on every U.S. coin produced since the Mint Act of April 2, 1792. Beside Washington's hair braid: national motto,

"In God We Trust." Below neckline: Quarter Dollar. On side of neckline: two initials, JF (John Flanagan), WC (William Cousins).

Reverse Design: At top: state name; beneath, date entered Union. At bottom: date of issue; beneath, motto "E Pluribus Unum" (Out of many, one), describing how the divided colonies became the United States of America. State design: *TO BE ANNOUNCED.*

Mintage Figures: *TO BE ANNOUNCED.*
Proof
Uncirculated "P"
Uncirculated "D"

Selected Specialty
Products Production   *Issue Price*   *Mintage or Sales Limit*

Design Commentary   *HEARING RESULTS TO BE ANNOUNCED.*
  from Citizens
  Commemorative Coin
  Advisory Committee
  (CCCAC) and Fine Arts
  Commission:

Grading Hints

Obverse: The high points of the coin's obverse are prone to wear; the field off Washington's nose, and the area behind the head curls, are prone to contact marks. Wear is most likely to be evident on the hair above Washington's ear and on the cheekbones.

Reverse: *DESIGN NOT FINALIZED.*

Highest Uncirculated Grade Reported (*TO BE ANNOUNCED*)

PCGS   *NGC*   *ANACS*

News or Other Notes (*To BE ANNOUNCED*)

Investment Potential (*COINS NOT YET STRUCK*)

Pricing Information (Typical MS-63 grade) from Circulation
(*To BE ANNOUNCED*)

COLORADO

State, Coin Date:	Colorado, 2006
Nickname:	Centennial State
Order in Union:	38 (1876)
Size:	104,100 sq. mi. (8th)
Population:	4 million (24th)
State Motto:	"Nil sine numine" (Nothing without Providence)
State Flower:	Rocky mountain columbine
State Bird:	Lark bunting
State Tree:	Colorado blue spruce
Selected Noteworthy Places:	Pike's Peak; Garden of the Gods (Colorado Springs); Mesa Verde (Anasazi Indian ruins); Cripple Creek

mining area; U.S. Air Force Academy; U.S. Olympic
Committee headquarters

Web Site: http://www.state.co.us

Additional Information: *To be announced.*

Coin Specifications

**Obverse
 Sculptor/Designer:** John Flanagan, (1931); revised by William Cousins,
assistant engraver, U.S. Mint, 1998.

Reverse Designer: *To be announced.*

Obverse Design: Portrait of George Washington, after Houdon, by John
Flanagan, modified by William Cousins (1997). Above
bust of Washington: United States of America. Beneath
Washington's chin: Liberty, which has appeared on
every U.S. coin produced since the Mint Act of April 2,
1792. Beside Washington's hair braid: national motto,
"In God We Trust." Below neckline: Quarter Dollar. On
side of neckline: two initials, JF (John Flanagan), WC
(William Cousins).

Reverse Design: At top: state name; beneath, date entered Union. At
bottom: date of issue; beneath, motto "E Pluribus
Unum" (Out of many, one), describing how the divided
colonies became the United States of America. State
design: *To be announced.*

Mintage Figures: *To be announced.*
Proof
Uncirculated "P"
Uncirculated "D"

Selected Specialty
Products Production   *Issue Price*   *Mintage or Sales Limit*

Design Commentary from Citizens Commemorative Coin Advisory Committee (CCCAC) and Fine Arts Commission:

HEARING RESULTS TO BE ANNOUNCED.

Grading Hints

Obverse:

The high points of the coin's obverse are prone to wear; the field off Washington's nose, and the area behind the head curls, are prone to contact marks. Wear is most likely to be evident on the hair above Washington's ear and on the cheekbones.

Reverse:

DESIGN NOT FINALIZED.

Highest Uncirculated Grade Reported (*TO BE ANNOUNCED*)

PCGS   NGC   ANACS

News or Other Notes (*TO BE ANNOUNCED*)

Investment Potential (*COINS NOT YET STRUCK*)

Pricing Information (Typical MS-63 grade) from Circulation

(*TO BE ANNOUNCED*)

NORTH DAKOTA

State, Coin Date:	North Dakota, 2006
Nickname:	Peace Garden State
Order in Union:	39 (1889)
Size:	70,704 sq. mi. (18th)
Population:	640,000 (47th)
State Motto:	"Liberty and Union, now and forever, one and inseparable"
State Flower:	Wild prairie rose
State Bird:	Western meadowlark
State Tree:	American elm
Selected Noteworthy Places:	Theodore Roosevelt National Park; the Badlands; Fort Abraham Lincoln State Park; International Peace Garden; Knife River Indian Villages
Web Site:	http://www.state.nd.us
Additional Information:	*TO BE ANNOUNCED.*

Coin Specifications

Obverse Sculptor/Designer:	John Flanagan, (1931); revised by William Cousins, assistant engraver, U.S. Mint, 1998.
Reverse Designer:	*TO BE ANNOUNCED.*
Obverse Design:	Portrait of George Washington, after Houdon, by John Flanagan, modified by William Cousins (1997). Above bust of Washington: United States of America. Beneath Washington's chin: Liberty, which has appeared on every U.S. coin produced since the Mint Act of April 2,

1792. Beside Washington's hair braid: national motto, "In God We Trust." Below neckline: Quarter Dollar. On side of neckline: two initials, JF (John Flanagan), WC (William Cousins).

Reverse Design: At top: state name; beneath, date entered Union. At bottom: date of issue; beneath, motto "E Pluribus Unum" (Out of many, one), describing how the divided colonies became the United States of America. State design: *TO BE ANNOUNCED.*

Mintage Figures: *TO BE ANNOUNCED.*
Proof
Uncirculated "P"
Uncirculated "D"

Selected Specialty
Products Production   *Issue Price*   *Mintage or Sales Limit*

Design Commentary   *HEARING RESULTS TO BE ANNOUNCED.*
  from Citizens
  Commemorative Coin
  Advisory Committee
  (CCCAC) and Fine Arts
  Commission:

Grading Hints

Obverse: The high points of the coin's obverse are prone to wear; the field off Washington's nose, and the area behind the head curls, are prone to contact marks. Wear is most likely to be evident on the hair above Washington's ear and on the cheekbones.

Reverse: *DESIGN NOT FINALIZED.*

Highest Uncirculated Grade Reported (*TO BE ANNOUNCED*)

PCGS   *NGC*   *ANACS*

News or Other Notes (*To be announced*)

Investment Potential (*Coins not yet struck*)

Pricing Information (Typical MS-63 grade) from Circulation
(*To be announced*)

SOUTH DAKOTA

State, Coin Date:	South Dakota, 2006
Nickname:	Coyote State
Order in Union:	40 (1889)
Size:	77,121 sq. mi. (17th)
Population:	740,000 (46th)
State Motto:	"Under God the people rule"
State Flower:	Pasqueflower
State Bird:	Chinese ring-necked pheasant
State Tree:	Black Hills spruce
Selected Noteworthy Places:	Badlands National Park, Crazy Horse State Memorial; Mount Rushmore; geographical center of the United States
Web Site:	http://www.state.sd.us
Additional Information:	*TO BE ANNOUNCED.*

Coin Specifications

Obverse Sculptor/Designer:	John Flanagan, (1931); revised by William Cousins, assistant engraver, U.S. Mint, 1998.
Reverse Designer:	*TO BE ANNOUNCED.*
Obverse Design:	Portrait of George Washington, after Houdon, by John Flanagan, modified by William Cousins (1997). Above bust of Washington: United States of America. Beneath Washington's chin: Liberty, which has appeared on every U.S. coin produced since the Mint Act of April 2, 1792. Beside Washington's hair braid: national motto, "In God We Trust." Below neckline: Quarter Dollar. On side of neckline: two initials, JF (John Flanagan), WC (William Cousins).
Reverse Design:	At top: state name; beneath, date entered Union. At bottom: date of issue; beneath, motto "E Pluribus Unum" (Out of many, one), describing how the divided colonies became the United States of America. State design: *TO BE ANNOUNCED.*

Mintage Figures:	*To be announced.*	
Proof		
Uncirculated "P"		
Uncirculated "D"		

Selected Specialty		
Products Production	*Issue Price*	*Mintage or Sales Limit*

Design Commentary   *Hearing results to be announced.*
  from Citizens
  Commemorative Coin
  Advisory Committee
  (CCCAC) and Fine Arts
  Commission:

Grading Hints

Obverse: The high points of the coin's obverse are prone to wear; the field off Washington's nose, and the area behind the head curls, are prone to contact marks. Wear is most likely to be evident on the hair above Washington's ear and on the cheekbones.

Reverse: *Design not finalized.*

Highest Uncirculated Grade Reported

PCGS   *NGC*   *ANACS*

News or Other Notes (*To be announced*)

Investment Potential (*COINS NOT YET STRUCK*)

Pricing Information (Typical MS-63 grade) from Circulation
(*TO BE ANNOUNCED*)

Mount Rushmore 50th anniversary U.S. mint commemorative.

MONTANA

State, Coin Date:	Montana, 2007
Nickname:	Treasure State
Order in Union:	41 (1889)
Size:	147,046 sq. mi. (4th)
Population:	880,000 (44th)
State Motto:	"Oro y plata" (Gold and silver)
State Flower:	Bitterroot
State Bird:	Western meadowlark
State Tree:	Ponderosa pine
Selected Noteworthy Places:	Custer Battlefield National Monument; Waterton-Glacier International Peace Park; Yellowstone National Park; Browning National Bison Range; Glacier National Park
Web Site:	http://www.mt.gov
Additional Information:	*TO BE ANNOUNCED.*

Coins Specifications

Obverse Sculptor/Designer:	John Flanagan, (1931); revised by William Cousins, assistant engraver, U.S. Mint, 1998.
Reverse Designer:	*TO BE ANNOUNCED.*
Obverse Design:	Portrait of George Washington, after Houdon, by John Flanagan, modified by William Cousins (1997). Above bust of Washington: United States of America. Beneath Washington's chin: Liberty, which has appeared on every U.S. coin produced since the Mint Act of April 2, 1792. Beside Washington's hair braid: national motto, "In God We Trust." Below neckline: Quarter Dollar. On side of neckline: two initials, JF (John Flanagan), WC (William Cousins).
Reverse Design:	At top: state name; beneath, date entered Union. At bottom: date of issue; beneath, motto "E Pluribus Unum" (Out of many, one), describing how the divided colonies became the United States of America. State design: *TO BE ANNOUNCED.*

Mintage Figures: *TO BE ANNOUNCED.*
Proof
Uncirculated "P"
Uncirculated "D"
Selected Specialty
Products Production   *Issue Price*   *Mintage or Sales Limit*

Design Commentary   *HEARING RESULTS TO BE ANNOUNCED.*
  from Citizens
  Commemorative Coin
  Advisory Committee
  (CCCAC) and Fine Arts
  Commission:

Grading Hints

Obverse: The high points of the coin's obverse are prone to wear;
                             the field off Washington's nose, and the area behind the
                             head curls, are prone to contact marks. Wear is most
                             likely to be evident on the hair above Washington's ear
                             and on the cheekbones.
Reverse: *DESIGN NOT FINALIZED.*

Highest Uncirculated Grade Reported (*TO BE ANNOUNCED*)

PCGS   **NGC**   **ANACS**

News or Other Notes (*TO BE ANNOUNCED*)

Investment Potential (*Coins not yet struck*)

Pricing Information (Typical MS-63 grade) from Circulation
(*To be announced*)

WASHINGTON

State, Coin Date:	Washington, 2007
Nickname:	Evergreen State
Order in Union:	42 (1889)
Size:	70,637 sq. mi. (19th)
Population:	6.7 million (15th)
State Motto:	"Alki" (Bye and bye)
State Flower:	Western rhododendron
State Bird:	Willow goldfinch
State Tree:	Western hemlock
Selected Noteworthy Places:	Klondike Gold Rush National Historic Park; Seattle Center and Space Needle; Columbia River National Scenic Area; Mount St. Helens National Monument; Mount Rainier
Web Site:	http://www.state.wa.gov
Additional Information:	*To be announced.*

Coin Specifications

Obverse Sculptor/Designer:	John Flanagan, (1931); revised by William Cousins, assistant engraver, U.S. Mint, 1998.

Reverse Designer: *TO BE ANNOUNCED.*

Obverse Design: Portrait of George Washington, after Houdon, by John Flanagan, modified by William Cousins (1997). Above bust of Washington: United States of America. Beneath Washington's chin: Liberty, which has appeared on every U.S. coin produced since the Mint Act of April 2, 1792. Beside Washington's hair braid: national motto, "In God We Trust." Below neckline: Quarter Dollar. On side of neckline: two initials, JF (John Flanagan), WC (William Cousins).

Reverse Design: At top: state name; beneath, date entered Union. At bottom: date of issue; beneath, motto "E Pluribus Unum" (Out of many, one), describing how the divided colonies became the United States of America. State design: *TO BE ANNOUNCED.*

Mintage Figures: *TO BE ANNOUNCED.*
Proof
Uncirculated "P"
Uncirculated "D"

Selected Specialty
Products Production   *Issue Price*   *Mintage or Sales Limit*

Design Commentary   *HEARING RESULTS TO BE ANNOUNCED.*
  from Citizens
  Commemorative Coin
  Advisory Committee
  (CCCAC) and Fine Arts
  Commission:

Grading Hints

Obverse: The high points of the coin's obverse are prone to wear; the field off Washington's nose, and the area behind the head curls, are prone to contact marks. Wear is most likely to be evident on the hair above Washington's ear and on the cheekbones.

Reverse: *DESIGN NOT FINALIZED.*

Highest Uncirculated Grade Reported (*To be announced*)

PCGS   *NGC*   *ANACS*

News or Other Notes (*To be announced*)

Investment Potential (*Coins not yet struck*)

Pricing Information (Typical MS-63 grade) from Circulation
(*To be announced*)

Ft. Vancouver commemorative half dollar.

IDAHO

State, Coin Date:	Idaho, 2007
Nickname:	Gem State
Order in Union:	43 (1890)
Size:	83,574 sq. mi. (14th)
Population:	1.3 million (40th)
State Motto:	"Esto perpetua" (It is perpetual)
State Flower:	Syringa
State Bird:	Mountain bluebird
State Tree:	White pine
Selected Noteworthy Places:	Hells Canyon, deepest gorge in North America; Sun Valley; Craters of the Moons National Monument; Yellowstone National Park; Nez Percé National Historic Park (two famous Nez Percé Indians were Chief Joseph and Sacagawea)
Web Site:	http://www.state.id.us
Additional Information:	Sacagawea dollar coin issued by U.S. Mint, starting 2000. Lewis and Clark commemorative gold dollars, 1903–04.

Coin Specifications

Obverse Sculptor/Designer:	John Flanagan, (1931); revised by William Cousins, assistant engraver, U.S. Mint, 1998.
Reverse Designer:	*TO BE ANNOUNCED.*
Obverse Design:	Portrait of George Washington, after Houdon, by John Flanagan, modified by William Cousins (1997). Above bust of Washington: United States of America. Beneath Washington's chin: Liberty, which has appeared on every U.S. coin produced since the Mint Act of April 2, 1792. Beside Washington's hair braid: national motto, "In God We Trust." Below neckline: Quarter Dollar. On side of neckline: two initials, JF (John Flanagan), WC (William Cousins).
Reverse Design:	At top: state name; beneath, date entered Union. At bottom: date of issue; beneath, motto "E Pluribus Unum" (Out of many, one), describing how the divided

colonies became the United States of America. State design: *TO BE ANNOUNCED.*

Mintage Figures:
Proof
Uncirculated "P"
Uncirculated "D"

TO BE ANNOUNCED.

Selected Specialty
Products Production

Issue Price　　**Mintage or Sales Limit**

Design Commentary
  from Citizens
  Commemorative Coin
  Advisory Committee
  (CCCAC) and Fine Arts
  Commission:

HEARING RESULTS TO BE ANNOUNCED.

Grading Hints

Obverse:

The high points of the coin's obverse are prone to wear; the field off Washington's nose, and the area behind the head curls, are prone to contact marks. Wear is most likely to be evident on the hair above Washington's ear and on the cheekbones.

Reverse:

DESIGN NOT FINALIZED.

Highest Uncirculated Grade Reported (*TO BE ANNOUNCED*)

PCGS　　　**NGC**　　　**ANACS**

News or Other Notes (*TO BE ANNOUNCED*)

Investment Potential (*COINS NOT YET STRUCK*)

Pricing Information (Typical MS-63 grade) from Circulation
(*TO BE ANNOUNCED*)

Yellowstone commemorative, U.S. Mint.

WYOMING

State, Coin Date:	Wyoming, 2007
Nickname:	Cowboy State
Order in Union:	44 (1890)
Size:	97,818 sq. mi. (9th)
Population:	481,000 (50th)
State Motto:	"Equal rights"
State Flower:	Indian paintbrush
State Bird:	Western meadowlark
State Tree:	Plains cottonwood
Selected Noteworthy Places:	Buffalo Bill Museum; Old Faithful (Yellowstone National Park); Grand Teton National Park; Fort Laramie National Historic Site; Devil's Tower National Historic Monument
Web Site:	http://www.state.wy.us
Additional Information:	*TO BE ANNOUNCED.*

Coin Specifications

Obverse Sculptor/Designer:	John Flanagan, (1931); revised by William Cousins, assistant engraver, U.S. Mint, 1998.
Reverse Designer:	*TO BE ANNOUNCED.*
Obverse Design:	Portrait of George Washington, after Houdon, by John Flanagan, modified by William Cousins (1997). Above bust of Washington: United States of America. Beneath Washington's chin: Liberty, which has appeared on every U.S. coin produced since the Mint Act of April 2, 1792. Beside Washington's hair braid: national motto, "In God We Trust." Below neckline: Quarter Dollar. On side of neckline: two initials, JF (John Flanagan), WC (William Cousins).
Reverse Design:	At top: state name; beneath, date entered Union. At bottom: date of issue; beneath, motto "E Pluribus Unum" (Out of many, one), describing how the divided colonies became the United States of America. State design: *TO BE ANNOUNCED.*

Mintage Figures: *TO BE ANNOUNCED.*
Proof
Uncirculated "P"
Uncirculated "D"

Selected Specialty Products Production	*Issue Price*	*Mintage or Sales Limit*

Design Commentary *HEARING RESULTS TO BE ANNOUNCED.*
from Citizens
Commemorative Coin
Advisory Committee
(CCCAC) and Fine Arts
Commission:

Grading Hints

Obverse: The high points of the coin's obverse are prone to wear; the field off Washington's nose, and the area behind the head curls, are prone to contact marks. Wear is most likely to be evident on the hair above Washington's ear and on the cheekbones.

Reverse: *DESIGN NOT FINALIZED.*

Highest Uncirculated Grade Reported (*To be announced*)

PCGS   *NGC*   *ANACS*

News or Other Notes (*To be announced*)

Investment Potential (*Coins not yet struck*)

Pricing Information (Typical MS-63 grade) from Circulation
(*To be announced*)

UTAH

State, Coin Date:	Utah, 2007
Nickname:	Beehive State
Order in Union:	45 (1896)
Size:	84,904 sq. mi. (13th)
Population:	2.1 million (34th)
State Motto:	Industry
State Flower:	Sego lily
State Bird:	Seagull
State Tree:	Blue spruce
Selected Noteworthy Places:	Temple Square and Mormon Tabernacle, Salt Lake City; Dinosaur and Rainbow Bridge National Monuments; Great Salt Lake; Zion National Park; Promontory Point continental railroad joining (1869)
Web Site:	http://www.state.ut.us
Additional Information:	*TO BE ANNOUNCED.*

Coin Specifications

Obverse Sculptor/Designer:	John Flanagan, (1931); revised by William Cousins, assistant engraver, U.S. Mint, 1998.
Reverse Designer:	*TO BE ANNOUNCED.*
Obverse Design:	Portrait of George Washington, after Houdon, by John Flanagan, modified by William Cousins (1997). Above bust of Washington: United States of America. Beneath Washington's chin: Liberty, which has appeared on every U.S. coin produced since the Mint Act of April 2, 1792. Beside Washington's hair braid: national motto, "In God We Trust." Below neckline: Quarter Dollar. On side of neckline: two initials, JF (John Flanagan), WC (William Cousins).
Reverse Design:	At top: state name; beneath, date entered Union. At bottom: date of issue; beneath, motto "E Pluribus Unum" (Out of many, one), describing how the divided colonies became the United States of America. State design: *TO BE ANNOUNCED.*

Mintage Figures: *To be announced.*
Proof
Uncirculated "P"
Uncirculated "D"

Selected Specialty
Products Production   *Issue Price*   *Mintage or Sales Limit*

Design Commentary   *Hearing results to be announced.*
  from Citizens
  Commemorative Coin
  Advisory Committee
  (CCCAC) and Fine Arts
  Commission:

Grading Hints

Obverse: The high points of the coin's obverse are prone to wear;
                           the field off Washington's nose, and the area behind the
                           head curls, are prone to contact marks. Wear is most
                           likely to be evident on the hair above Washington's ear
                           and on the cheekbones.
Reverse: *Design not finalized.*

Highest Uncirculated Grade Reported (*To be announced*)

PCGS   *NGC*   *ANACS*

News or Other Notes (*To be announced*)

Investment Potential (*COINS NOT YET STRUCK*)

Pricing Information (Typical MS-63 grade) from Circulation
(*TO BE ANNOUNCED*)

OKLAHOMA

State, Coin Date:	Oklahoma, 2008
Nickname:	Sooner State
Order in Union:	46 (1907)
Size:	69,903 sq. mi. (20th)
Population:	3.4 million (27th)
State Motto:	"Labor omnia vincit"
	(Labor conquers all things)
State Flower:	Mistletoe
State Bird:	Scissor-tailed flycatcher
State Tree:	Redbud
Selected Noteworthy Places:	National Cowboy Hall of Fame; Pioneer Women's Museum; Will Rogers Memorial; Indian Territory, home to five tribes: Cherokee, Choctaw, Chicaww, Creek, and Seminole (after they arrived from Trail of Tears 1826–46); Cherokee heritage center
Web Site:	http://www.state.ok.us
Additional Information:	*TO BE ANNOUNCED.*

Coin Specifications

Obverse Sculptor/Designer:	John Flanagan, (1931); revised by William Cousins, assistant engraver, U.S. Mint, 1998.

Reverse Designer:	*TO BE ANNOUNCED.*
Obverse Design:	Portrait of George Washington, after Houdon, by John Flanagan, modified by William Cousins (1997). Above bust of Washington: United States of America. Beneath Washington's chin: Liberty, which has appeared on every U.S. coin produced since the Mint Act of April 2, 1792. Beside Washington's hair braid: national motto, "In God We Trust." Below neckline: Quarter Dollar. On side of neckline: two initials, JF (John Flanagan), WC (William Cousins).
Reverse Design:	*TO BE ANNOUNCED.*

Mintage Figures:	*TO BE ANNOUNCED.*
Proof	
Uncirculated "P"	
Uncirculated "D"	

Selected Specialty		
Products Production	*Issue Price*	*Mintage of Sales Limit*

Design Commentary from Citizens Commemorative Coin Advisory Committee (CCCAC) and Fine Arts Commission:	*HEARING RESULTS TO BE ANNOUNCED.*

Grading Hints

Obverse:	The high points of the coin's obverse are prone to wear; the field off Washington's nose, and the area behind the head curls, are prone to contact marks. Wear is most likely to be evident on the hair above Washington's ear and on the cheekbones.
Reverse:	*DESIGN NOT FINALIZED.*

Highest Circulated Grade Reported (*To be announced*)

PCGS   **NGC**   **ANACS**

News or Other Notes (*To be announced*)

Investment Potential (*Coins not yet struck*)

Pricing Information (Typical MS-63 grade) from Circulation
(*To be announced*)

NEW MEXICO

State, Coin Date:	New Mexico, 2008
Nickname:	Land of Enchantment
Order in Union:	47 (1912)
Size:	121,598 sq. mi. (5th)
Population:	1.8 million (37th)
State Motto:	"Crescut eyundo" (It grows as it goes)
State Flower:	Yucca
State Bird:	Roadrunner
State Tree:	Piñon
Selected Noteworthy Places:	Aztec Ruins National Monument; Carlsbad Caverns; Gila Cliff Dwellings National Monument; Santa Fe; White Sands National Monument
Web Site:	http://www.state.nm.us
Additional Information:	*TO BE ANNOUNCED.*

Coin Specifications

Obverse Sculptor/Designer:	John Flanagan, (1931); revised by William Cousins, assistant engraver, U.S. Mint, 1998
Reverse Designer:	*TO BE ANNOUNCED.*
Obverse Design:	Portrait of George Washington, after Houdon, by John Flanagan, modified by William Cousins (1997). Above bust of Washington: United States of America. Beneath Washington's chin: Liberty, which has appeared on every U.S. coin produced since the Mint Act of April 2, 1792. Beside Washington's hair braid: national motto, "In God We Trust." Below neckline: Quarter Dollar. On side of neckline: two initials, JF (John Flanagan), WC (William Cousins).
Reverse Design:	At top: state name; beneath, date entered Union. At bottom: date of issue; beneath, motto "E Pluribus Unum" (Out of many, one), describing how the divided colonies became the United States of America. State design: *TO BE ANNOUNCED.*

Mintage Figures: *TO BE ANNOUNCED.*
Proof
Uncirculated "P"
Uncirculated "D"

Selected Specialty
Products Production   *Issue Price*   *Mintage or Sales Limit*

Design Commentary   *HEARING RESULTS TO BE ANNOUNCED.*
  from Citizens
  Commemorative Coin
  Advisory Committee
  (CCCAC) and Fine Arts
  Commission:

Grading Hints

Obverse: The high points of the coin's obverse are prone to wear;
                  the field off Washington's nose, and the area behind the
                  head curls, are prone to contact marks. Wear is most
                  likely to be evident on the hair above Washington's ear
                  and on the cheekbones.
Reverse: *DESIGN NOT FINALIZED.*

Highest Uncirculated Grade Reported (*TO BE ANNOUNCED*)

PCGS   *NGC*   *ANACS*

News or Other Notes (*TO BE ANNOUNCED*)

Investment Potential (*COINS NOT YET STRUCK*)

Pricing Information (Typical MS-63 grade) from Circulation
(*TO BE ANNOUNCED*)

ARIZONA

State, Coin Date:	Arizona, 2008
Nickname:	Grand Canyon State
Order in Union:	48 (1912)
Size:	114,006 sq. mi. (6th)
Population:	4.6 million (21st)
State Motto:	"Ditat deus" (God enriches)
State Flower:	Giant cactus (saguaro)
State Bird:	Cactus wren
State Tree:	Paloverde
Selected Noteworthy Places:	Grand Canyon National Park; Petrified Forest National Park; Navajo National Monument; London Bridge; Tombstone; painted desert
Web Site:	http://www.state.az.us
Additional Information:	*TO BE ANNOUNCED.*

Coin Specifications

Obverse Sculptor/Designer:	John Flanagan, (1931); revised by William Cousins, assistant engraver, U.S. Mint, 1998.

Reverse Designer: *To be announced.*

Obverse Design: Portrait of George Washington, after Houdon, by John Flanagan, modified by William Cousins (1997). Above bust of Washington: United States of America. Beneath Washington's chin: Liberty, which has appeared on every U.S. coin produced since the Mint Act of April 2, 1792. Beside Washington's hair braid: national motto, In God We Trust." Below neckline: Quarter Dollar. On side of neckline: two initials, JF (John Flanagan), WC (William Cousins).

Reverse Design: At top: state name; beneath, date entered Union. At bottom: date of issue; beneath, motto "E Pluribus Unum" (Out of many, one), describing how the divided colonies became the United States of America. State design: *To be announced.*

Mintage Figures: *To be announced.*
Proof
Uncirculated "P"
Uncirculated "D"

Selected Specialty Products Production	*Issue Price*	*Mintage or Sales Limit*

Design Commentary from Citizens Commemorative Coin Advisory Committee (CCCAC) and Fine Arts Commission: *Hearing results to be announced.*

Grading Hints

Obverse: The high points of the coin's obverse are prone to wear; the field off Washington's nose, and the area behind the head curls, are prone to contact marks. Wear is most likely to be evident on the hair above Washington's ear and on the cheekbones.

Reverse: *Design not finalized.*

Highest Uncirculated Grade Reported (*To be announced*)

PCGS   **NGC**   **ANACS**

News or Other Notes (*To be announced*)

Investment Potential (*Coins not yet struck*)

Pricing Information (Typical MS-63 grade) from Circulation
(*To be announced*)

ALASKA

State, Coin Date:	Alaska, 2008
Nickname:	Last Frontier
Order in Union:	49 (1959)
Size:	615,230 sq. mi. (1st)
Population:	609,000 (48th)
State Motto:	"North to the future"
State Flower:	Forget-me-not
State Bird:	Willow ptarmigan
State Tree:	Sitka spruce
Selected Noteworthy Places:	Mount McKinley (Denali) National Park; Portage glacier; Russian Orthodox Cathedral, Sitka National Historic Park; Klondike Gold Rush National Historic Park
Web Site:	http://www.state.ak.us
Additional Information:	The state mineral of Alaska is gold, something very important to the growth and past of America's most northerly state. Originally Russian, it was sold by the czar to the United States in 1867 for $7.2 million.

Coin Specifications

Obverse Sculptor/Designer:	John Flanagan, (1931); revised by William Cousins, assistant engraver, U.S. Mint, 1998.
Reverse Designer:	*TO BE ANNOUNCED.*
Obverse Design:	Portrait of George Washington, after Houdon, by John Flanagan, modified by William Cousins (1997). Above bust of Washington: United States of America. Beneath Washington's chin: Liberty, which has appeared on every U.S. coin produced since the Mint Act of April 2, 1792. Beside Washington's hair braid: national motto, "In God We Trust." Below neckline: Quarter Dollar. On side of neckline: two initials, JF (John Flanagan), WC (William Cousins).
Reverse Design:	At top: state name; beneath, date entered Union. At bottom: date of issue; beneath, motto "E Pluribus Unum" (Out of many, one), describing how the divided colonies became the United States of America. State design: *TO BE ANNOUNCED.*

Mintage Figures: *TO BE ANNOUNCED.*
Proof
Uncirculated "P"
Uncirculated "D"

Selected Specialty
Products Production   *Issue Price*   *Mintage or Sales Limit*

Design Commentary   *HEARING RESULTS TO BE ANNOUNCED.*
  from Citizens
  Commemorative Coin
  Advisory Committee
  (CCCAC) and Fine Arts
  Commission:

Grading Hints

Obverse: The high points of the coin's obverse are prone to wear; the field off Washington's nose, and the area behind the head curls, are prone to contact marks. Wear is most likely to be evident on the hair above Washington's ear and on the cheekbones.

Reverse: *DESIGN NOT FINALIZED.*

Highest Uncirculated Grade Reported (*TO BE ANNOUNCED*)

PCGS   *NGC*   *ANACS*

News or Other Notes (*TO BE ANNOUNCED*)

Investment Potential (*COINS NOT YET STRUCK*)

Pricing Information (Typical MS-63 grade) from Circulation
(*TO BE ANNOUNCED*)

HAWAII

State, Coin Date:	Hawaii, 2008
Nickname:	Aloha State
Order in Union:	50 (1959)
Size:	6,459 sq. mi. (47th)
Population:	1.2 million (41st)
State Motto:	"The life of the land is perpetuated in righteousness"
State Flower:	Yellow hibiscus
State Bird:	Hawaiian goose
State Tree:	Kukui (candlenut)
Selected Noteworthy Places:	*USS Arizona* (Pearl Harbor) National Monument; Diamond Head; Iolani Palace; Polynesian cultural center; National Cemetery of the Pacific (Punchbowl crater)
Web Site:	http://www.state/hi.us
Additional Information:	Hawaii had its own coinage during the 19th century.

The cent (1847), nickel (pattern, 1881), dime, quarter, half dollar, and dollar (1883) all bear a rich history. "After a quick survey of state agencies that might be involved in America's 50-State Quarters program, I unfortunately have nothing to report to you . . . other than that no plans are in the works at this time. Since we are the 50th state, and our quarters are the last to roll out of the Mint in 2008, specific design plans in 2000 would be premature for Hawaii. Good luck with your publishing project!"—Wally Inglis, director of information services, Office of the Gov.

Coin Specifications

Obverse Sculptor/Designer: John Flanagan, (1931); revised by William Cousins, assistant engraver, U.S. Mint, 1998.

Reverse Designer: *TO BE ANNOUNCED.*

Obverse Design: Portrait of George Washington, after Houdon, by John Flanagan, modified by William Cousins (1997). Above bust of Washington: United States of America. Beneath Washington's chin: Liberty, which has appeared on every U.S. coin produced since the Mint Act of April 2, 1792. Beside Washington's hair braid: national motto, "In God We Trust." Below neckline: Quarter Dollar. On side of neckline: two initials, JF (John Flanagan), WC (William Cousins).

Reverse Design: At top: state name; beneath: date entered Union. At bottom, date of issue, beneath motto "E Pluribus Unum" (Out of many, one), describing how the divided colonies became the United States of America. State design: *TO BE ANNOUNCED.*

Mintage Figures:
Proof
Uncirculated "P"
Uncirculated "D"

TO BE ANNOUNCED.

Selected Specialty Products Production	Issue Price	Mintage or Sales Limit

Design Commentary from Citizens Commemorative Coin Advisory Committee (CCCAC) and Fine Arts Commission: *HEARING RESULTS TO BE ANNOUNCED.*

Grading Hints

Obverse: The high points of the coin's obverse are prone to wear; the field off Washington's nose, and the area behind the head curls, are prone to contact marks. Wear is most likely to be evident on the hair above Washington's ear and on the cheekbones.

Reverse: *DESIGN NOT FINALIZED.*

Highest Uncirculated Grade Reported (*TO BE ANNOUNCED*)

PCGS	NGC	ANACS

News or Other Notes (*TO BE ANNOUNCED*)

Investment Potential (*COINS NOT YET STRUCK*)

Pricing Information (Typical MS-63 grade) from Circulation
(TO BE ANNOUNCED)

Hawaii 1928 commemorative half dollar.

SELECTED BIBLIOGRAPHY

Periodicals Consulted

COINage magazine (various issues)
Coin World (various issues)
The Congressional Record (various)
Numismatic News (various issues)
The Numismatist (various issues)

Important Works of the Author Utilized

Ganz, "Toward a Revision of the Minting and Coinage Law of the United States," 26 Cleveland State Law Review, pp. 175–257 (1977).

Ganz, "Valuation of Coin Collection," 5 Proof of Facts, 3rd ed., p. 577 (1989).

Ganz, *The Official Guide to U.S. Commemorative Coins* (Bonus Books, 1999).

Ganz, *The World of Coins and Coin Collecting,* 3rd ed., (Bonus Books, 1998).

Ganz, *Planning Your Rare Coin Retirement* (Bonus Books, 1999).

Pricing and Grading Guides

NumisMedia Fair Market Value Price Guide (various issues, 1999–2000).

The Teletrade Real Price Guide, 12th ed., 1998–1999 (Teletrade, 2000).

The PCGS Population Report (Collector's Universe, 2000; various).

United States Coins Census Report (Numismatic Guaranty Corporation, 2000; various).

Travers, ed., *Official Guide to Coin Grading and Counterfeit Detection* (House of Collectibles, 1997).

Yeoman, *A Guide Book of United States Coins* (Bressett, ed.) (various editions).

Official Documents

Minutes of the Citizens Commemorative Coin Advisory Committee, 1993–date.

Minutes and Hearings (transcripts) before the Commission of Fine Arts, 1910–date.

United States Mint Annual Report, 1993–1999.

Annual Report of the Citizens Commemorative Coin Advisory Committee to the Congress of the United States, 1994, 1995, 1996, 1997, 1998.

Hearing on the U.S. Mint's Commemorative Coin Program Before the Subcommittee on Domestic and International Monetary Policy of the House Committee on Banking and Financial Services, 104th Cong., 1st session (Serial 104–25) (July 12, 1995).

Statistical Abstract of the United States 1996–1997 (116th ed., 1996).

Department of the Treasury, U.S. Mint, 50 State Quarters Information Kit (1998).

Public Laws

Pub. L. 104-329, 110 Stat. 3514, Oct. 24, 1996 (U.S. Commemorative Coin Act of 1996).

Pub. L. 105-124, 111 Stat. 2534, Dec. 1, 1997 (50 State Commemorative coin 1999).

Pub. L. 105-176, 112 Stat. 104, May 29, 1998 (50 State Commemorative coin).

Official Web Sites

Official web site of each of the fifty states, and each of America's six territories and commonwealths.

Correspondence

E-mails and letters from governors of the fifty states.

Almanacs

N.Y. Times Almanac (1999).
The World Almanac (2000).

Auction Catalogs

Heritage Numismatic Auctions (various)
Bowers & Merena Galleries (various)

Price Lists

Fred Weinberg, Inc.

APPENDIX

How to Care for Your 50 State Quarters

Now that you've decided to collect America's state quarters, it is important for you to learn how to care for your coins.

How you preserve your coins can have a substantial impact on their premium value.

Even coins that are put away in a desk drawer and never touched again can be damaged over time. The wood of the drawer can be a source of a gaseous element that combines with moisture in the air to create a damaging sulfide reaction on the surface of coins.

Coins that are put into drawers, socks, or jars have a different problem, as they can acquire nicks, dings, or scratches through contact. That can result in a substantial diminution of premium value.

Use of a coin holder may have its own problems, if you are not careful. There are some elaborate-in-appearance commercial holders that have coins placed in cardboard frames with acetate shields covering the coins. If the coin is not seated properly in the cardboard cut-out, the acetate passing over the coin can, under some circumstances, cause "slide marks" that lower a coin's value.

Or suppose you take a coin out of its carefully crafted holder and drop it on the floor. That could cause soft metal on the coin to be moved, thus lowering the value. Perhaps when you pick the coin up, you don't hold it by the edge (as it should be held), and instead allow your fingers to grasp the coin's surface. The natural oil from your fingers can damage the coin's surface by eventually etching smudges and your fingerprints on the coin. Hold the coin by the edge only, using your thumb and index finger.

What are the answers that you should look for in the battle to preserve a coin's condition and ultimately its premium value? First, the enemy of all coins is air and moisture. Spittle from talking that lands on a coin's surface will eventually blacken it; so take special care not to talk over your coins (or to cover your mouth if you do). High humidity in some areas of the country can also cause damage to metal, much as outdoor furniture may eventually rust.

If your coins are stored in a sealed container such as a safety deposit box, a moisture-absorbing packet can be very useful. These are the same packages that are found in the stereo box that you just opened, or in some other electronic devices, to protect them until consumers open the package. They are available commercially at many hardware stores.

When handling the coin, do so either while wearing fingertip sheaths or disposable polyethylene gloves. That helps to prevent fingerprints later appearing on the coin. Also, place coins that you are handling over a soft velvet or foam pad: If you drop a coin accidentally using this method, serious economic loss will be minimized.

There are a number of inexpensive commercial products that you can use to satisfactorily store your coins. There is the acid-free paper two-by-two paper holder (two inches by two inches, square), which looks like a miniature envelope. These usually cost less than two or three cents apiece and can conveniently hold a coin without damaging it. You can write a description of the contents with a soft pencil.

There are also cardboard two-by-two holders with cellophane inserts that cover the coin; they are usually held together with a staple (staple carefully, as many a coin has been damaged by a staple mark that overshot the intended target). These are usually available at 5 cents apiece, or less.

There are also soft vinyl holders. Be cautious that you do not place a state quarter in a soft vinyl holder that contains polyvinyl chloride (PVC). The chemicals in the PVC respond to heat, and time, and can leach onto the surface of the coin, damaging it, and destroying the value of an otherwise fine coin. Some rigid, vinyl-type holders in clear plastic have no PVC and work quite well in holding coins. They are 2 x 2 inches as well in size, generally. The cost of both types is usually under six cents apiece.

There are vinyl pages that hold two x two holders (again watch for PCV that can leach onto the surface) as well as coin wallets with pockets that range from eighteen to sixty coins. This works well enough, provided you insert it in a safe holder.

There are plastic holders represented by their manufacturers to be inert and that fit tightly around the coin, preventing air from circulating freely. One of the better known is the Mylar "Kointain," manufactured by E&T Kointainer Co. These are about 12 cents apiece.

More rigid plastic containers, two x two in size, and made from poured molds that allow for the coin to be fitted, are commercially available. The cost of these plastic holders are about 70 cents apiece.

There are also commercially produced holders that the various grading services use. These are of an inert plastic for the holder and the insert. The added benefit is that the coin is also graded for you. There are a variety of rates that can be charged for this, but generally under $25.

John Albanese, in conjunction with Lucent Technologies-Bell Labs, has a product called Intercept Shields. The manufacturer says that this acts almost as a magnet for airborne particulate matter protecting the coin from damage. The product is sold as a component of the grading service of Independent Coin Grading Company (ICG) of Englewood, Colorado.

For the fun of it, the exposed holders that are being given away by the American Numismatic Association, the Professional Numismatists Guild, the American Numismatic Society, and the U.S. Mint can be described as cardboard with a backing: The coin fits into a slot and can be seen from one side only. It is very similar to the blue Whitman folders that have been around for a generation. The flaws in this are that the coins are exposed to the elements and handling by third persons, sometimes fall out of their holders, and are not at all recommended to store valuable high-grade coins. That said, I have one at home and one in the office, and am enjoying using it to collect the series out-of-pocket change without a lot of regard for premium value or condition.

For further information on coin preservation, read *The Coin Collector's Survival Manual*, fourth edition, by Scott A. Travers (Bonus Books, 2000, $16.95).

INDEX

About the Author

DAVID L. GANZ, forty-nine, managing partner and principal litigator in the law firm of Ganz & Sivin, P.A., in Fair Lawn, New Jersey, and Ganz & Hollinger, P.C., in New York City, has a practice that is focused on litigation, guardianship, real estate, and general corporate work. He is also an award-winning writer on a variety of topics, and the elected 29th Mayor of Fair Lawn, New Jersey.

A prolific author in a variety of different fields, his books include: *14 Bits: A Legal & Legislative History of 31 USC §§324d-i* (1976); *The World of Coins & Coin Collecting* (first published in 1980, 3rd revised edition, 1998); *Planning Your Rare Coin Retirement* (1998); *The 90 Second Lawyer* (1996); *The 90 Second Lawyer Guide to Buying Real Estate* (1997); *How to Get an Instant Mortgage* (1997); and *The Official Guide to Commemorative Coins* (1999).

He has also written a number of law review articles and book chapters in important works on real estate and other areas. He previously edited a book on America's coinage laws (1792–1894) (1991). He has also been an award-winning columnist and contributing editor for *COINage* magazine since 1974, a columnist for *Numismatic News,* the weekly periodical, since 1969, and winner of the Numismatic Literary Guild's highest achievement award, the Clemy.

A graduate of the School of Foreign Service at Georgetown University, he has a law degree from St. John's University Law School and did postgraduate legal studies in the master's of law program at New York University. He also studied international law at Temple University Law School in Rome, Italy, while working for the coins and medals office of the Food & Agriculture Organization of the United Nations. In 1994 he was awarded the Order of St. Agatha (Commander) by the Republic of San Marino.

He has been asked to testify before the Subcommittee on Consumer Affairs and other subcommittees of the House Banking Committee on more than a dozen occasions since 1974, most recently in July 1995. He is qualified in the first panel of certified arbitrators for the U.S. District Court for the Eastern District of

New York and New Jersey, and he is an arbitrator and mediator in the Superior Court program in Bergen County, New Jersey. In 1996 he became one of only seventy-one certified mediators of the U.S. District Court for the District of New Jersey mediation program.

In his spare time, he is a coin collector. A life fellow (one of 200 voting members) of the American Numismatic Society, he was appointed by President Richard Nixon to the 1974 Annual Assay Commission, the oldest continually functioning committee in the federal government (dating to the founding of the Mint in 1792). He served from 1985 to 1995 as an elected member of the Board of Governors of the American Numismatic Association, the largest, educational nonprofit organization of collectors in the world. He became the organization's 48th president in July 1993, serving until August 1995.

In December 1993, Treasury Secretary Lloyd Bentsen appointed him a charter member of the Citizens Commemorative Coin Advisory Committee, where he was the first and strongest proponent of circulating commemorative coinage and the 50-state quarters program. He was reappointed in 1995 for a second one-year term, leaving office in February 1996. He chaired the World Mint Council in 1994 and 1995 at its meetings held in conjunction with the American Numismatic Association annual convention. In 1995 more than twenty-four nations' ministers attended Council meetings in Anaheim.

He has served as a consultant to the Canadian Olympic Coin Program (1973–76), the Moscow Olympic Coin Program (1976–80), for Occidental Petroleum and Lazard Frères in their 1981–82 Olympic Coin program effort, the 1985–86 Statue of Liberty Centennial Celebration, and many others. His legislative expertise has been tapped by Olin Brass, Memorial Mission Hospital (Asheville, N.C.), The Platinum Guild, the Dutch Mint, the Portuguese State Mint, and others on coin and related matters over the course of the past twenty years.

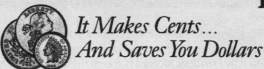